Gestures and Acclamations in Ancient Rome

Ancient Society and History

Gestures and

GREGORY S. ALDRETE

Acclamations in Ancient Rome

The Johns Hopkins University Press
Baltimore and London

© 1999 The Johns Hopkins University Press
All rights reserved. Published 1999
Printed in the United States of America on acid-free paper
9 8 7 6 5 4 3 2 1

The Johns Hopkins University Press
2715 North Charles Street
Baltimore, Maryland 21218-4363
www.press.jhu.edu

All illustrations except Figures 12, 16, 17, and 18 were drawn by Alicia
Nowicki. Those of the standing togate orator illustrating various gestures
were adapted from Fig. 99 in *Ancient Greek, Roman and Byzantine
Costume and Decoration* by Mary Houston (London: A. and C. Black
Limited, 1959).

Library of Congress Cataloging-in-Publication Data will be found
at the end of this book.
A catalog record for this book is available from the British Library.

ISBN 0-8018-6132-2

To my parents

Contents

Contents

Figures

Acknowledgments

A book, like a person, has a genealogy, and the roots of this one run all the way back to my days as an undergraduate when I first became interested in the topics of delivery and crowd response. This book is an adaptation of my dissertation, written for the Department of History at the University of Michigan. Later, the process of revision benefited greatly from my spending a summer as a member of a National Endowment for the Humanities seminar held at the American Academy in Rome.

Such a lengthy undertaking creates the pleasant necessity of thanking a number of people. I am grateful to Peter Brown, Erich Gruen, and Edward Champlin for providing inspiration and for serving as role models during my time as an undergraduate. I am indebted to David Mattingly and John Humphrey for giving me a respect for the importance of archaeology in studying the ancient world. Of those who directly advised me on this project, I must particularly thank my dissertation committee, Bruce Frier, Sally Humphreys, Elaine Gazda, and, most of all, my chairperson, Ray Van Dam, for all his support and guidance. The directors of the NEH Summer Seminar, Bettina Bergmann and Christine Kondoleon, offered much helpful advice, as did the other members of the seminar.

The process of writing was aided at various stages by a Rackham Merit Fellowship and a Hewlett International Dissertation Grant from the University of Michigan, and the fellowship from the National Endowment for the Humanities. I am also grateful to the staffs of the American Academy in Rome and the Vatican Library for their assistance.

I would also like to acknowledge David West Reynolds, whose conversation and friendship consistently provided both intellectual stimulation and enjoyment. Finally, special thanks are due to Alicia Nowicki, who not only carefully proofread innumerable drafts and drew the illustrations, but who also has shared many years of happy companionship with me.

Introduction

This work is a study of communication, how Roman speakers communicated with their audiences, and how in turn audiences were able to reply and convey their reactions back to the speakers. Such an interaction implies a system of rules to govern and facilitate the communicative process; further, for the system to function properly, each side had to know what the rules were or, at the very minimum, be conditioned to act in certain more or less predictable ways. Ideally, there would have been both self-conscious knowledge of the rules and at least a tacit agreement to abide by them. This book is an attempt to discern some of those rules and patterns of behavior and to assess how effectively they were put into practice in the late republic and early empire. It focuses on two particular forms of communication, one nonverbal, used primarily by speakers, and one verbal, mainly used by audiences. The first half of the book investigates the use of gesture and the second does the same for acclamations. These were not the only methods available, but have been selected because in this period they shared the characteristics of flexibility and versatility and, more importantly, were truly interactive forms of communication that encouraged a two-way dialogue between speaker and listener.

Various public spectacles dominated the urban life of Rome in the late republic and early empire. These events included not only entertainments such as gladiatorial combats, beast hunts, chariot races in the circus, and theatrical performances, but also funerals, triumphs, religious ceremonies and festivals, holidays, court trials, voting procedures, and assemblies. These activities had several elements in common. First, they were a part of a specifically urban experience; they occurred in cities and particularly at the capital city, Rome. Second, they were all staged in highly visible public settings such as the streets, spaces, and public buildings of the city. Religious ceremonies, for example, usually did not take place inside the temples but in front of them, on the imposing flights of steps that formed such an essential part of Roman temple architecture. Even criminal trials were held not in an enclosed space, but rather in the open air, often in the Forum itself. Third, the audience for these events could be both very large in numbers and quite diverse in composition. Finally, all these activities to a greater or lesser degree involved speechmaking: orations directed both toward the immediate participants and at whatever bystanders were present.

These events ran the gamut from politics to entertainment and from celebration to mourning. In Roman society such urban rituals cannot be divided into categories such as secular and religious. Athletic games were held to celebrate religious festivals, observing court cases was a popular form of entertainment, the senate often convened in temples, and funerals were accompanied by gladiatorial combats. Life at Rome was intensely and relentlessly public, and because of this, for ambitious members of Rome's upper class, "politics" encompassed much more than those activities thought of by modern readers as strictly political. For these men, every individual appearance in public was suffused with political importance. Increasing or at least maintaining their authority and prestige, their power and influence, summed up in the uniquely Roman term, *dignitas*, was a full-time and obsessive occupation. *Dignitas*, however, was labile and had to be constantly renewed. One of the primary ways this could be accomplished was through participation in the urban life of the city, by being seen and heard prominently taking part in the many public spectacles and rituals. Since oratory, the art of speaking before an audience, was at the center of all these public events, oratory was at the center of politics and of urban life.

The two main sections of this book share the same structure and each consists of two chapters. In each case the first chapter is descriptive and offers a survey of the different ways that the Romans used gesture or acclamations at Rome in the late republic and early empire. The second chapter in each section examines the wider social context for that form of communication, and some of the implications attendant upon its use.

Part One, "Speakers," focuses on how orators at Rome employed gestures to aid communication with their audiences. Chapter 1 offers a descriptive typology of the very different purposes that gesture could serve in the course of an oration. Among modern scholars, oratorical delivery has been somewhat neglected as a topic of inquiry, but to the ancients it was of vital interest. Ancient rhetoricians considered the delivery of a speech to be the single most important component of oratory because of its power to sway an audience's emotions. Gesture and voice tone were conventionally regarded as forming the main elements of delivery. A complex and versatile vocabulary of hand and body gestures developed, which prospective orators had to master in order to present their speeches most persuasively. Certain gestures possessed such specific emotional connotations that an orator could suggest these emotions to his audience through his body language. Because of the richly symbolic landscape in which most speeches were delivered, by using pointing motions an orator could draw on this environment to enhance or supplement his words. Gesture also served a metronomic function, emphasizing the innate rhythmic qualities of many orations. In all these functions, as well as a few others, gesture constituted a significant nonverbal component of ancient oratory that could augment, supplement, or even take the place of an orator's words.

Chapter 2 sets the complex system of oratorical gesture into the broader context of Roman urban society. The accounts of gesture in literary sources are compared with depictions of oratorical gesture in a variety of artistic media, including state and private statues and reliefs and imperial coinage. The chapter next considers the extent to which audiences in the city of Rome would have been able to understand and interpret the nonverbal language used by orators and offers some reasons why this knowledge may have been surprisingly widespread. Many of the most popular forms of entertainment, including pantomime, mime, and the theater, employed gestural systems comparable in intricacy with that used by orators. The link between actor and orator is particularly significant, and evidence suggests that each studied the other and that they even borrowed specific gestures from one another in order to hone their performative skills. Because of the gulf in status separating them, however, the similarities between actor and orator were a source of great anxiety to aristocratic orators. Finally, this chapter addresses some of the practical problems faced by orators in ancient Rome, which probably resulted in an increased reliance on gesture in order to converse with large audiences.

After having examined one of the techniques by which speakers could communicate at public gatherings, I turn to the audience itself and to the primary method available to it for responding to speakers and making known its own desires and opinions. The focus of Part Two is narrower in that it centers on a special type of interaction, that between the emperor and the urban plebs in the early empire. This particular discourse has been selected because it most vividly illustrates the versatility and power of acclamations. A brief transitional chapter links Parts One and Two. As a prelude to the discussion of the role of acclamations in emperor-pleb relations, it outlines how both emperors and plebs used gestures in their interactions. Thus in the early empire gesture became a tool of both speakers and audiences.

Chapter 3 enumerates the various types of acclamations used by the urban plebs, and the situations in which their use was judged most appropriate. It opens by considering the changed political circumstances of the empire and how acclamations took on a new, more influential significance at the very time when formal and informal power was being concentrated in the person of the emperor. The most common and least volatile purpose of acclamations was to greet and praise the emperor whenever he made a public appearance. This greeting could take a variety of forms ranging from simple applause to complex chants, but it was a mandatory acknowledgment of his presence. Audiences could also react with acclamations during the course of an oration and in this way express their approval or disapproval of the speaker's message. In addition, because of their versatility acclamations offered a way for the plebs to present petitions to, or even make criticisms of, the emperor. Often this type of acclamation was coupled with praise and was delivered at public entertainments. An elaborate but informal set of rules and expectations quickly developed around imperial appearances at entertainments, and to some degree these events became the designated setting for the people to express their opinions to the emperor.

Chapter 4 builds on this description of the ways in which acclamations were used in order to explore the characteristics of this method of communication and the implications of these characteristics for the distribution and maintenance of power in early imperial Rome. Audiences at Rome were fluent in the language of acclamations because they had learned a series of formulas that could be adapted to various situations. Spontaneous demonstrations were possible largely because of this body of shared knowledge. Moreover, many acclamations were based on easily learned rhythmic patterns that further enhanced their flexibility and ease of memorization and use. These characteristics enabled the urban plebs to improvise upon the basic formulas and to convey a variety of messages. The use of acclamations brought with it benefits and risks for both emperor and plebs. The shouts of the people were an important component in establishing and maintaining the emperor's legitimacy and prestige, but their protests could also undermine his position. Acclamations were a way for the people to participate in politics and gain material benefits, but there was always the danger of pushing the emperor too far and incurring his anger, which was sometimes accompanied by lethal retaliation.

A Note on Sources and Methodology

Since this study extends from the very late republic through the early empire, roughly from Cicero's ascendancy to Trajan, I have tried to rely as much as possible on contemporary sources. Thus, Cicero, Tacitus, Pliny, Suetonius, Juvenal, and Martial figure prominently in the citations. The accounts of some later authors, most notably Dio Cassius, have also been used. Where possible, I have also incorporated nonliterary evidence to supplement or corroborate the material supplied by the ancient authors. The rhetorical manuals of Cicero and Quintilian offer in-depth treatment of gesture, but much of the evidence presented in these and in later chapters is admittedly anecdotal. Moreover, no single ancient author wrote an extended commentary on the use and characteristics of acclamations. Therefore, my method has been to build up an accumulation of evidence from a variety of literary sources, which, when considered as a whole, will have cumulative force. Whereas one stray incident involving gesture or acclamations may represent an aberration, a collection of such incidents is indicative of a meaningful pattern.

Such an approach has its perils, however. Using and mixing together multiple sources to argue a point carry the danger that passages may be cited out of context, or that such a format will not take into account the peculiar biases inherent in any source. The various authors wrote from widely disparate social, political, and economic perspectives, with dramatically different goals and aspirations, in both prose and verse, and in a variety of literary forms from history and biography to satire and the difficult-to-categorize works of Suetonius. Indiscriminately mingling individual anecdotes from Tacitus's historical works with the comic fiction of Juvenal is obviously problematic. Several justifications of this method may, however, be offered.

First, the multiplicity of voices ensures that no one author's viewpoint dominates my analysis. Second, there is the apparent paradox that because most of the texts I use were not written specifically on the topics in which I am interested, their comments on these topics are more reliable. Much of the cited material is casually mentioned by authors such as Tacitus in the course of discussions about other subjects. Whereas any comments he might make explicitly about the power of the senate, for example, obviously need to be weighed in light of his broader agenda and personal prejudices, a stray comment about a type of gesture that a senator made while speaking does not carry as heavy an ideological baggage. In other words, the anecdotal nature of the evidence is frequently a strength rather than a weakness, since what an author briefly says about a gesture while discussing something else may represent a nugget of unselfconscious truth couched within a conscious fabrication. By the same token, accounts such as that of Suetonius or even the *Historia Augusta* can contain relevant information. Since this study is not so much about specific public events, but rather about how communication at such events in general was conducted, even wholly fictitious accounts may contain important information about how communication was conducted at similar historically real occurrences.

Abbreviations

Abbreviations used for primary source authors and works are generally those found at the beginning of the *Oxford Latin Dictionary* of P. Glare and the *Greek-English Lexicon* of H. Liddell and R. Scott. Where Latin and Greek quotations differ from the standard versions in the Oxford Classical Texts, it will be indicated in the text. Most translations are based on those in the Loeb series, although usually modified by me.

In reference to coins, the following abbreviations are used:

BMC   H. Mattingly, *Coins of the Roman Empire in the British Museum*, 6 vols. (1923–50)

RIC   H. Mattingly and E. Sydenham, *Roman Imperial Coinage*, 9 vols. (1923–81)

Strack   P. L. Strack, *Untersuchungen zur römischen Reichsprägung des zweiten Jahrhunderts*, 3 vols. (1931–37)

In general, for titles of periodicals listed in the bibliography I have employed the standard abbreviations in *L'Année Philologique*.

PART 1

SPEAKERS

> Action is eloquence, and the eyes of th' ignorant
> More learnèd than the ears.
> —Shakespeare, *Coriolanus* 3.2

One

Eloquence without Words: Uses of Gesture in Roman Oratory

The primary purpose of upper-class Roman education was to prepare young men for public life, and because of the central place that oratory held in this life, the central goal of this education, particularly from the late republic onward, was to produce effective public speakers.[1] Roman boys proceeded from the study of literature, which included memorizing and reciting long passages of poetry, to the crowning phase of their education, the study of rhetoric. Their initial lessons in rhetorical composition involved imagining themselves in the place of a famous mythological or historical figure at some crucial episode in his life and writing an appropriate oration. Eventually the students moved on to essays on historical themes or problems and ultimately to preparation for delivering original declamations in the lawcourts.

For these later stages of their training they had access to a body of handbooks written about the art of rhetoric, which typically outlined the characteristics of the ideal orator. A great deal is known about what qualities were thought to make up the perfect orator, since several didactic handbooks of rhetoric are extant from the late republic and early empire. The most significant of these are the extremely detailed *Institutio Oratoria* by Quintilian, and three manuals by the man usually considered to be the greatest Roman orator, Marcus Tullius Cicero: the *De Oratore*, the *Brutus*, and the *Orator*. The figure of Cicero dominates the study of rhetoric, since not only were the power and skill of his oratory widely recognized, but he also represented the heights attainable in Roman society for one who could master the art of public speaking. Indeed, his skill at oratory was primarily responsible for his rise to prominence. Cicero was a *novus homo*, a "new man," an outsider who was not a member of one of Rome's powerful families and who had no famous ancestors. He was able to overcome this considerable handicap and eventually rise to the highest elected magistracy almost entirely as a result of his mastery of the skills of public speaking.

Although speeches such as those that made Cicero's reputation were originally given orally in public, many modern analyses of Roman rhetoric tend to treat existing speeches only as written documents, focusing on the technical rhetorical components of the structure and word choice of the speeches, while largely ignoring their actual delivery. The difficulty of reconstructing this aspect of ancient oratory is reflected in the standard modern text on Roman rhetoric, which devotes less than twenty pages out of nearly seven hundred to the topic of delivery.[2] When we turn to the ancient sources themselves, a very different picture of Roman rhetoric emerges. Their attitude is best exemplified by an anecdote that Cicero, Quintilian, and nearly every other commentator on oratory repeated concerning Demosthenes, the greatest Greek orator. When asked to list the three most important elements of rhetoric, Demosthenes replied that the single most important element of great oratory was delivery, the second was delivery, and the third was also delivery.[3] Roman rhetoricians conventionally divided their discipline into five portions: invention (*inventio*), arrangement (*collocatio*), style (*elocutio*), memory (*memoria*), and delivery (*actio*).[4] Delivery itself was formally defined as having two components, voice tone and gesture.[5] Gesture, therefore, formed an integral part of ancient oratory, which in turn was one of the most prominent features of life at Rome.[6]

Roman rhetoricians, while deeply indebted to their Greek predecessors, probably elaborated the most on earlier theory when discussing the topic of delivery. In his work on rhetoric, Aristotle emphasizes the importance of delivery but repeats several times that the subject has not yet been addressed in any rhetorical treatise (Arist. *Rh.* 3.1.3, 3.1.5). Furthermore, for Aristotle, delivery is chiefly a matter of voice tone, and his comments on gesture are mostly restricted to facial expression and a few instinctive gestures, such as shaking the fists when angry (3.1.4, 3.7.10, 3.16.10). The first author to address delivery in detail was apparently Theophrastus of Eresus, who composed a now lost work on the subject. Although the extent of his treatment and its influence on later Roman writing are difficult to assess, Theophrastus did include bodily movements in his analysis.[7]

When one turns to Roman rhetoric and attempts to recreate the gestures used by Roman orators, by far the most useful resource is the rhetorical handbook of Quintilian.[8] He devotes much of the penultimate section of his work to an extraordinarily detailed description of oratorical gestures and their proper use. He bluntly asserts that a mediocre speech accompanied by excellent delivery will be infinitely more effective in influencing its audience than even the best speech if poorly delivered, an idea echoed by other writers (Quint. *Inst.* 11.3.5; Cic. *Orat.* 56, *De Orat.* 213). The story of Demosthenes practicing his speeches with a mouth full of pebbles in order to clarify his enunciation is well known, but he also practiced all of his speeches before a full-length mirror because he realized that what his body said was as important as his words (Quint. *Inst.* 11.3.68). Quintilian noted that gestures could convey meaning without words and constituted an entire language that the orator can and must master in addition to his control of words. He commented that for the mute, gestures took the place of language, and for the orator, they were no less valuable (11.3.65–66). Cicero too spoke of the *sermo corporis*, the "language of the body," which was at least as influential in swaying an audience as the words of the oration (Cic. *Orat.* 56). The idea in antiquity of the existence of a natural language of gesture can perhaps be found in Lucretius's account of the early days of humanity. He described an era before the development of speech when communication was accomplished nonverbally through gestures and inarticulate noises (Lucr. *De Rerum Natura* 5.1031).

When a Roman spoke before an audience, he was simultaneously communicating in two languages, one verbal and one nonverbal, and the messages the two conveyed could be identical, complementary, or different. For Roman orators gesture was a powerful rhetorical tool with which to reinforce and gloss the verbal component of their performances. This chapter will consider the different ways in which Roman orators used gesture in their public speeches, the rules set down in the rhetorical handbooks that governed this usage, and the possibilities that this nonverbal language offered for augmenting the persuasive power of a speech.

Emotion

Gestures were routinely used by orators to complement the meaning of their words. This was probably the most important function of gesture and usually took the form of adding emotional coloring to an oration. Certain gestures were associated with various emotions so that as an orator spoke, his body offered a separate and continuous commentary on what emotions the words were intended to provoke. In the *De Oratore* Cicero likened the constituent parts of the human body to the strings of a lyre and suggested that just as various notes tend to evoke various emotions in a listener, certain gestures, expressions, and movements will elicit specific emotional responses in an observer (Cic. *De Orat.* 3.216). The orator's goal was to identify these emotional "lyre strings" and learn how to "play" his own body to arouse the desired responses in his audience. It is further stated that men more often make decisions based on emotions such as hate, love, sorrow, rage, fear, and hope than on logic, authority, or the law. Due to this tendency, the orator is advised not to dwell on erudite philosophical arguments but instead to direct his appeals to the feelings and emotions of his listeners: "nothing else is more important" (2.178). The ultimate goal of oratory was to persuade an audience, and in order to do this, it was vital to incite the emotions of the audience in a way favorable to the speaker's cause. According to Cicero, "To sway [the audience's emotions] is victory; for among all things it is the single most important in winning verdicts" (*Orat.* 69).[9] The perceived ability of gestures to stimulate emotions made the systematic study of bodily movement a central focus of rhetorical training.[10]

In his discussion of gesture Quintilian proceeded from the head to the feet, describing how each part of the body can be used, what motions are regarded as permissible, and what emotion is expressed by each movement (Quint. *Inst.* 11.3.68–149). He offered a code with rules as rigid as those for the composition of a speech, in which each twitch of an eyebrow or bend of a finger had a specific and widely recognized emotional content. The head received considerable attention, and he stressed especially the eyes and the power of the gaze to convey a variety of feelings. A glance could express emotions such as grief, happiness, anger, and pride, and an orator could also use his glance to direct supplications or threats toward others. Quintilian instructed the orator to be aware of the importance of the gaze, since his audience will focus its attention on the speaker's eyes (11.3.72–77). Whereas certain emotions conveyed by the eyes could enhance the appeal of an oration, others could detract from it. Thus, an orator should never allow his gaze to suggest lasciviousness or sloth, and his eyes should never appear fixed or glazed. In order to make full use of the power of the eyes one should not squint, and "no one but an idiot" would speak with them closed (11.3.76). Quintilian also discussed in detail the proper use of the eyebrows, lips, neck, and even the nostrils. Most of the directions concerning these parts of the head consist of negative injunctions, such as to avoid waggling one's eyebrows indecorously, raising one while lowering the other, wrinkling or twitching the nostrils, snorting loudly, picking one's nose, protruding or smacking the lips, licking them frequently, or letting them curl or droop in an unsightly fashion (eyebrows: 76–80; neck: 82–83; lips and nostrils: 80–81).

While the directions concerning the head and particularly the eyes were quite detailed, overwhelmingly the most attention was given to the movements of the fingers and arms. The gestures made with these parts of the body were both the most important and the most versatile, and it is not surprising that iconographic depictions of orators on sculptural reliefs, on coinage, and in statues all stressed arm and hand gestures.[11] Quintilian introduced his ac-

Figure 1. Gesture for use during exhortation

Figure 2. Gesture for use while presenting arguments

count of hand gestures by comparing the eloquence achieved with words to the range of expression available through gestures. He flatly asserted that "the hands may almost be said to speak. Do we not use them to demand, promise, summon, dismiss, threaten, supplicate, express aversion or fear, question or deny? Do we not use them to indicate joy, sorrow, hesitation, confession, penitence, and measure quantity, number, and time?" (11.3.86–87). An orator spoke with both his mouth and his hands, and he had to learn how to make his nonverbal vocabulary as eloquent as his verbal.

Quintilian described specific gestures by which to express a spectrum of emotions with the hands and arms. He enumerated nearly two dozen hand gestures, including some that were minor variations upon a set of basic finger positions. The arrangement of the fingers ranged from the simple, such as holding up the hand with the fingers slightly cupped, which was a gesture used to accompany words of exhortation, to the very complex, such as gripping the top joint of the index finger with the tips of the thumb and middle finger while curving the remaining two fingers slightly toward the palm but not touching it, and with the little finger curved to a more pronounced degree than its neighbor (simple: 11.3.103; complex: 11.3.95; see Figs. 1, 2). This awkward curling of the fingers was one of the prescribed gestures to use while making arguments, and Quintilian also offered minor variations that rendered it more emphatic. The emotions for which he provided precise hand gestures include wonder, admiration, surprise, approval, adoration, assent, praise, indignation, fear, regret, anger, aversion, reproach, commiseration, and horror.

Some of the gestures used to express these emotions seem natural and almost universal. For example, to clench the hand and press it to the chest denoted profound grief or anger (Fig. 3). Quintilian commented that while holding his hand in this position, an orator might speak a despairing line such as, "What should I do now?" (11.3.104). Some gestures seem to have derived their meaning from cultural beliefs or attitudes. For example, to express horror of a person or idea the orator was instructed to turn both of his palms to the left (11.3.114; Fig. 4). Since the left hand or side often had negative connotations, there was probably a link between these beliefs and this gesture. Similarly, to indicate aversion, the right hand was thrust out to the left while the left shoulder was brought forward and the head turned to the right (11.3.113; Fig. 5). In this case the emotional meaning of aversion was literally acted out by the orator's physically turning away from his left side. Conversely, to demonstrate adoration, the orator could employ the common ges-

Figure 3. Gesture denoting anger or grief

ture of religious invocation and stretch out both arms toward the person or object of veneration (11.3.115; Fig. 6). Other motions seem rather more arbitrary in meaning, such as moving the hand toward the mouth while converging the fingertips, a gesture that Quintilian said should be used to denote either mild surprise, indignation, or entreaty (11.3.103; Fig. 7). Ideally, the orator's body language should provoke the appropriate emotion in his listeners and thus render them amenable to his message. Even Cicero himself admitted to being susceptible to a skilled practitioner of gestures, as when he conceded to another orator that "your wagging finger made me tremble with emotion" (Cic. *De Orat.* 2.188).

Figure 4. Gesture denoting horror

All the rhetorical handbooks caution that motions should not become overly violent or excessive, causing a speaker to flail about ungracefully. Quintilian offered several examples of orators indulging in excessive gesticulation and commented that it is hazardous to stand too near such a man because of the danger of being struck by his sudden and violent motions (Quint. *Inst.* 11.3.118). On the whole, gestures should be fairly restrained with most of the actions being performed by the right arm and hand, and the left employed only for particularly emphatic movements. The left hand should never be used alone but only

11

Figure 5. Gesture denoting aversion

in conjunction with the right, and motions that proceeded from the speaker's left to right were judged to be most aesthetically pleasing (11.3.112–15). Furthermore, the range of motion for the arms should be contained within the space between the waist and the level of the eyes. Several gestures broke this rule yet were still approved, such as the outstretched arms of invocation or the raised right arm of exhortation. This last gesture was permissible as long as the orator did not attempt to augment the effect by causing his open hand to tremble, an addition that Quintilian derided as a theatrical trick inappropriate for orators. Most impor-

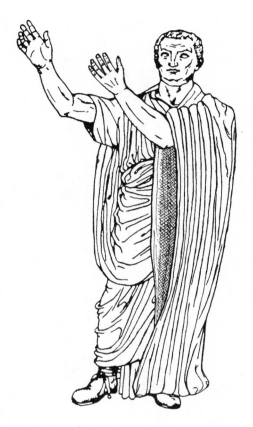

Figure 6. Gesture denoting adoration or invocation

tant among these more emphatic gestures was the practice of violently slapping the thigh with the palm of the right hand in order to express anger or indignation, and indeed, this was a favorite action of Cicero's (11.3.123; see also Plut. *G. Gracch.* 2). In general, according to Quintilian, gestures such as these, which involved greater physical movement or extended dramatically beyond the trunk of the orator's body, were best reserved for "topics of importance, or themes of joy or horror" (Quint. *Inst.* 11.3.116).

Many of the hand positions were static. Once the desired gesture had been formed, the orator held his fingers and arms completely

13

Figure 7. Gesture denoting mild surprise, indignation, or entreaty

rigid. For others, movement of the fingers was an integral component of the signal, without which it was not complete. The prescribed gesture to express a feeling of wonder illustrates the
gracefulness inherent in some of these motions. The orator held up
his right hand with all of the fingers extended and then curled them
back into the palm one by one, beginning with the little finger.
Once all the fingers had been brought to the palm, the movement
was then reversed by opening the fingers again, but in reverse
sequence, while at the same time gently rotating the entire hand
(11.3.100; Fig. 8). Some gestures combined a static finger position
with movements of the entire arm. When an orator wished to

portray modesty, he converged the tips of the thumb and the next three fingers, and then moved his hand toward the area of his mouth or chest. Once he had drawn his hand near his mouth, the orator then allowed his arm and hand to relax downward toward the ground (Fig. 9). This, according to Quintilian, was the gesture made by Cicero during the opening of his *Pro Archia* when he spoke the self-deprecating line, "If I have any talent, I know how little it is" (11.3.96–97; *Pro Arch*. 1.1).

In general, motion was divided into six types, forward, backward, to the right, to the left, and up and down, each of which "has significance," though the meanings are not specified (Quint. *Inst.* 11.3.105). Quintilian suggested that circular movements really constitute a seventh kind of motion and should be added to the list (11.3.105).[12] Sometimes the meaning of a single gesture could vary according to the context in which it was made. To cup the hand and lightly touch the chest with the fingertips could indicate exhortation, reproach, or commiseration depending upon the situation (Fig. 10). This motion seems to have been reserved for particularly emphatic situations, since Quintilian noted that an orator should use this gesture sparingly, "on rare occasions" (11.3.124).

Although an orator should exercise some restraint in his movements, not to gesticulate enough indicated a lack of emotional engagement on the part of the orator and was seen as a grave error. In a revealing passage Cicero berated one orator for not using enough gestures: "And you, Marcus Calidius, . . . there was no sign of agitation, neither in your mind nor your body. Did you strike your forehead? Did you slap your thigh, or at the very least stamp your foot? In fact, so far from inflaming my emotions, I nearly fell asleep on the spot" (Cic. *Brut.* 278). This passage explicitly links gesture and emotion. In addition, Cicero spoke approvingly even of very sudden and violent motions, such as foot stamping and striking the head, because such dramatic gestures were particularly effective in exciting the emotions of the audience.

Adding to the complexity of the system was the fact that multiple gestures sometimes had the same emotional meaning, although the different gestures in such a set often seem to have been used to indicate varying intensities of emotion. An orator had to match the

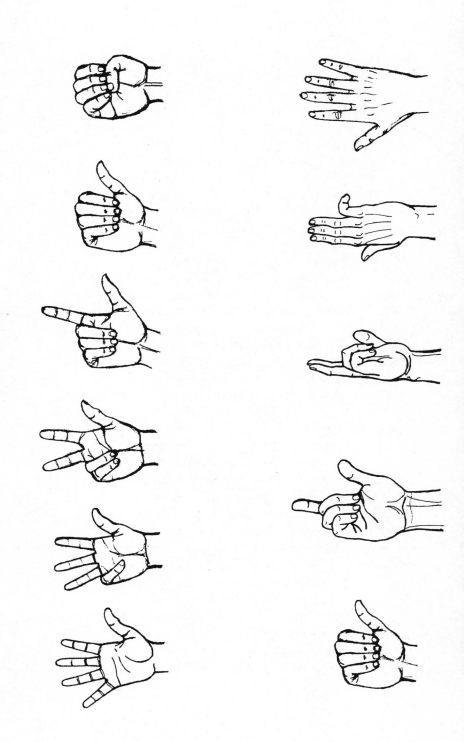

emotional content of his words with the proper gesture, one that not only expressed just the appropriate feeling, but also denoted the desired nuance of emotional intensity. An orator's motions also had to be timed to coincide exactly with his words. The movement of the hand had to begin when the corresponding verbal sentence or phrase began and end exactly when it ended, so that there would not be jarring discontinuities between the emotions or ideas articulated in the words and those expressed by the hands. Orators were warned neither to anticipate their words with their gestures nor to allow their words to outpace their gestures (Quint. *Inst.* 11.3.106).

The vocabulary of gesture that prospective orators had to learn was clearly a complex one in which the correct finger posture had to be combined with the appropriate motions in order to convey the desired emotion. The system was elaborate, but because of the perceived link between gesture and emotion, it offered yet one more method by which an orator could hope to persuade his audience. Furthermore, since the goal of oratory was to appeal to the emotions of the listener, gesture provided a direct path for the speaker to work on the emotions of his audience. Adding an emotional gloss to the verbal content of a speech was an important function of gesture in Roman oratory, but it was not the only purpose for which Roman orators used their nonverbal vocabulary.

Indication

Another gesture that orators used was the most basic of human motions, pointing. Roman orators used their hands to point at themselves, at objects and places, or at another person about whom they were speaking. A simple motion toward the chest without actually making contact was the prescribed manner for referring to oneself, and directly pointing at someone else was acceptable as well (Quint. *Inst.* 11.3.89). Orators could also use indicative motions to refer to objects and locations. The Roman indicative gesture was the same as ours: the index finger was extended rigidly while

Figure 8 (opposite). Gesture denoting wonder

Figure 9. Gesture denoting modesty or deprecation

the others were folded under the thumb (11.3.94; Fig. 11). Pointing at the ground, however, signified insistence, and a variation of the pointing motion made toward the shoulder indicated affirmation. Pointing with the thumb was considered unbecoming for an orator, although Quintilian admitted that this vulgar gesture was widely used (11.3.104). He asserted that pointing motions are employed by orators as a substitute for adverbs and pronouns in order to indicate places and people (11.3.87). An imaginative orator could use such gestures to point out features of the physical surroundings, which were exploited to enhance or support the message of the speech. Pointing motions either could be used in conjunction with the words of an oration, or such a gesture could even take the place of the words and refer to an object or person not verbally mentioned. The physical environment where speeches and assemblies were held could therefore function both as a complementary and an alternative language for communication.

The buildings and spaces themselves that formed the back-

Figure 10. Gesture denoting exhortation, reproach, or commiseration

ground or setting were often loaded with symbolic meanings or powerful associations, either due to the nature of an edifice itself or to elements of its decorative scheme. An orator speaking in a temple, for example, could simply gesture toward the cult statue to allude to virtues associated with that deity. The area of the Forum in which most public speeches were delivered was a space bounded by and composed of a vast assemblage of potent visual symbols of Roman religion, culture, and history. Roman orators speaking in this space were surrounded by statues, temples, war trophies, altars, sacred sites, monuments, buildings, and other physical objects possessing powerful emotional associations with Roman religion

19

Figure 11. Gesture used for pointing at persons, places, or things

and identity. The pediment, roof, and steps of Roman temples, such as the Temple of Jupiter Capitolinus, were festooned with statues of gods and deities.[13] By a simple pointing motion, a speaker could use these settings to emphasize, elaborate upon, or even convey messages.

The senate house, where so many memorable orations occurred, was an officially consecrated sacred space. Unfortunately, little is known of the interior decoration of the Curia Hostilia in which most of Cicero's speeches to the senate were delivered, since it was completely burned down in 52 B.C. by Clodius's followers (Cic. *Mil.* 90; Asc. *Mil.* 29; Dio 40.49.2–3). One side of this senate house had featured a painting of the Romans victorious over the Carthaginians, and this memento of a notable victory could have served as a convenient reference for orators (Pliny *Hist. Nat.* 35.22; Cic. *In Vat.* 9.21). The new senate house, the Curia Julia, contained a large statue of Victory and several paintings.[14] This statue of Victory, dedicated by Augustus in 29 B.C., was a famous monument and remained in the senate house for several centuries (Dio 51.22.1–2; Pliny, *Hist. Nat.* 35.27).[15] The paintings portrayed an old man leaning on a stick, a two-horse chariot, and a depiction of Nemea clutching a palm branch and seated upon a lion, the symbolic representation of victory at the Nemean Games (Pliny *Hist. Nat.* 35.27, 131).[16] Two years later a golden shield was set up in the curia honoring Augustus and inscribed with the virtues of *clementia, iustitia,* and *pietas* (*Res Gest.* 34.2).[17] All of these monuments would have offered useful reference points for orators.

During the late republic and early empire many meetings of the senate were also held in temples, including the Temples of Castor, of Concord, and of Jupiter Optimus Maximus on the Capitoline Hill. This last temple was so stuffed with military trophies, statues, and religious offerings that at one point many of them had to be cleared out (Livy 40.51.3). Included among these was a portrait statue of Scipio Africanus (Val. Max. 8.15.1). The Temple of Concord had been the site of the trial of the Catilinarian conspirators, and during the imperial period at least some senate sessions were held there.[18] This temple amply illustrates the richness of imagery available to orators in such surroundings. After its restoration by Tiberius, the interior contained statues of Vesta, Juno, Latona and her children, Diana, Asclepius, Hygieia, Mars, Mercury, Ceres, Jupiter, and Minerva, two statues of Apollo, paintings of Marsyas, Liber Pater, and Cassandra, a gem collection, and four obsidian elephants.[19] The exterior was equally elaborate and featured more statues of gods, perhaps including the Capitoline triad, Ceres, Diana, and Victories on the roof, as well as statues of Hercules and Mercury flanking the steps.[20] A Tiberian sestertius captures the busy exterior of this temple and gives a vivid impression of the elaborateness of Roman temple facades (Fig. 12).[21] Such a cornu-

Figure 12. Sestertius of Tiberius with Temple of Concord
(Courtesy of Fototeca Unione, American Academy in Rome, 3549)

copia of potent symbols could be, and certainly was, exploited by orators such as Cicero.[22]

Orations given before the senate in these temples could draw on a rich array of visual symbols, but orators speaking to the plebs in the Forum had access to an even more abundant variety of monuments. Just as there was a choice of places where the senate could convene, there were various platforms from which an orator could address crowds in the area of the Forum. The old republican rostra was in the area of the Comitium at the northwest end of the Forum. There may also have been some sort of platform during the republican period on the site where the later Rostra Augusti was built, and perhaps another at the opposite end of the Forum where the Temple of the Deified Caesar stood.[23] After the naval victory at Antium in 338 B.C. the eponymous captured ships' beaks were affixed to a platform in the Forum (Livy 8.14.12; Pliny *Hist. Nat.* 34.20). Renovations of this platform were begun by Julius Caesar, who moved it to its present location, and the work was finished posthumously by Octavian (Dio 43.49, 56.34). He dedicated it in 42 B.C. from which time it was known as the Rostra Augusti (Diod. 12.26; Asc. *Mil.* 12). The old rostra was decorated with numerous statues of famous Roman heroes (Cic. *Sest.* 38.83). A group of half-size statues commemorated ambassadors who had been slain while on state service, including Tullus Cloelius, Lucius Roscius, Spurius Nautius, and Gaius Fulcinius, all killed by the Fidenates; Publius Junius and Tiberius Coruncanius, both murdered by the Illyrian queen Teuta; and Gnaeus Octavius, an ambassador to the Seleucid king Antiochus IV (Pliny *Hist. Nat.* 34.23–24; Livy 4.17, 8.13; Cic. *Phil.* 9.7.16). At least some of these statues seem to have been moved from the old to the new rostra, and it is sometimes difficult to determine exactly which would have been present at any given time. Because the statues listed by Pliny were still visible in his time, these were clearly moved from rostra to rostra during the various reconstructions and renovations. Also on or around the rostra were equestrian statues of Sulla, Pompey, Julius Caesar, and Octavian (Vell. Pat. 2.61; App. *BC* 1.97).

In the Comitium were many other statues, including ones of the augur Attus Navius, the philosopher Pythagoras, the Greek leader Alcibiades, Hermodorus the interpreter of the Twelve Tables, the Roman champion Hostius Hostilius, and the mythical hero Horatius Cocles.[24] Nearby were columns with statues celebrating the naval victories of Maenius over the Antiates and of Gaius Duilius over the Carthaginians and a rostrated column bearing a golden statue of Octavian.[25] Some other monuments in or near this area were a copy of the Twelve Tables, and statues of Romulus, Camillus, Hercules, Lucius Minucius, a prefect of the grain supply, Quintus Marcius Tremulus, victor over the Samnites, and three Sibyls.[26] Additional important statues and monuments adorned the central area of the Forum, including the Lacus Curtius, the Lapis Niger, a statue of Marsyas, and the Ficus Navia as well as the sacred vine and fig and olive trees.[27] By the mid-second century B.C. commemorative statues in the area of the Forum had proliferated so much that the censors Publius Cornelius Scipio and Marcus Popilius found it necessary to remove all statues in the area that had not been authorized by a decree of the people or the senate.[28] A not insubstantial part of the crowd at public speeches in the Forum consisted of statues of great heroes of Roman history, and nearly every historical or religious allusion in a speech could have been matched to a corresponding statue or monument.

The Roman reverence for tradition and the past is well known and is summed up by a popular Roman phrase, *mos maiorum*, "the custom of our forefathers." This antiquarian ethos pervaded Roman society in a variety of ways, such as the practice at funerals of parading the *imagines* of illustrious ancestors. Veneration of the past extended to the great figures in Rome's history, who were frequently invoked as *exempla* of virtues and as models of proper behavior to be emulated. Literature and art were filled with allusions to the heroes of Rome's past, both historical and mythological. The supposed achievements and virtues of these men were codified during the early empire in literary works such as Livy's history and Virgil's poetry and in stone in public monuments such as the Forum of Augustus, whose colonnades were crammed with statues of *summi viri*, famous men both mythological and historical from Rome's past.[29] The area of the Forum was packed with images of these men, and so too were the speeches of the orators who spoke there.

Although explicit literary references to exploitation of features of the environment are scarce, enough exist to indicate that Cicero and others did take advantage of the symbolic richness of their surroundings and made direct verbal and nonverbal allusions to them. A famous example that seems to have particularly impressed the ancient rhetoricians occurred in a speech by Gaius Gracchus in which he emphasized his unhappy situation by repeatedly asking, "Where can I turn?" After each repetition he suggested a destination that should have offered him refuge, such as the Capitol or his home, and then explained why he could not go there. Gracchus acted out his pleas by stretching out his arms toward each failed sanctuary in turn. This incident is cited by both Quintilian and

Cicero as a masterful use of gesture to arouse sympathy in the audience (Quint. *Inst.* 11.3.115; Cic. *De Orat.* 3.214). Cicero himself repeated the tactic in his *Pro Milone* when, according to Quintilian, he invoked the hills and groves of Alba with a similar gesture of his arms (Cic. *Pro Mil.* 85; Quint. *Inst.* 11.3.115). Later in this passage Cicero directly called upon Jupiter Latiaris, whose temple was also located on the Alban mount.[30] The appeal to the god which begins with the address, "You, Jupiter . . . ," was another obvious occasion for Cicero to hold out his arms to the god in a posture of religious invocation (Cic. *Pro Mil.* 85).

Cicero's Catilinarian orations demonstrate how an orator could exploit the site of a speech to embellish its persuasiveness.[31] To deliver the first *Catilinarian*, Cicero convened the senate in the Temple of Jupiter Stator, an act that in itself was meaningful, since the temple commemorated the salvation of Rome from an enemy, and in the speech Cicero represented Catiline as another enemy threatening the city. Twice in the speech Cicero directly addressed the cult statue of Jupiter within the temple, including a formal prayer seeking the god's assistance (Cic. *Catil.* 1.11.33). These appeals, and particularly the prayer, would have been accompanied by appropriate gestures. Cicero chose this temple for the location of his oration at least partly so that he could take advantage of its symbolic association of preserving the city from enemies, and in addition he was able to make use of the potent visual aids within the temple, most notably the cult statue itself. Cicero's speeches often contained direct appeals and prayers either to the gods collectively or to specific deities. Particularly for speeches in the Forum there would have been visible to Cicero and his audience a statue or temple of the appropriate god to whom he could direct his words. For example, in the *Pro Lege Manilia* given from the rostra, Cicero included in his closing statement the invocation, "I appeal to the gods, and particularly to the ones who watch over this sacred site" (Cic. *Man.* 24). The many similar passages in his other speeches presented numerous opportunities for accompanying gestures of invocation.

When possible, Cicero even altered his surroundings in order to use them to advantage in his speeches. Just before his third oration against Catiline, which was delivered to the people in the Forum, Cicero had a newly completed statue of Jupiter erected so that it was prominently visible from the Forum. In the course of his speech he alluded to the statue and got rhetorical mileage out of it by asking those in the crowd how they could stand by and not take action when under the very eyes of the god. He elaborated on the shame they would feel if the god were allowed to continue to witness the plots of Catiline and no one opposed him. In one passage he referred to "that statue which you now see," and certainly accompanied his words with a pointing gesture toward the statue (Cic. *Catil.* 3.7.20). In this example Cicero had maximized the effectiveness of his oration by arranging for an appropriate prop to be set up in the Forum. Just as a modern speaker might employ posters or slides for the purpose of providing illustrations for his talk, so Cicero ensured that he would have a visual aid available to supplement the verbal component of his performance. Of course, Cicero's visual aid was far more potent than any slide, since it was not merely an object to look at but was itself the sacrosanct visible manifestation of a god.

An orator's exploitation of his environment did not always have to be serious or reverential; he could make reference to the surroundings for humorous purposes as well. Cicero in the *De Oratore* has Gaius Julius Caesar Strabo, one of the characters in this dialogue, deliver an analysis of the use of humor by orators. In the course of a speech against Helvius Mancia, Strabo recounts how he spoke the words, "Now I will demonstrate what type of man you are," at which point Mancia demanded, "Show me, I beg you!" (Cic. *De Orat.* 2.266). In reply, Strabo said nothing but merely pointed at a Cimbrian shield captured by Marius that hung below the shops on the northeast side of the Forum in front of the Basilica Aemilia. This particular shield bore a painting of a grotesque Gaul with a twisted body, flabby cheeks, and protuberant tongue. The gesture caused the audience to erupt into laughter at Mancia's expense because the figure bore a striking resemblance to Mancia.[32] This incident demonstrates not only the range of uses to which a clever orator could put his surroundings, but also how a skilled orator could deal with hecklers and turn their comments against them.

These shops, the *tabernae novae,* and their counterparts on the opposite side of the Forum, the *veterae,* were yet another source of visual aids.[33] Although sections of shops burned down repeatedly and were rebuilt in various forms, making it impossible to determine exactly what decor they had at a given time, there was a tradition of decorating the shops with triumphal shields. In 310 B.C. the predecessors of the *novae,* called the *argentariae,* were all presented with the beautiful gilded armor and shields that had been captured from the Samnites. This armor had caused such a sensation when paraded at the triumph celebrating the victory that it was given to the *tabernae* owners to be displayed permanently in the Forum by being hung on their shops (Livy 9.40). How much of this survived until the late republic is unknown, but as illustrated by Cicero's story, the tradition of placing triumphal shields on these structures was alive and well at least as late as the time of Marius, and offered a range of interesting visual images ripe for exploitation by any orator ingenious enough to find a way to make use of them.

Orators' speeches were often compared with theatrical presentations, and this metaphor is valid not just because both orators and actors performed before audiences and used stylized gestures, but also because both gave thought as to how best to use the "stage" on which they would appear, and then provided that stage with appropriate props.[34] Cicero explicitly equated a *contio,* a public assembly, with a stage that offered rich opportunities for manipulation and pretense (Cic. *De Amic.* 97). Probably the most famous use of a prop by an orator was the fresh Libyan figs that Cato the Elder pretended to drop "accidentally" from the folds of his toga at the completion of his speech urging the destruction of Carthage. After some senators marveled at their size and beauty, Cato was casually able to add the capstone of his argument—that Carthage was only three days' sail from Rome (Plut. *Cato Maior* 27). Aulus Gabinius also seems to have prepared a visual prop to reinforce the message of his words when in 67 B.C. he denounced the extravagant luxury of Lucius Lucullus in a speech while displaying a picture of Lucullus's sumptuous mansion (Cic. *Sest.* 43.93).

In court cases great emotional reactions could be produced by displaying sensational objects related to crimes. Although he expressed neither a favorable nor a negative opinion concerning the decorum of this strategy, Quintilian related that he had witnessed others bringing a variety of objects into the court, including "swords encrusted with blood, bits of bone taken from wounds, and the bloodstained clothing of the victim" (Quint. *Inst.* 6.1.30). Furthermore, he had seen victims remove their dressings in court in order to show their wounds or take off their clothes to bare their scourged bodies to the gaze of the jury. Visual aids, he noted, have "enormous" effects on the observers, and he favorably recounted the exhibition of Julius Caesar's bloody garments at his funeral as an example of the effective use of the clothing from a murder victim. The power of such displays is suggested by the fact that the famous riot culminating in the spontaneous cremation of Caesar's corpse seems to have been sparked not so much by Marcus Antonius's eloquence, but by the exhibition of Caesar's bloody clothing and a wax effigy of his body replete with wounds.[35] Quintilian did not approve, however, of the practice of bringing into the court a picture painted on wood or canvas depicting the crime actually being committed (6.1.32). The fictional recreation of real crimes in pictures and their display seem to have crossed over the line of the permissible in Quintilian's view, although he himself freely admitted that others did not feel such a constraint and that this practice was a well-known trial stratagem.

Orators sometimes went to great lengths to supply their stages with visual aids. After hearing rumors that Nero intended to have him murdered, Galba determined to revolt and have himself proclaimed emperor. As carefully as any actor, he chose the stage for his inauguration and then supplied it with visual props. Since he was a governor in Spain, he regularly conducted judicial affairs from the tribunal in New Carthage, so he chose this as the site for his oration. On the appointed day he mounted the tribunal as if he were going to conduct his usual business, but instead gave an address deploring the condition of the empire under its current ruler who had committed so many crimes. To provide a visual reminder of some of these offenses, he had as many portraits and statues of eminent men who had been murdered by Nero as he could find set up on the front of the tribunal. These inanimate symbols of the victims of

Nero's depredations were supplemented by a living one in the form of a young nobleman whom Galba had had brought from exile in the Balearic Islands "for that very purpose," and whom Galba also displayed on the tribunal alongside the statues (Suet. *Galba* 10). Together the living and inanimate statues served throughout his speech as silent witnesses to Galba's accusations and as graphic reminders of the scope of Nero's crimes.

Perhaps portraits such as these, or Gabinius's picture of Lucullus's mansion, were acceptable because no one could argue that Nero had not killed the men or that the mansion was not luxurious. On the other hand, displaying depictions of crimes that showed the defendants committing the misdeed meant assuming the verdict of the trial before it had been given. Thus, reminders of undisputed facts may have been permissible, but suppositions were not. An image of a dead man also played a prominent role in the trumped-up trial of Rabirius in 63 B.C. for the murder of Saturninus thirty-seven years earlier. The prosecutor, T. Labienus, attempted to resuscitate enthusiasm for Saturninus by parading an *imago* of Saturninus about the city, a performance that culminated when Labienus propped it up on the rostra next to himself during his speech to the people at a *contio* (Cic. *Pro Rab.* 24–25). In instances such as these, Cicero's equation of the *contio* with a stage is certainly justified by the elaborate care that these orators took in preparing and incorporating visual aids into their rhetorical performances.

Galba's employment of a living person as a visual aid was not unprecedented. In the late republic it was a standard practice in the lawcourts to parade the family of the accused before the jury, particularly young children or aged parents, in order to provoke sympathy. In his theoretical works on oratory Cicero readily admitted that this is an effective strategy that he himself had used, even going so far as to cradle a baby in his arms while delivering the peroration. He additionally recounted a case in which he "filled the Forum with sobs and laments" by holding aloft the young son of the defendant (Cic. *Orat.* 38.131). In his extant speeches there is ample evidence of such appeals to pity as well as of the lengths to which an orator would go to summon up sympathy for a defendant's family. In the *Pro Sestio*, for example, Cicero composed his oration to exploit the fact that Publius Sestius had a youthful son, Lucius, who was prominently displayed at the trial and to whom Cicero repeatedly referred. Early in the speech he drew the audience's attention to Lucius "whom you see here" (Cic. *Sest.* 3.6). Later, Cicero even employed Lucius as a speaking prop by forcing him to read out in his, "boyish voice" an honorary decree given to the elder Sestius (4.10). Finally, in his closing statements Cicero shamelessly invoked Lucius a final time: "I am suddenly checked in the very midst of my speech by the sight of my friends. I see Publius Sestius. I see his son, still in childhood, turning toward me with his eyes brimming with tears" (69.144). Each of these verbal references was certainly accompanied by a pointing motion to draw the gaze of the audience to the object of his words and thereby evoke its pity.[36]

In the early empire Augustus used gestures to draw attention to Germanicus's children who were displayed to the crowd at a public entertainment in order to reinforce his legislation aimed at encouraging Romans of the upper classes to have more children (Suet. *Aug.* 34). During his speech to the people in which he announced that he intended to renounce his power, Vitellius also used the device of holding up his small son while commending the boy's safekeeping to the care of his audience, both singling out individuals and asking them collectively to take pity on his young children (Tac. *Hist.* 3.68).

Most orations at Rome probably did not call for such elaborate preparations as those made by Galba, since the veritable forest of statues of famous Romans that cluttered the center of Rome was a ready source of visual aids. A statue of Julius Caesar was exploited by Octavian, who wished to emphasize his status as Caesar's adopted son during the struggle for power following the assassination of Caesar in March 44 B.C. In November of the same year Octavian convened a *contio* of the people to be held in the Forum. In his oration Octavian stressed the achievements of Caesar and presented himself as Caesar's legitimate heir (App. *BC* 3.41.169). At the moment when he was enumerating Caesar's honors, Octavian extended his hand toward the statue of Caesar situated nearby, which probably depicted Caesar crowned with a star, symbolizing his divinity. The statue of Caesar may have been the one that Octavian himself had erected in the Forum a few months earlier. The star on Caesar's brow represented the comet that had appeared during the games held by Octavian in July, which was widely interpreted as a sign of Caesar's divinity (Pliny *Hist. Nat.* 2.93–94). By the use of his pointing gesture, Octavian was thus able to create a potent combination of verbal and visual imagery, simultaneously invoking the memory of Caesar and using it to strengthen his own position. This gesture was described by Cicero in one of the last letters he wrote to Atticus (Cic. *Ad Att.* 16.15). It is suggestive of the importance of such gestures to rhetoric that so skilled an orator as Cicero would explicitly comment on the gestures used by fellow orators, and, indeed, the pointing incident is the only part of this speech that Cicero mentions at all. Cicero's reaction to Octavian's use of the statue is also revealing. He ends his account of the incident with the comment, "What a speech!"

In 92 B.C. Crassus ridiculed the overweening aristocratic pride of an adversary, probably Domitius Ahenobarbus, by pretending to swear first by "your rank" and then by "your lineage." Crassus melodramatically ended by solemnly referring to "your statues" and accompanied his words by stretching out his arm toward them, causing the audience to burst into derisive laughter (Cic. *De Orat.* 242). Interestingly, the narrator of this anecdote seemed to consider Crassus's performance a bit vulgar, due to its reliance on the undignified ploy of voice mimicry, until Crassus's gesture, which was judged to be quite witty.[37] In a similar but more reverential use of statuary, the orator Gaius Albucius Silus gave a speech that invoked the memory of Marcus Brutus and lavishly praised him in a location from which "his [Brutus's] statue was visible" (Suet. *De Rhet.* 6). The fact that the brief secondhand account of this oration bothers at all to note that Brutus's statue was visible indicates the importance attached to the use of visual aids. As these examples illustrate, statues could be used for a variety of purposes, most notably to summon forth a range of responses including pity, reverence, shame, derision, sympathy, and even humor. Orators plainly chose the site of a speech to take advantage of specific honorific monuments, and in the course of the speech the standard way to draw the audience's attention to the statue was not by words but by pointing at it. In most of these incidents the orator did not specifically instruct his listeners to look at the statue, but instead described or invoked the memory of the person in words while simultaneously indicating the statue with a gesture.

A clever orator could even use visual aids to convey messages that he did not explicitly verbalize. Early in the reign of Tiberius, Marcus Hortalus, a destitute grandson of the renowned orator Hortensius, appeared before the senate in order to apply for a grant of money to save his famous family from extinction. On this occasion the senate had convened in the Latin Library on the Palatine, which was decorated with bronze portrait medallions of notable orators. In order to arouse the sympathy of the senate and remind them of his family's glorious past, Hortalus repeatedly glanced at the medallion of his illustrious ancestor Hortensius. He also directed his gaze at the portrait of Augustus, who had previously given one million sesterces in order to revive his family's fortune (Tac. *Ann.* 2.37–38). Thus, completely without words, he was able to use the physical environment both to recall the glorious past of his family and to remind the senate that Augustus had deemed his family worthy of being saved. This is a particularly subtle use of a nonverbal rhetorical strategy, since Hortalus did not even use an obvious physical gesture and never actually pointed at the portraits with his hands. Just his gaze alone, in the form of repeated glances, was sufficient to carry his message to his audience. In Quintilian's catalog of how an orator should use each part of his body, the power and versatility of the eyes was second only to that of the hands. He noted that, by themselves, the eyes can express "supplication, threats, flattery, sorrow, joy, pride, or submission," and that a gaze can convey a great deal of meaning and sometimes can even be more persuasive than an orator's words (Quint. *Inst.* 11.3.72).[38] Hortalus's employment of his gaze to enhance his appeal certainly exemplified the strategy that Quintilian would later systematize in writing. Unfortunately for Hortalus, while his oratorical skill succeeded in arousing the sympathy of the senate, it did not move the miserly Tiberius, who rejected his appeal.

The availability of visual aids could even become a cause for contention between rival orators. On one occasion, Cicero accused his opponent of conniving to prevent the trial from being held during the Ludi Romani because he feared that Cicero would be able to exploit the presence of carts carrying statues of the gods that were used in the festivities (Cic. *Planc.* 83). Cicero even admitted that this had been a shrewd move since he had indeed planned to make these carts a centerpiece of his oration.

The value and reliance that orators placed upon being able to use the environment to appeal to the emotions of their audiences are vividly revealed by the comments of Cicero on an occasion when he could not make use of the accustomed surroundings in the Forum and had to deliver a speech in the confines of a private house. This was Cicero's speech in favor of King Deiotarius of Armenia Minor, the *Pro Rege Deiotaro*, delivered in front of Julius Caesar and a few others in Caesar's house in 45 B.C. In this instance Cicero did not select the place and hence could not control it or alter it to augment the power of his oration. His response to this constraint was to draw attention to it explicitly and hope that his audience would sympathize with his predicament. Thus he inserted into the opening section of this speech a lament that his oration would have been much more powerful and convincing if he had been allowed to deliver it in the space of the Forum, where he could have excited the emotions of a large crowd and where "I would look at the senate house; I would look across the Forum; I would invoke heaven itself. In this environment . . . it would be impossible for my oration to fail" (Cic. *Deiot.* 5–6). Here a nonverbal aspect of delivery, the use of the orator's gaze, which Hortalus employed so effectively, was explicitly mentioned as a powerful oratorical tool, and the invocation of heaven could well be a reference to the practice of speakers alluding to and pointing to the temples and altars present in the Forum, a strategy of which Cicero seems to have been especially fond.

It is also interesting that Cicero included the crowd in the list of factors that could be used to increase the effectiveness of an oration. This remark reinforces the idea that speeches were interactive events in which the interjections and reactions of the audience were important components of the performance itself.[39] This attitude also is mirrored in Cicero's theoretical works on oratory, in which he declared that "a speaker can no more be eloquent without a large audience than a flute player can perform without a flute" (Cic. *De Orat.* 2.338). For Cicero and other Roman orators, the audience was an integral part of the performance. Later in the *Pro Rege Deiotaro* he returned to this theme to protest that his oratorical powers were hobbled by his surroundings, and he specifically drew attention to the situation's negative effects on the most powerful of the five canonical components of rhetoric, delivery. He ended his comments on this subject with the plaintive line, "My delivery [*actio*] is crippled by its surroundings" (Cic. *Deiot.* 7).

For skilled speakers such as Cicero the physical location in which an oration was given was itself a significant and valued rhetorical resource, and one that orators carefully considered when composing and delivering their speeches. Orators sometimes supplied their own visual props, a practice that seems to have been acceptable within certain limits, but it was preferable to make use of objects already in the visible surroundings. In particular, the areas in and around the Roman Forum with their concentration of temples, statues, and monuments provided a space that was rich with sites of the greatest historical resonance and offered a fertile environment of verbal and nonverbal allusions that orators could exploit. In order to understand fully the rhetorical effectiveness of ancient Roman oratory in all its aspects, it is essential to consider not just the oration itself, but the context of its delivery and the interrelationship between words and environment.

Mimicry, Accompaniment, Rhythm, and Signaling

The utility of gesture was not limited just to adding emotional commentary and drawing attention to elements of the environment. Gestures served a number of other functions. Chief among these is that they kept pace with the rhythm of an orator's words and that they provided a visual accompaniment by which the audience could more easily follow the cadences of the spoken component of an oratorical performance. In sheer numbers, such time-keeping motions probably accounted for the majority of an orator's gestures during a speech. Orators also used several rarer and more specialized gestures, the two most significant being to mimic or act out scenes described by the orator and to give prearranged signals to members of the audience. This final section on oratorical uses of gesture considers all of these topics.

The most obvious use of gestures was to mirror the words of a speech. Such gestures were often in the form of mimicry or acting out a motion described in words. Examples mentioned by the ancient sources include suggesting a sick man by imitating the posture of a doctor bending over and taking the arm of a patient in order to feel the pulse, or miming a musician by making string-plucking motions as if playing upon a lute. These overtly theatrical gestures were judged to be inappropriate, however, for extremely formal orations, especially pleading in the lawcourts (Quint. *Inst.* 11.3.88–91). It is repeatedly emphasized that an orator should not resemble an actor too closely; for example, an advocate speaking on behalf of a client who had been falsely beaten is sternly warned not to make his body writhe as though cringing from blows. In formal oratory the speaker's motions should reflect the thoughts expressed but not precisely mirror the words. The distinction between permissible instances of mimicry and those which sacrificed the orator's dignity is difficult to discern from the limited number of examples in the sources, which seem to make this determination on a case-by-case basis.

One specialized form of mimicry that was clearly acceptable, however, even in formal law cases, was προσωποποιία, the impersonation of others. An orator could assume the persona of a historical or contemporary figure and deliver an invented speech in the first person. Quintilian noted that an orator could also pretend to be a god or mythical figure, or even the personification of a place or entire peoples (9.2.29–31). The fictitious speech had to be plausible, however, and the orator was warned to be careful not to strain credibility by attributing improbable words to the impersonated character. According to the rhetorical handbooks, the speech had to be something that the person could reasonably have said, and if it was done well, an impersonation could be a potent rhetorical device. In addition to using appropriate words, the orator also had to mimic the voice tone and gestures of the assumed persona

(11.1.39–42). This sort of performance approached perilously close to the assumption of roles by stage actors and was described as a "bold" strategy for an orator.

Probably the most famous usage of this device is the brilliant middle passage of Cicero's *Pro Caelio* when he pretended first to be the stern censor, Appius Claudius Caecus, and then daringly assumed a very different persona, that of a contemporary, his personal enemy Publius Clodius (Cic. *Pro Cael.* 33–36). Later he offered a pair of contrasting fathers drawn from Roman comedy, first an irritable, crotchety old man from Caecilius, and then a forgiving, kindly father from Terence (37–38). Cicero's tour de force of acting in this speech was much admired in antiquity and seems to have represented the ideal for the proper use of προσωποποιία (Quint. *Inst.* 3.8.54, 12.10.61). Also memorable were instances when Cicero assumed the role of the person whom he was defending and spoke in his voice, as when he assumed the role of Milo in the *Pro Milone*. In this case it was believed that the speech was almost more moving if given by an advocate pretending to be his defendant than if the defendant had given it himself, because the advocate could present arguments that the defendant would be prevented by modesty from mentioning (6.1.29–31). In reference to the effectiveness of this section of the *Pro Milone*, Quintilian drew an explicit analogy to the stage "where the actor's voice and delivery produce greater emotional effect when he is speaking in an assumed role than when he speaks in his own character" (6.1.26).

There were also hand and arm movements appropriate to specific parts of a speech, including gestures to be used during the *exordium*, while arguing, while praising, while pleading, and even one to be used when making denunciations. The gesture used to accompany the *exordium* was identified as one of the most frequently made gestures in the orator's repertoire and consisted of touching the middle finger to the thumb and extending the other three (Fig. 13). The hand was then moved gently forward to the right and left (11.3.92). This gesture is an example of the complexity of the system outlined by Quintilian, since not only does he describe a variety of different gestures, but he also notes that by altering the speed with which a gesture was made and its range of

Figure 13. Gesture for use during the *exordium*

motion, the same gesture could have multiple meanings or purposes. If an orator made the *exordium* gesture more quickly and extended his arm further, then it became the gesture for making a statement of facts. If the gesture was made with great vigor and speed, it became an appropriate gesture to be used while refuting or reproaching an adversary (11.3.92). This strategy of modulating the speed of a gesture in order to express slightly different meanings was used to give versatility of denotation to several basic gestures.[40]

A somewhat similar gesture that an orator could use when stating facts consisted of making a circle with the thumb and forefinger and extending the remaining three fingers (11.3.101; Fig. 14). If the three fingers were folded into the palm, the gesture then became one suited to accompany a list of enthymemes, a type of syllogism (11.3.102; Fig. 15). When presenting arguments, the orator should grasp the outermost joint of the index finger on either side with the thumb and middle finger while allowing the other two fingers to curve slightly (Fig. 2). This gesture also had a more emphatic varia-

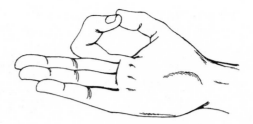

Figure 14. Gesture for use while stating facts

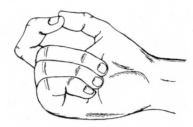

Figure 15. Gesture for use while presenting enthymemes

tion in which the last two fingers were contracted further (11.3.95). Just as rhetorical theory dictated that the various types of speeches should have certain components, it also prescribed distinctive types of gestures to accompany these divisions. When an orator was speaking, his progress through an oration could be measured not just by verbal structure but by changes in the types of gestures that he used.

Another important purpose of gestures was to serve a metronomic function, keeping time with the cadence of the words.[41] Quintilian observed that even common speech contains subtle stresses, which he compared with metrical feet, and which one's gestures naturally reflect (11.3.108). Rhythm was a significant consideration in the composition of speeches, so much so that in Cicero's last work on rhetoric, the *Orator*, the longest single section concerned the proper use of rhythm (Cic. *Orat.* 164–236). Ideally the orator's gestures should conform to the rhythm of his words but in a way that was very subtle and natural. It was a grave error to be

seen obviously beating time with one's gestures (59).[42] Nevertheless, many orations were deliberately composed to be rhythmic in
nature and sometimes even to rhyme or resemble verse.[43] The
frequent injunctions against excessively rhythmic orations suggest
that they were popular with audiences, an idea supported by the
advice given to a novice orator in Lucian's satire on teachers of
rhetoric to employ the rhythmic cadences and the postures of a
mime in order to achieve popularity (Luc. *Rh. Pr.* 15). As with so
many other of the rhetorician's rules, the key to the proper use of
rhythm in a speech was moderation; an oration should have some
repetition of stressed syllables, but not so much that the speech
took on a singsong nature. In one rhetorician's words, the speech
should "approximate a poetic rhythm" without actually possessing
one (*Rhet. Her.* 4.32). Cicero somewhat paradoxically advised that
an orator's prose should have rhythm but not actual meter, while
conceding that there are no rhythms except for those found in
poetry (Cic. *Orat.* 187–88). Similarly, while an orator should avoid
blatant metronomic motions, his hand and arm movements should
nevertheless begin and end simultaneously with the verbalized
thought that they accompany (Quint. *Inst.* 11.3.106).

With gestures serving all these functions, it seems that a Roman
orator would have been constantly in motion. Although he personally disapproved of so reductive a formula, Quintilian noted that
some orators plan to use one gesture for every three words in an
oration (11.3.107). He then went on, however, to cite a famous line
from one of Cicero's speeches, *Pro Ligario* 1.1, and indicated each
place where the ideal orator would make a gesture. The sentence
has seventeen words and Quintilian (11.3.108) prescribed no less
than eight gestures, each gesture marked here by a set of brackets:
"<Novum crimen> <Gai Caesar> <et ante hanc diem> <non
auditum> <propinquus meus> <ad te> <Quintus Tubero>
<detulit>" (<Of a new crime,> <Gaius Caesar,> <and one that
before today> <had never been heard of,> <my relative,>
<Quintus Tubero,> <has accused> <you>). Each gesture would
have begun as Cicero spoke the first syllable of the phrase within
the brackets and would have ended at the instant he finished enun-
ciating the last syllable within those brackets. Quintilian did not

specify what the gestures actually were, but did state that the rationale for the division of words into gestures was based on the rhythms and stresses of the spoken sentence. In this example, gestures seem to be serving primarily a metronomic function. The gestures Cicero would have made are probably some of those used to accompany specific parts of the oration, in this instance very likely one of the varieties of *exordium* gestures. The same gesture may have been used several times throughout this line, and the divisions referred to repetitions of a prescribed motion such as moving the hand across the body while held in the *exordium* position. An orator performing this line in this way would appear very much like a conductor of an orchestra, who uses his hands to control the tempo of the music, just as the orator parallels the tempo of his words with the movements of his hands.

Despite the apparent rigidity of Quintilian's directions concerning this line, he stressed that an experienced orator will use the correct gestures naturally, almost without conscious thought. Even if an orator's gestures were carefully rehearsed, it was vital that he give the impression that they were spontaneous. Quintilian admitted that young, inexperienced speakers will often have to plan their hand and body movements as they compose their speeches, but he assumes that eventually the use of gestures will become instinctive (Quint. *Inst.* 11.3.109; cf. Cic. *Brut.* 141). One reason novice orators may have erred in composing excessively metrical speeches was because such overtly structured sentences would have been easier to coordinate with metronomic gestures. Probably an even worse error than making a speech overly rhythmic was to do so and then allow one's gestures to become unsynchronized with one's words. Roman crowds had trained ears that would have quickly noted such a discrepancy, resulting in a shower of verbal abuse. Cicero noted that "if an actor makes a motion that is a little bit out of rhythm, or speaks a single syllable that is too long or too short, then he is hissed and he is booed" (Cic. *Parad.* 3.26). Despite the difficulties of this system, Quintilian ultimately stressed that above all an orator's motions should appear dignified and natural.

Roman orators were expected to gesture almost constantly throughout their orations. Indeed, the directions for performing the line from the *Pro Ligario* include no moment when the orator is not gesticulating. Further evidence for the frequency and vigor of orators' gestures was provided by Quintilian's remarks concerning clothing. He elaborately described how the toga should be donned and meticulously arranged with every fold in its proper place at the beginning of a speech (Quint. *Inst.* 11.3.137–47). By the middle of a speech he expected that due to the orator's exertions the folds of the toga would begin to become disarranged and would start to slide off the left shoulder.[44] He even suggested that the toga would begin to stick to the throat and upper chest as the orator began to sweat, and that it was permissible to pluck it away with the left hand. Finally, he approvingly noted that by the close of an oration sweat should pour off the orator, his clothing should be disheveled, and his toga should be falling off on all sides. This progressive disintegration of the orator's attire was not merely a natural consequence of the vehemence of his gestures, but was actually another deliberate rhetorical strategy calculated to appeal to the emotions of the audience. Quintilian indicated that all the visual aspects of an orator's delivery, including both his gestures and his appearance, work together to appeal to the emotions, so that the orator has to be conscious of them. By the end of an oration, an orator should give every appearance of being exhausted by his effort; he should "display signs of fatigue" and even his "disordered hair makes an additional appeal to the emotions" (11.3.147–48). There could be no clearer evidence of the fact that Roman orators used gestures constantly and vigorously than that speeches were expected to leave them sodden with sweat, their clothing thoroughly disarranged by their exertions.

Although it is certainly not an approved practice in the rhetorical handbooks, some orators made gestures with their clothing in order to give secret signals to their supporters in the audience. In an alleged plot to seize power in 65 B.C. Julius Caesar was supposed to give the signal to begin a massacre of the senate. The chosen sign was for Caesar to let his toga slide off his shoulder. Since this was apparently a frequent occurrence during orations, it would seem that this signal appealed to the conspirators as an innocuous gesture that would not arouse alarm in the intended victims (Suet. *Jul.* 9.2).

Another famous example of a prearranged gesture involving the speaker's clothing occurred during a court case at which Pompey was present. Clodius shouted out a series of insulting questions, such as "What is the name of the lecherous imperator?" After he asked each question, he signaled to his partisans in the crowd by shaking the folds of his toga, at which sign his followers would shout out the planned response, "Pompey!" (Plut. *Pomp.* 48). Once again, an orator is making use of an approved gesture involving clothing described by the rhetorical handbooks in order to give a secret signal to partisans in the audience. The motions approved by Quintilian for controlling the toga during an oration seem to have been particularly suitable for exploitation as such prearranged signals because, while they were common and approved gestures, they did not have a specific meaning.

Such signals were obviously far removed from the dictates for the use of gesture laid out in Quintilian's treatise, but just as plainly they were one of the many ways Roman orators actually used gesture during their speeches. This chapter has attempted to offer a kind of typology of gesture in Roman oratory as derived from the literary sources, particularly the rhetorical works of Cicero and Quintilian. The descriptions of the use of gesture in these works are less schematic than their presentation in this chapter. No ancient rhetorical manual presented gesture in this format or self-consciously divided its usage into distinct categories such as "emotion" or "indicative gestures." The rhetorical handbooks mostly jumble these categories together. The most elaborate of these, Quintilian's *Institutio Oratoria*, used the simple principle of starting at the top of the head and proceeding down the body, listing the possible uses to which each part could be put. Both he and Cicero did treat the subject of rhythmic gestures as a distinct topic. While admittedly the divisions in this chapter are somewhat arbitrary, the material has been presented in this way in order to illustrate most clearly the broad range of purposes that gesture served in enhancing the delivery of a speech and in making that delivery as persuasive as possible to its audience. This presentation makes one point very clear. Gestures were an indispensable part of oratory and served many purposes. Hand and body motions could mirror the verbal component of an oration, impart emotional shadings to the words, serve as an alternative language for communication, and enhance the innate rhythmic nature of many orations. Gesture truly offered a way for Roman orators to achieve eloquence not only with their words but also with their entire bodies.

Two

Gesture in Roman Society

he rhetorical handbooks of Cicero and Quintilian paint a vivid picture of orators' use of gesture as a central component of speechmaking in a variety of contexts, from speeches in the senate to public spectacles of all kinds. This image is consistently reinforced by comments in other literary sources ranging from the historical works of Tacitus to the anecdotes of Suetonius. Several questions naturally follow from this interpretation. First, can the literary evidence for the existence and widespread use of a supplementary nonverbal language for communication be substantiated by other kinds of evidence? Second, did orators really use all of these complex motions, or are the descriptions in the rhetorical handbooks an unrealistic ideal that bore little relation to everyday practice? Third, to what extent was the audience at these speeches able to understand and interpret correctly the gestures of Roman orators? Certainly those among the audience who were themselves senators or equestrians or who had received a Roman education emphasizing rhetoric had the requisite knowledge, but what about the majority of the inhabitants of Rome, including the urban plebs, slaves, and resident foreigners? A corollary to this question is, how was gesture used by ordinary members of Roman society, and was there overlap with the orator's system of gesture? An important consideration for all these questions is, how did the role of gesture in oratory change over time, and especially over the period covered by the works of Cicero and Quintilian?

Finally, and most basically, why did such an elaborate system develop in the first place? Were there conditions present at Rome that encouraged or even necessitated the use of a nonverbal language? This chapter considers these questions in order to offer a social context for the use of gesture by orators in late republican and early imperial Rome.

Oratorical Gesture in Art

The literary evidence is amply supported by various iconographic representations of the use of gesture. Statues, coins, reliefs, and wall paintings often portray gesticulating figures, including magistrates, emperors, actors, and orators. Much of this material has been usefully collected in the fundamental study of gesture in Roman art by Richard Brilliant. He gathers examples of gestures in all forms of visual media from the early republic through the later empire and offers a good general overview of their treatment in art. I cite only a few obvious representative examples here since his book amply illustrates the fact that gesture permeates Roman art. Brilliant is most concerned with tracing stylistic developments over time and how such changes were reflected in iconographic images of the emperor up through the later empire.

One of the earliest artistic depictions of a gesticulating orator is the famous statue now in Florence, the "Arringatore," a bronze statue of a togate magistrate with uplifted right arm, which is dated to the late second century or early first century B.C.[1] Later statues of orators provide visual counterparts to the verbal descriptions of Quintilian and Cicero. From the first century A.D. the bronze portraits of Marcus Calatorius and Mammius Maximus from Herculaneum and the marble statue of Marcus Nonius Balbus from Pompeii all show standing figures with carefully arranged togas partially draped over the left arm, while the right makes a gesture. The arm and hand positions are different in each case, but all seem to be oratorical motions.[2] How these men chose to be portrayed in a lasting memorial such as a statue is a revealing indication of what they considered important, and in view of the centrality of oratory to politics, it is no surprise that they frequently chose oratorical poses for their statues. The ubiquity of gestures made by these bronze and marble orators that perfectly conform to the rules laid out by the rhetorical handbooks further attests to the use and importance of gesture in oratory.

Emperors, too, were often sculpted as if delivering a speech, as exemplified by statues of Tiberius and Titus; even the statue of Augustus from Prima Porta appears to be in an oratorical pose.[3] Although Augustus's right hand was broken and restored, the present position of the fingers appears to reflect the original statue, and the gesture is very similar to the one prescribed by Quintilian for presenting arguments except that Augustus's middle finger is curved slightly toward the palm rather than with its tip against the first joint of the index finger. There are also marble reliefs of *adlocutiones*, scenes of emperors addressing a crowd. Two such portraits of Hadrian are the Anaglypha of Hadrian (Fig. 16) and the *adlocutio* relief from the Arco di Portogallo (Fig. 17).[4] In many instances the speaker clutches in his left hand a scroll, which is perhaps the text of the speech he is delivering. Although memorization was one of the components of formal rhetoric, many orators, most notably Augustus, frequently read their speeches from a written text. In his catalog of Augustus's habits, Suetonius noted that it was the princeps's invariable routine whenever he had to speak to the senate, people, or army, to compose his speech ahead of time and then to read it aloud. He frequently extended this practice to conversations with individuals and even to communications with his wife, Livia (Suet. *Aug.* 84).

In the relief of Hadrian from the Arco di Portogallo the emperor gestures only with his right arm, while an unrolled scroll is plainly visible in his left hand, suggesting that he is reading its contents to the audience. Part of the emperor's left hand, including the hanging portion of the scroll, is a later restoration. The portion of the scroll lying along the wrist and arm, however, is original and is sufficient to indicate that the relief was intended to show an orator holding up

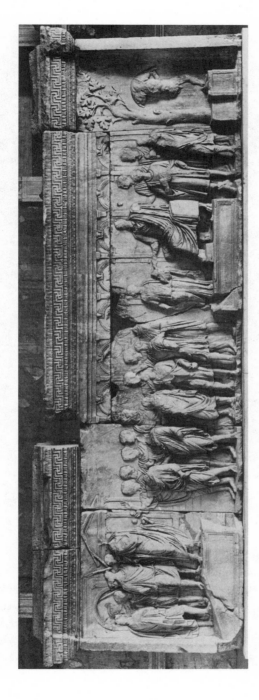

Figure 16. *Adlocutio* relief from the Anaglypha of Trajan/Hadrian, Curia, Rome
(Courtesy of Fototeca Unione, American Academy in Rome, 3546)

Figure 17. *Adlocutio* relief from the Arco di Portogallo, Museo del Palazzo dei Conservatori, Rome
(Courtesy of Fototeca Unione, American Academy in Rome, 4262)

a text in front of himself.[5] If this practice was widespread, as these sculptures imply, another reason for the rhetorical handbooks' injunctions concerning the dominance of the right hand in gesticulation may have been that the left was often employed to hold the manuscript of the oration from which the speaker read.

Figure 18. Sestertius of Hadrian with *adlocutio* from Rostrum Aedes Divus Iulius (Courtesy of Fototeca Unione, American Academy in Rome, 6132)

Finally, emperors or members of the imperial family in oratorical poses and *adlocutio* scenes are common subjects on Roman coinage. Augustus, Germanicus, Vespasian, Trajan, and Hadrian all appear in a similar pose on coins, standing clad in a toga with the right arm raised in an oratorical gesture.[6] *Adlocutio* scenes were also a popular subject for depiction on coins, particularly scenes of the emperor speaking before an assembly of soldiers. Caligula, Nero, Galba, Nerva, and Hadrian all appear on coins on which they are shown standing on a platform delivering a speech accompanied by gestures to a crowd of soldiers, while Trajan and Hadrian (Fig. 18) are pictured addressing a civilian crowd in urban surroundings.[7] The

49

many religious festivals of Rome were occasions for imperial speeches and for interactions between emperor and plebs in which gestures played an important role, and such scenes also appear on coins.[8] Gestures are a common feature of Roman art in a variety of media, and enough specific depictions of motioning speakers exist to substantiate the interpretation that the rhetorical handbooks' emphasis on gesticulation accurately represented the everyday practice of Roman orators.

Extent of Knowledge of Oratorical Gesture

Incidental literary references in Roman historical works and even in fiction also suggest that the knowledge and use of formal rhetorical gestures were widespread, even among the poorer classes. In Apuleius's colorful novel *The Metamorphoses*, when a lowly night watchman began to tell a story to his friends, he first extended his right arm and made what the novelist called "the orator's gesture" (Apul. *Met.* 2.21). Such incidents challenge the idea that the rather intricate rules of rhetoric were the exclusive preserve of the nobility and imply that this knowledge penetrated much deeper into Roman society. Obviously such knowledge was common among Roman elites because their education was centered around learning the art of rhetoric. Among the urban plebs, too, the level of sophistication about oratory may have been surprisingly high. One explanation is the sheer ubiquity of occasions at which the plebs would have been subjected to gesticulating orators. In addition to political events such as *contiones*, most of the varied civic rituals of Rome included speech-making. Another reason is the highly public nature of all of these urban events, from entertainment to religion, and from politics to judicial matters. Anyone conducting business, or even just passing through one of the ceremonial centers of Rome, such as the Forum, would probably have witnessed at least one orator in action.

Observing speakers and evaluating their performances, particularly those of orators arguing cases in the lawcourts, were popular forms of entertainment.[9] Court cases in ancient Rome were held in the open air where large crowds of the curious could watch, and because of the large size of the juries and the noise of the environment, advocates often had to stand on elevated platforms and speak as loudly as possible, thus making it easy for bystanders to see and hear the proceedings. There does not seem to have been a mandatory site for trials, so that the praetor in charge could convene them almost anywhere, but the most popular locations were in the Forum, a space capable of holding a large audience and containing many rostra and temple platforms from which the orators could speak.[10] Particularly in the litigious late republic, there were days when the Forum was "full of courts," each with its attendant excitable crowd of magistrates, advocates, juries, partisans, and bystanders (Cic. *Verr.* 2.5.143). Even in the early empire, cautioned Quintilian, a speaker in the Forum had to be prepared to cope with the noise and distractions of "lawsuits on every side" (Quint. *Inst.* 10.3.30). Under these circumstances sensational trials could and did degenerate into riots, and in more than one case troops had to be posted, or the trial moved, when bystanders became too incensed.[11] Just as with any other spectator sport, the Roman lawcourts had their aficionados who would have become experts on all the nuances of their "sport," meaning in this instance all the subtleties of the art of rhetoric, including, of course, gestures. In addition to those who enjoyed the spectacle of trials as a form of entertainment, the courts were also full of *laudiceni*, or "dinner clappers," those who made or supplemented their living by going from trial to trial and selling their applause to the highest bidder.[12] Both of these groups naturally would have acquired considerable expertise on forensic oratory and how to interpret its gestures.

Another route by which the average inhabitant of Rome would have acquired knowledge of gestures was through certain forms of theatrical entertainment. While gladiatorial games and chariot races have captivated the attention of writers both ancient and modern, these were exceptional events and in the early empire were usually held only on holidays or special occasions. Gladiatorial shows in particular were rare, held perhaps only two or three times a year.[13] Far more common were performances in the theater, such as pantomime dances, mime shows, Atellan farces, and theatrical plays.

Roman pantomime was a stylized form of dance, in which the

masked actors did not speak and instead used gestures to communicate.[14] The pantomime dancer was trained in "a code of gestures
that, as though by the letters of the alphabet, instructs the viewer's
sight; without writing it performs what writing has set forth" (Cassiodorus *Variae* 4.51.9). In the words of an admiring observer of
one such show, pantomime performers, like orators, "talked with
their hands" (Luc. *De Salt.* 63). This is the assessment of a certain
Demetrius who, doubting the versatility of gestures, challenged a
dancer to perform without the accompaniment of either songs or
music and still convey the full meaning of the piece. The dancer
rose to the challenge and was so successful in portraying all the
nuances of the performance using only gestures that Demetrius was
completely won over.

A popular anecdote involving pantomime dances concerned a
Pontic ruler who visited Rome during the reign of Nero and witnessed such a show. Although he could not understand the words of
the songs and speeches accompanying the dance, he was able to
follow the performance and understood everything by watching the
gestures of the dancers. Astonished by this, the king asked Nero to
let him take one of the pantomimes back to his kingdom in the
belief that the dancer's gestures were so eloquent that he would be
able to dispose of his interpreters and use the dancer to communicate with his linguistically varied neighbors (Luc. *De Salt.* 64). Even
more amazing was a certain Memphis, a "philosopher-pantomime"
(φιλόσοφον ὀρχηστὴν), who was supposedly able to explicate
the nuances of Pythagorean philosophy, "explaining in silent mimicry all of its doctrines more clearly than those who claim to teach
eloquence" (Athenaeus 1.20.C–D). These anecdotes are found in
satirical sources and, to some degree, are plainly exaggerations.
However, satire depends on the presence of a basic element of truth
that the audience can easily recognize, even if it is in a highly
distorted form. Thus, even if hyperbolic or apocryphal, these stories suggest that a sophisticated level of communication was possible through gesture at Rome.

Additionally, the complexity of pantomimic gesture was emphasized in nonsatirical sources as well. Quintilian himself mentioned
a contest during the reign of Augustus between two pantomimes

who competed by gesturing in turn (Quint. *Inst.* 6.3.65). Even the Stoic Seneca was impressed by the nonverbal communication skills of these entertainers: "We admire professional pantomime dancers because their hands represent every incident and its accompanying emotions, and their gestures flow as fast as words" (Sen. *Ep.* 121.6). Not only does this observation stress the versatility and speed of gestures and their ability to convey a wide range of meanings, but it also once again links gestures with emotion. The Romans seem to have believed that certain gestures constituted a natural language in which the signifiers were based not on meaning but on emotion. These comments show that a complex nonverbal vocabulary was not confined to the elites but rather that all sectors of the populace were accustomed to watching and being able to interpret such a language.

The most popular form of entertainment among the poorer classes of Rome was the mime show, which was often denounced by upper-class moralists as obscene and degrading. These farces did contain a large element of double entendres, slapstick violence, and depictions of sexual promiscuity and took as their subjects short vignettes on nearly any topic, often sensationalistic stories of urban and rural life.[15] Unlike pantomime dancers, mimes did not wear masks and they spoke in prose or verse, but nevertheless many of their jokes were conveyed by wild gesticulations. Quintilian warned orators not to make use of any of the grotesque facial expressions used by the mimes, and also to avoid the more vulgar of the gestures that provided much of the humor in these shows (Quint. *Inst.* 6.3.29). The Atellan (or Oscan) farce, which seems to have been an indigenous Italian form of entertainment, was similar in tone to the mime shows with an emphasis on stock characters and ribald jests, and again Quintilian inveighed against orators indulging in the kinds of double entendres popular in these farces (6.3.47).[16] Finally, actors of tragedies and comedies on the stage also used gestures in their performances to convey meaning and emotion.[17]

The rhetorical handbooks energetically attempted to distance the upper-class orator's use of gesture from that of theatrical performers. The reasons for this are obvious considering the huge gulf in status between aristocratic orators and performers of the stage. Few groups in Roman society were more maligned than the supposedly debased and degenerate actors.[18] The actors and dancers of Rome were ostentatiously expelled from the city on numerous occasions by various emperors who desired to give the impression that they were taking steps to improve the moral climate of the city, although usually these performers of the stage quickly returned. Tiberius, for example, in A.D. 23 expelled pantomime dancers from all of Italy (Tac. *Ann.* 4.13; Suet. *Tib.* 37). In A.D. 56 Nero expelled them again (Tac. *Ann* 13.24). During his reign, Domitian banned them from appearing in public, and Trajan expelled them yet again around A.D. 100 (Suet. *Dom.* 7; Pliny *Pan.* 46). Pantomime dancer, and mime in particular, were professions with pejorative connotations, and any similarities they shared with the members of the Roman elite would have made the latter very uncomfortable.[19]

Quintilian stated that "the orator should be as different from a pantomime dancer as possible," yet in methods and goals the two groups had much in common (Quint. *Inst.* 11.3.89). Both attempted to communicate with an audience with the primary purpose of producing a desired emotional reaction. Lucian recorded that the goal of the dancer was to present emotions to his audience (Luc. *De Salt.* 67). This claim may be compared with numerous similar ones made in rhetorical handbooks, such as the statement in the *De Oratore* that "nothing is as important in oratory as for the orator to win the goodwill of his hearer" by arousing his emotions (Cic. *De Orat.* 2.178). Orator and actor shared numerous additional characteristics, including the use of props and scenery, and both tried to manipulate their audiences by employing amateur and professional claques.[20] In addition to the above similarities, many of the actual gestures used by these two groups were the same.

The Illustrated Terence Manuscripts

Several extant manuscripts of Terence's plays include illustrations showing actors performing most of the scenes in the works. In every scene actors are depicted making a variety of gestures.[21] The four main manuscripts (C, Vaticanus 3868; P, Parisinus 7899; F, Ambrosianus H 75 inf.; O, Bodleianus Auct. F. 2, 13) clearly derive from a common original, and range in date from the ninth through the twelfth centuries A.D.[22] The earliest of the manuscripts, C (ninth century), has the most detailed and carefully drawn illustrations.[23]

L. Jones and C. R. Morey, who have extensively studied these manuscripts, note that, due to the handling of the figures and because the medieval artists eschewed contemporary artistic conventions, the illustrations "have the air of meticulous copies after an antique model."[24] Although the costume of the actors, the backgrounds, and the artistic techniques vary considerably from manuscript to manuscript, the gestures remain constant. This suggests that even though the medieval copyists altered some aspects of the scenes to conform to current artistic conventions, the gestures were faithfully reproduced. Since, according to the analysis of Jones and Morey, the goal of the copyists seems to have been to produce "an unusually careful rendition of the antique model," at least as far as the gestures were concerned, these miniatures may offer a guide to theatrical practices at least as early as the era of the original. That the artists considered these gestures to be the most important feature of the drawings is indicated by the fact that in P, F, and O, the hands of the actors are often grossly exaggerated in size and are also the most detailed part of the drawings (Figs. 19, 20).[25] It was a standard convention in ancient art to depict more important individuals, such as the emperor, as larger than the other people in a scene. In these manuscripts this convention has been extended to include individual parts of a person's body. The hands and arms are the significant limbs for conveying rhetorical meaning, so they are correspondingly larger to indicate their importance. The artists went out of their way to render precisely the exact finger positions of the performers, which at times are quite complex.

Estimates for the date of the original illustrations range from the fifth century A.D. to contemporaneous with the composition of the plays. After lengthy discussion Jones and Morey settle on the fifth century as the original date.[26] They summarize earlier arguments concerning the original date of the illustrations, many of which

Figure 19. Miniature for act 2, scene 2, lines 315–47, from the illustrated manuscript of the *Phormio* of Terence, Parisinus 7899

Figure 20. Miniature for act 4, scene 4, lines 682–712, from the illustrated manuscript of the *Phormio* of Terence, Parisinus 7899

favor a considerably earlier date, and reject the majority of the arguments. Ultimately, however, they concede that the dating issue depends upon whether one believes the actors' gestures are related to those described by Quintilian.[27] The consensus of later scholars is that the original from which all the extant copies derive dates from the fifth century. Whether this fifth-century manuscript was itself a copy of an earlier work is open to speculation. Even if the original was made several centuries after Terence, the theatrical vocabulary of gesture clearly developed much earlier and fifth-century theater would probably have been heavily dependent on earlier forms.

The reliability of the gestures in the miniatures has sometimes been questioned on the grounds that Terence was probably not being performed as late as the fifth century. This statement is probably true, but it is not a valid reason for rejecting the gestures as representative of theatrical practice, since many forms of theater, including pantomime and mime shows, were still flourishing and popular among urban inhabitants. In the middle of the fourth century there were still thousands of male and female dancers active at Rome, and throughout the fifth and sixth centuries, rulers continued in vain to attempt to regulate the supposedly immoral influence of the ever popular mimes, pantomimes, and actors.[28] The absence of any sort of a *scaenae frons* and the fact that the actors were often drawn in the order in which they speak in a scene rather than in the way that the actors would have been arranged during a stage performance indicate that the miniatures are not meant to be taken literally as scenes from an actual staging of Terence. The artist may well have used his personal experiences of observing theatrical performers in order to draw his actors in easily recognizable poses, making gestures that match the emotional content of their speeches in a specific scene.

In the illustrations for these plays, many of the gestures made by these comic actors are exactly those used by orators as described by Quintilian. These include gestures denoting specific emotions as well as motions to be used during various parts of a speech, such as the narration. Because these illustrations may offer the most complete visual counterpart to Quintilian's handbook, it is worth examining them in some detail. The very distinctive gesture used to accompany the statement of facts, which Quintilian describes as "the first finger touching the right-hand edge of the thumbnail with its extremity while the other fingers are relaxed," occurs frequently in the illustrations (Quint. *Inst.* 11.3.101). Clear examples include

GETA SERVUS   DEMEA   SENEX

Figure 21. Miniature for act 5, scene 6, lines 889–98, from the illustrated manuscript of the *Adelphi* of Terence, Vat. Lat. 3868, folio 63r

its use by Demea in a panel from the *Adelphi*, or by Chremes in the *Phormio* (Fig. 21).[29] This gesture appears in five out of six of the plays, and sometimes seems to be used by the actors during explanatory speeches, which roughly correspond to its oratorical usage. This correspondence is by no means perfect, however, and it is impossible to determine a consistent meaning for this gesture in the plays. Jones admits that this gesture is "very unusual" and indeed exactly matches Quintilian, but says that because it is hard to ascertain its significance in the plays, this correspondence is meaningless.[30] According to Quintilian, the same gesture can also be used to express approval or to indicate the distinction between different points in an argument (11.3.101). The multiplicity of meanings ascribed to this motion may help to account for its widespread use, or it may simply have acquired somewhat different connotations in its theatrical usage. While the gestures drawn in these panels may have been derived from oratory or vice versa, their meanings did not always translate exactly.

Whatever its precise meaning, this gesture is found frequently in the *Eunuchus* where it is made by Thais in act 3, scene 2, and act 4, scene 6, and by Pythias in act 4, scene 5. In one remarkable illustration, Parmeno, Thraso, and Gnatho make the gesture in unison, although why they are doing so is not clear in the context of the

Figure 22. Miniature for act 5, scene 8, lines 1031–49, from the illustrated manuscript of the *Eunuchus* of Terence, Vat. Lat. 3868, folio 33v

scene (Fig. 22).[31] In F, only Parmeno is making this gesture, which leads Jones to believe that F is more accurate, since in this scene the three men should be having different emotional reactions and hence would be unlikely to be making the same gesture. The use of this gesture occurs in so many varying contexts in the plays that without further evidence, all interpretations must remain speculative. Other instances of this gesture are found in the *Heauton Timorumenos* 3.3 (made by Chremes) and 2.4 (Bacchis), in the *Adelphi* 3.4 (Hegio) and 5.4 (Demea), and in the *Hecyra* 4.3 (Laches).[32]

Pointing motions with the index finger extended and the other fingers curled into the palm are also common in all the plays, and are used by the actors both to point at someone to whom they are speaking or referring and to add emphasis to their words by directing the index finger straight up (Figs. 23, 24).[33] The clenched fist denoting anger or grief is another motion that appears many times throughout the plays, and at least this gesture plainly had the same meaning for actor and orator. Thus in act 5, scene 1 of the *Eunuchus* when Thais hears of the rape of her sister, she makes this gesture as she angrily upbraids her servant Pythias for not having protected her sister. In 4.2 as Phaedria hurries alone through the countryside "in a very unhappy state of mind," he delivers a monologue lamenting that he must "spend several days here cut off from my love" and wondering, "Will I not even be allowed to see her?" (Ter. *Eu.* 634–

Figure 23. Miniature for act 5, scene 7, lines 1025–30, from the illustrated manuscript of the *Eunuchus* of Terence, Vat. Lat. 3868, folio 33v

Figure 24. Miniature for act 5, scene 2, lines 767–98, from the illustrated manuscript of the *Hecyra* of Terence, Vat. Lat. 3868, folio 75r

39). He is shown in the illustration for this scene in a grieving posture with his fist clenched and held against his upper chest. In the next scene his woes are compounded when he learns that his eunuch has committed the crime, and again he is drawn in the same posture. Similarly, in the *Andria*, the gesture of the fist against the chest is made by Simo when he believes that his slave has betrayed him, and by Pamphilus upon learning that his father has arranged

Figure 25. Miniature for act 1, scene 5, lines 236–300, from the illustrated manuscript of the *Andria* of Terence, Vat. Lat. 3868, folio 7r

Figure 26. Miniature for act 2, scene 1, lines 231–314, from the illustrated manuscript of the *Phormio* of Terence, Vat. Lat. 3868, folio 80r

his marriage to someone other than his beloved (Fig. 25).[34] Finally, in the *Phormio* Demipho becomes enraged upon learning that his son has married without his permission and bitterly clenches his fist and shakes it at his unfaithful slave, Geta (Fig. 26).[35]

There also may be several depictions of the end position of the "modesty" motion in which the fingers are converged while the hand is drawn near to the mouth or chest (Quint. *Inst.* 11.3.96–97).

61

Figure 27. Miniature for act 4, scene 4, lines 610–35, from the illustrated manuscript of the *Adelphi* of Terence, Vat. Lat. 3868, folio 59

Jones protests that it is impossible to identify a gesture involving movement from the static views found in the panels. There is some truth to this, but since we will never have a videotape of an ancient play, it seems extreme not even to consider the possibilities suggested by the evidence that we do have.[36] In the plays, the gesture often appears in scenes in which characters are apologetic or expressing regret. This is slightly different from its oratorical meaning of humility, but perhaps not such a far leap, since the characters in all these scenes have been humbled by some negative experience. In the miniatures, the modesty gesture is difficult to separate from the closed-fist anger pose, but it is distinguishable in the better manuscripts by the hand being raised to the level of the face and, most importantly, by the fingers being extended rather than clenched.[37] In the illustration for act 4, scene 4 of the *Adelphi*, Aeschinus's fingers are clearly separated and extended toward his face (Fig. 27).[38] In this scene he is on the way to try to placate Sostrata by explaining his actions, so a gesture indicating humility seems appropriate. In the same play, Sannio makes this gesture while he is being abused by Syrus for having been cheated in a preceding scene (Fig. 28).[39]

Figure 28. Miniature for act 2, scene 2, lines 209–53, from the illustrated manuscript of the *Adelphi* of Terence, Vat. Lat. 3868, folio 53v

Pamphilus is shown in this pose while delivering a long, sorrowful monologue describing his mistreatment and ill fortune in act 3, scene 3 of the *Hecyra* (Fig. 29).[40] Demipho similarly makes this gesture while lamenting the lack of justice in the world in act 5, scene 2 of the *Phormio*. Reinforcing the interpretation that this gesture represents humility is its use by a slave such as Syrus (*Ha.* 4.4).[41]

Overall, the most common gesture in the panels consists of the right arm being outstretched with the index and middle fingers extended and held together, while the thumb and other fingers are curled into the palm. The characters generally seem to direct this gesture toward another character, and sometimes two actors are shown making it at one another, as do Demipho and Chremes in the *Phormio* (Fig. 30).[42] This is not one of the gestures described by Quintilian, but it is very similar to the Christian motion of benediction, when made with the palm held outward as in the above scene. The actors also often hold their palms directed inward, which is very different from the Christian gesture, as does Geta in another scene from the *Phormio*.[43] These gestures occur so frequently in the panels that their meaning is uncertain, but they may have been used to add emphasis to narration or argument.[44] Another recurrent gesture not mentioned by Quintilian is for one of the characters in a

PAMPHILUS ADULESCENS

Figure 29. Miniature for act 3, scene 3, lines 361–414, from the illustrated manuscript of the *Hecyra* of Terence, Vat. Lat. 3868, folio 70r

DEMIPHO SENEX   CHREMES II

Figure 30. Miniature for act 4, scene 1, lines 567–90, from the illustrated manuscript of the *Phormio* of Terence, Vat. Lat. 3868, folio 84v

Figure 31. Miniature for act 4, scene 2, lines 577–606, from the illustrated manuscript of the *Hecyra* of Terence, Vat. Lat. 3868, folio 72v

scene to raise his right arm with the little finger extended and the rest curled inward, as does Laches in the *Hecyra* (Fig. 31).[45] Jones suggests that this is a stage convention that denotes that the actor making the gesture is overhearing the conversation of other actors on the stage but that they are not aware of this fact.[46]

Additional evidence that there was widespread knowledge of a common vocabulary of gestures can be found in scenes from the *Eunuchus* and the *Hecyra* in which Thais in the former and Sostrata in the latter make the so-called *pudicitia* gesture (Figs. 32, 33).[47] This is made by bending the left arm across the waist with the palm held open and facing downward while the right elbow rests on the back of the left hand. The right arm is bent upward toward the face with the forefinger extended and the others curled inward. The forefinger typically ends up at the level of the chin or cheek and often lightly touches the face. In extant depictions it is always made by Roman women and seems to be an exclusively feminine gesture. The meaning conventionally ascribed to this pose is that it signifies the woman's modesty or fidelity.[48] This matches Sostrata's use of it, since in this scene her husband suspects that she has caused turmoil in the household, and in a soliloquy she asserts that she has been a faithful wife: "So help me heaven, concerning this accusation of my husband I am innocent. But it's not easy to clear oneself" (Ter. *Hec.*

Figure 32. Miniature for act 2, scene 3, lines 274–80, from the illustrated manuscript of the *Hecyra* of Terence, Vat. Lat. 3868, folio 68r

Figure 33. Miniature for act 4, scene 7, lines 771–817, from the illustrated manuscript of the *Eunuchus* of Terence, Vat. Lat. 3868, folio 29v

276–77). In the illustration for this scene she is appropriately drawn making the gesture that signals feminine humility and virtue. The pose appears most frequently on funerary reliefs of freed slaves.[49] Interestingly, this gesture seems to have transcended status distinctions, since a famous statue of a woman now in the Vatican also depicts her in this pose.[50] It was also in use for a considerable period of time, as it was a staple on funeral reliefs at least from the late republic through the early empire. Its appearance in the illustrations for the comedy *Eunuchus* is intended to be humorous because Thais, the woman making this gesture, is the antithesis of modesty and fidelity, a prostitute. Not only is this an example of the widespread use of gesture in Roman society, but it also suggests that this nonverbal vocabulary was so well known that it could be intentionally misused for satiric or ironic purposes, since the joke depended upon the audience first correctly interpreting the gesture and then realizing its inappropriateness.

The illustrated Terence manuscripts provide a visual analogue to the rhetorical handbooks and even help to make many of the convoluted descriptions in Quintilian intelligible. Not only do the actors employ many of the same motions as orators, but they follow other rhetorical dicta as well. The right arm is the dominant limb of gesticulation, and indeed, the left is never shown gesturing alone, but only in concert with the right. The left is often shown being used to manage the actor's clothing, just as the orator was supposed to control his toga with the left hand. Whatever differences there were between actor and orator, they plainly shared to some extent a common vocabulary of gestures.

Orators, Actors, and the Trend toward Theatricality

Due to these similarities, it is not surprising that orators often found it useful to study the thespian arts in order to improve their own rhetorical skills. Demosthenes supposedly greatly enhanced his oratorical delivery by studying under the actor Andronicus (Quint. *Inst* 11.3.7). Cicero was friends with the actors Quintus Roscius Gallus and Clodius Aesopus and often praised their talents in his letters and speeches (e.g., Cic. *Sest.* 56–58, *Ad Fam.* 9.22). In his youth, Cicero feared that his delivery was deficient, so he regularly attended their performances on the stage to rectify this weakness (Plut. *Cic.* 5.3). Cicero's knowledge of theatrical gestures was also sharpened by contests with Roscius in which each attempted to portray a certain thought, Cicero with words and Roscius with gesture (Macr., *Sat.* 3.14.11–12). Just as Demosthenes was said to have performed his speeches in front of a mirror before delivering them in public so as to improve his gestures, so too Roscius carefully practiced every gesture he planned to make on the stage beforehand in private so as to perfect its appearance and persuasiveness (Val. Max. 8.7.7). Cicero described the oratorical style of Julius Caesar with thespian metaphors and characterized his demeanor in court trials as being infused with "a charm suggestive of the stage" (Cic. *De Orat.* 3.8.31). The great orator Quintus Hortensius was one of the most avid students of gesture, since he devoted more time to developing his delivery and planning his body movements than he did to composing the speech and practicing his elocution (Val. Max. 8.10.2). His theatrical delivery drew censure on the grounds that he too closely resembled an actor because he "used energetic hand gestures excessively," and on one occasion he was taunted by being addressed as Dionysia, a notable dancing girl (Aul. Gel. 1.5).[51] Other orators were also ridiculed for their delivery. Gaius Scribonius Curio habitually swayed from side to side so alarmingly and employed such violent gestures while orating that one wit commented that his thrashing was an effective method of driving away flies, and another likened his appearance to someone speaking from a wave-tossed boat (Cic. *Brut.* 216–17). Sextus Titius's overly languid and supple gestures caused a popular dance to be labeled "the Titius" (225). The frequent criticisms leveled against orators who too exactly resembled actors indicate the thin line that divided performances on the rostra from those in the theater and the close affinity between the gestures used by orator and actor. Nonetheless, as the examples of Cicero and Hortensius make clear, it was not just inferior orators who studied the stage and incorporated its techniques.

The rhetorical handbooks labored to draw distinctions between orators' gestures and those employed by theatrical performers. Motions that acted out scenes described in a speech were to be strictly avoided. An orator also should never pretend to be another person by imitating his mannerisms or posture (Quint. *Inst.* 11.3.88–90). The rationale behind these directions is plain, since assuming the personae of others is the basis of the actor's art. In the other direction, theatrical commentaries did not seem to have any qualms about equating their own art with rhetoric. Lucian compared rhetoric with pantomime and asserted that the dancer "tries to show character and emotion, of which the orators are also fond" (Luc. *De Salt.* 35).[52] In the *De Oratore*, Cicero offers an extended analysis of the proper use of humor in a speech delivered by the character of Gaius Julius Caesar Strabo. The orator is cautioned that, while it is easy and tempting to provoke laughter through mimicry, he must be careful to indulge in such humor selectively and should practice restraint in voice and gesture when he does attempt impersonations so as not to appear too similar to an actor. If an orator is too extravagant in his caricatures, he then loses all dignity and resembles a "buffoon or a pantomime." Ideally, an orator should borrow "only a hint of mimicry so that the listener will imagine more than he actually sees." A vigorous caricaturist may be quite amusing, but "not in the way I would have an orator be amusing" (Cic. *De Orat.* 2.237–52).

Quintilian several times describes a specific gesture that he instructs orators to avoid using because it "is a vulgar gesture rather than artistic," or "is an exclusively theatrical trick," or "is appropriate only for the stage," or "is in general use, but is not suitable to an orator," or most plainly, "is better suited to the comic actor than to the orator" (Quint. *Inst.* 11.3.102, 123, 103, 104, 125). The frequency of such asides is suggestive of the rhetorician's eagerness to attempt to establish a distance between his craft and that of the actor. Despite these injunctions, the "high" art of oratory and the "low" art of the stage did influence each other, as evidenced by Cicero and others observing as well as studying under actors. Orators, politicians, and even emperors, including Julius Caesar Strabo, Julius Caesar, Augustus, Lucius Cornelius Balbus, and Seneca, were known to have been keenly interested in the theater and to have written plays. It has been suggested that their works indicate "a process of cross-fertilization between oratory and theatrical rhetoric."[53] This cross-fertilization certainly occurred, but not merely because aristocrats wrote plays but also because they shared a nonverbal vocabulary with the actor and refined their delivery by studying the actor's craft.

In addition to vulgar gestures to avoid, Quintilian noted some that had become permissible for the orator and at least once commented, "I do not see why some object," in reference to a certain gesture that he now deemed acceptable for the orator (Quint. *Inst.* 11.3.103). This gesture consisted of moving the hand with the fingertips converged toward the mouth to express surprise, or sometimes indignation or entreaty. It may have originated as a common gesture among the people, as when members of a crowd in Apuleius's novel were astonished by the dazzling beauty of a young girl: they expressed their admiration by "bringing their right hands to their lips with the outstretched thumb and forefingers touching" (Ap. *Met.* 4.28).[54] This anecdote also illustrates that the vocabulary of oratorical gesture was not static but grew over time as gestures were incorporated from everyday life and the stage. Gestures passed the other way as well, as in the case of the "orator's gesture" made by Apuleius's rustics. Certainly, the perceived pomposity of aristocratic orators would have offered fertile subject matter for the mime to parody, and in so doing he would have incorporated some of their gestures into his own repertoire. The skilled delivery of notable orators was admired by serious actors as well. Just as the performances of great actors were observed by orators in order to gain inspiration, so too actors attended the performances of the greatest orators. Roscius and Aesopus always went to the courts when Quintus Hortensius was pleading in order to observe and copy his eloquent gestures (Val. Max. 8.10.2).

An interesting change in Quintilian's attitude toward the theater occurs over the course of his discussion of gesture. At the very beginning of his section on gesture, he drew favorable analogies between the motions of the actor and the orator and stressed their similarities. He even paralleled his statement that a poor speech accompanied by great delivery is better than a great speech with poor delivery by observing that a worthless work of literature appears sublime when performed by a great actor, but even classic works suffer if read in the library (Quint. *Inst.* 11.3.4). He emphasized the point that actors, like orators, use gesture to appeal to emotion. Directly mirroring the statements of Cicero and himself concerning the central importance of arousing the emotions of the audience with gesture, he stated that "the movements of the dance are full of meaning and appeal to the emotions without any aid from words" (11.3.65). The story that Demosthenes studied under an actor to improve his delivery is also repeated without negative comment (11.3.7). Toward the end of Quintilian's discussion, however, his comments distinguishing acting from oratory become more frequent, and he concludes the entire section with an emotional outburst against delivery. After meticulously presenting dozens of pages of precise instruction for using gestures, he seems to contradict his own previous advice by saying that "we need not study all the details of gesture or voice tone," and that "there is good reason for condemning delivery involving much gesturing or tone variations" (11.3.181, 183).

A work that began by asserting the overwhelming importance of delivery in great oratory abruptly ends by condemning it. The reasons offered for this statement are telling: "I am not trying to form a comic actor, but an orator" (11.3.181). He protests against the comparison by asserting that oratory, unlike acting, is "serious," and concludes with the somewhat pompous statement that if orators imitate the performers of the stage, "we may master the skills of the actor, but we shall lose the authority [*auctoritas*] that should characterize the man of dignity and virtue" (11.3.182, 184). Quintilian was the first Latin rhetorician to treat gesture in detail, and perhaps the very process of itemizing the use of gesture by senatorial and equestrian orators made plain the close resemblance between their art and that of the despised thespians, thus prompting this curious epilogue as a final attempt to deny the obvious similarities. There is a constant tension in the rhetorical handbooks between the desire to make an oration as persuasive as possible by inflaming the emotions of the audience through impassioned delivery and the fear that employing such methods will compromise aristocratic dignity.[55] The line between a brilliant orator and a buffoonish one was very fine, a reality acknowledged by ancient practitioners of rhetoric. Pliny the Younger voiced this idea in one of his letters when he stated that "the orator should be hot and excited, even up to the boiling point, and allow his emotions to lead him on. For eloquence is one of the arts that gains much from taking chances" (Pliny *Ep.* 9.26).

The similarities between orator and actor may have become more pronounced over time. Quintilian himself claimed that the style of delivery practiced in his time was more animated than that of earlier generations (Quint. *Inst.* 11.3.184). In the earliest complete Latin work on oratory, the *Ad Herennium*, the system of gesture described was certainly much less sophisticated and elaborate than

71

that in Quintilian's work (*Rhet. Her.* 26–28). The author of the *Ad Herennium* closely linked gesture with the other component of delivery, voice tone. He described almost no specific gestures, and instead listed the seven voice tones used in oratory and commented mostly on the speed and vigor of the motions appropriate to each. For example, he suggested that an orator, when speaking in the hortatory tone, should use slow and deliberate gesticulations (*Rhet. Her.* 27). Cicero's discussions of gesture were likewise much sketchier and give the impression that the use of gesture was not as fully developed and formalized as it later became. He stressed that while gestures were necessary and powerful, the orator should perform them with moderation and avoid excess (Cic. *Orat.* 59). The development of gesture can be traced by the evolution of attitudes toward dramatic motions. For example, slapping the thigh was a startling innovation when performed by Gaius Gracchus, was later acceptable to Cicero, and by Quintilian's time was commonplace.[56] Although incomplete, this evidence hints that, perhaps beginning in the late republic, oratorical delivery rapidly began to incorporate more and more physical movements, many of them co-opted from gestures already in use in Roman society, particularly on the stage. While both Cicero and Quintilian were deeply concerned with effective oratorical delivery, the differences in specificity and range of gestures found in their handbooks are startling. The system described by Cicero is easily recognizable as the same one still in use at the time of Quintilian, but it had grown enormously in complexity and versatility.

In rhetorical writings throughout the rest of antiquity, gestures never again received the same intense attention they were given by Quintilian. Gestures certainly continued to be a part of public speaking during the middle and later empire, but the overall impression is that, just as oratory itself became more stilted and formalized without the creative spur of sensational trials and meaningful public debates, so too the use of gestures became more rigid and less innovative. The Greek and Roman rhetoricians of the Silver Age and the Second Sophistic rarely describe specific gestures, although they continue to place great importance on oratorical delivery. The true eventual inheritors of the vibrant tradition of oratorical gesture are not found in the secular world, but rather in the ecclesiastical. Late antique and medieval writers from Augustine to Amalarius of Metz and Hugh of Saint-Victor emphasize the role of gesture in effective speaking and preaching and some of them provide catalogs of gesture every bit as elaborate as Quintilian's.[57]

The period of rapid development of oratorical gesture seems to have peaked in the early empire, and the increase in the visual theatricality of oratory was often depicted as being symptomatic of oratory's decline. In a letter written in the second century A.D., Fronto lamented the decrease in rhetorical ability in the rulers from Tiberius to Vespasian by saying that these emperors were reduced to communicating "either by gestures like actors, by nods of the head like the mute, or through intermediaries like foreigners" (Fron. *Ver.* 2.1.7). These comparisons were clearly intended to be sarcastic exaggerations, but his choice as comparisons of people who employ nonverbal forms of communication is interesting. Perhaps, as suggested by the increased attention given to gesture in the rhetorical handbooks, oratory over this period was incorporating more and more of the actor's gestural vocabulary, and the actions of an aristocratic or imperial speaker did begin to resemble more and more those of an actor or a mime. Quintilian's concern that oratory and acting were becoming too similar may thus be justified by a genuine trend toward theatricality on the part of orators.[58] The aristocratic consensus on this trend was that it represented a moral decline in the art of rhetoric. Whatever the artistic merits of this development, it probably had the practical effect of making oratory more accessible to the urban plebs of Rome, steeped as they were in the eloquent nonverbal language of the theater.

Practical Considerations

Rhetorical gestures, then, pervaded all levels of Roman society and were not an exclusive preserve of the nobility. That gestures should have been so prevalent in Roman urban life is not too surprising. Rome's political and social life revolved around face-to-face public interactions, of which speechmaking before large audiences was the central feature. To fulfill their goals, events such as debates, trials, demonstrations, parades, and *contiones* all had to be witnessed by as many people as possible. While Rome was by no means a democracy in the pure sense, the political process was democratic, since all citizens were theoretically able to cast votes to elect magistrates and pass legislation, although in practice the system favored the wealthy and the urban.[59] Much recent scholarship on the Roman Republic has emphasized the significant role that the people played in political decision making and in various urban rituals, both those of an overtly political nature and those which were at least nominally for other purposes.[60] Yet this intensely verbal and public society functioned under a significant constraint not shared by modern societies. The Romans lacked the electric microphones and speakers that today are integral parts of all speeches and performances before large audiences. This lack of artificial methods of voice amplification practically ensured that nonverbal forms of communication would develop and flourish in an attempt to compensate for the limitations imposed on oratory by the capacity of the human voice.

The invention of the microphone in the late nineteenth century revolutionized public speaking by making it possible for huge crowds to hear accurately the words of a single speaker. The microphone was invented seemingly independently by several men, among them Alexander Graham Bell in 1876, Thomas Edison in 1877, Emile Berliner circa 1877, and David Hughes in 1878. The initial application of this technology was as a telephone transmitter. Widespread use of the amplified microphone as an aid to public speaking followed much more slowly, and was not common until the early decades of the twentieth century. A side effect of this technological advance has been a greatly decreased interest in the subject of oratorical delivery.

This development can be traced in the attention devoted to the subject by scholars. Interest in ancient oratorical delivery, and gestures in particular, flourished until the twentieth century and produced many serious studies. As early as 1644 the first of these studies was published in English, John Bulwer's *Chirologia: Or the Naturall Language of the Hand . . . Whereunto is added Chironomia: or the Art of Manuall Rhetoricke.*[61] The use of an elaborate system of gestures in learned oratory in the early modern period was so well known that the practice was even parodied in contemporary popular literature. Rabelais's satire *Gargantua and Pantagruel* contains a rhetorical debate between Panurge and a "great English scholar" conducted not with words but entirely through gestures.[62] Of course, the gestures used by Panurge are largely farcical and obscene, but the caricature Rabelais presents of the pompous scholar who uses a stylized language of gesture to communicate was clearly expected to be a familiar figure to his audience. One fascinating study from the beginning of the nineteenth century attempts to recreate the gestures of Roman actors by observing and analyzing the gestures of contemporary Neapolitans as observed in everyday life in the streets of the city.[63] The interest in classical rhetorical gesture, as reflected in these monographs, abruptly ceases in the last decade of the nineteenth century, and there were no extended treatments of the subject at all between the 1890s and the 1980s.[64] This startling lacuna in what had been up to that point a continuous and lively topic of scholarly inquiry is highly suggestive, since it exactly coincides with the widespread use of the electric microphone and amplifier in speechmaking.[65]

The current pervasive use of the microphone and amplifier has rendered gesture partially redundant as a form of communication. As a significant side effect, orators have become less visible to their audiences. Not only does the microphone, particularly the early bulky models, partially obscure the speaker, but it also necessitates a stand to hold it near to the speaker's head. These stands often take the form of podia that completely hide the orator's body, frequently up to the level of his or her chest. Furthermore, an orator's movements are severely restricted by the necessity of maintaining an even distance from the microphone while talking so as to ensure uniform voice volume. Audiences have become conditioned to focus more on listening to a speaker than on watching him. The emphasis on listening over observing may also have been hastened by the widespread broadcast of speeches over radio in the early and middle parts of the twentieth century, as exemplified by Franklin D. Roosevelt's popular "fireside chat" broadcasts and Churchill's wartime radio speeches. The typical twentieth-century orator, his body rooted in place, unable to move his head more than a few inches, with both his head and body concealed behind a microphone and its stand, is far removed from the image of Cicero striding freely about the rostra.

Interestingly, modern technology is now sufficiently advanced that it is possible to use very tiny microphones or directional ones that do not hide the speaker. Coupled with the omnipresence of television, which allows mass audiences to see the speaker plainly, this technology has led to a huge increase in the attention paid to physical appearance and body language. In contemporary American politics, how a politician appears and the visual impression produced by his oratorical delivery are often more important than the content of his speech. This renewed attention to oratorical delivery is perhaps most vividly embodied in the much commented upon fact that one of the most popular U.S. presidents of the past three decades, and one of the only ones to win reelection, was trained not as a politician but as an actor.[66]

For the Romans, who lacked artificial means of voice amplification, the problem of effective communication at large gatherings was serious since the active public culture of Roman cities demanded a way to communicate at public spectacles. The problem was particularly acute in the city of Rome itself for several reasons. The city was the center of both religious and political ritual, each of which required frequent ceremonies of considerable complexity involving large numbers of participants and observers. Rome also had an unusually heterogeneous population, which included many different cultural and linguistic groups.[67] The influx of slaves in the late republic, many of whom were later freed, certainly brought linguistic, cultural, and ethnic variety to Rome. Rome's conquests brought people to the city as captives from all over the Mediterranean basin as well as from its northern and southern hinterlands. In addition, Rome was the center of long-distance trade in the Mediterranean, which also contributed to the city's diversity. Seneca complained that Rome "contained more foreigners than citizens," and while this statement is hard to take literally, it points to the existence of a large presence of foreigners among the population (Sen. *Ad Helviam de Consolatione* 6.5). Rome, particularly from the middle republic on, was a chaotic Babel of differing languages and peoples in which Germans from the northern forests mingled with Numidians from the African deserts and Jews from Alexandria. This diversity may have been one reason for the extreme popularity of pantomime and mime shows, since most of the witticisms of the actors were expressed nonverbally through gestures. Thus, as in the case of the Pontic ruler at the pantomime show, even those who were not fluent in Latin could enjoy the performance. In this context the "language" of gesture may have constituted a common language for the city's inhabitants that transcended status and ethnicity.

Adding to an orator's difficulties in making himself heard was the reality that Roman audiences were not passive listeners; they actively and vocally reacted to the speaker's message as well as making known their own desires through shouts, clapping, and chants. At an oration given in the Forum (such as during a law trial) there would also have been considerable background noise from other trials, from people conducting business in the area, and from those passing through or simply loitering about. The public setting of most orations meant that speakers had to deal with all the noises of a major city and its inhabitants. In addition to man-made noises, speakers had to contend with nature as well. An orator had to be prepared to speak in any sort of climate since he could be called upon to deliver his speech in a strong wind or downpour, which certainly would have added to the difficulties of his task. Quintilian confirms this observation when he instructed would-be advocates that they cannot just desert a client if the weather is inclement, but that they always have to be ready to perform in all conditions, even under a glaring "sun, or on a windy, a wet, or a sweltering day" (Quint. *Inst.* 11.3.27).

Most problematic of all, however, was the sheer size of the city. By the late first century B.C. the population of Rome approached one million people, and perhaps topped this in the early empire.[68] Among premodern cities the size of Rome was unique, as it was at least twice as large as any other contemporary city. No other city reached an equivalent size for almost another two thousand years, until London's population reached one million in the early nineteenth century.[69] By comparison, in the classical Greek world, Athens, the largest democratic Greek city-state, had only a fraction of Rome's population, even at its height.[70] The various permanent buildings constructed at Rome in the early empire to house public entertainments testify to the size of the crowds that were routinely gathered at Rome during this time. The largest, the Circus Maximus, could hold a quarter of a million spectators, the Flavian amphitheater known as the Colosseum probably could accommodate just over fifty thousand, and each of the three permanent theaters seated between five and twelve thousand. Voting assemblies, funerals, festivals, and special games were sometimes held in open fields such as the Campus Martius, which could have accommodated immense crowds. Finally, the Roman Forum, although cluttered with monuments, had enough open space for a gathering of several tens of thousands.

On memorable occasions, the Forum area seems to have been filled to capacity. During his delivery of the fourth *Catilinarian* Cicero remarked that "the Forum is crowded with people, the temples round about are jammed tight, all the approaches to this shrine and this place are packed with spectators" (Cic. *Cat.* 4.14). At the beginning of his *Pro Lege Manilia* he similarly noted that "the Roman people filled the Forum, and crammed every available corner in each of the temples that overlook this platform [the rostra]" (Cic. *Man.* 14). Due to the uniquely large size of the crowds possible at events in Rome, the voice alone was not sufficient for communication. All these factors placed a premium on an orator's ability to project his voice above the din so that his words could be heard by his entire audience. In the absence of artificial means of voice amplification, the Romans explored other ways of conveying information at public gatherings.

The main method by which verbal messages were transmitted to large crowds was through the use of heralds, who were routinely employed by emperors and magistrates and were present at court cases. Heralds also played prominent roles in the interactions between emperors and plebs at public entertainments.[71] Heralds had special training that enabled them to increase the range at which their voices could be heard. By positioning a series of heralds around a space, the emperor could have his messages relayed to distant members of an audience or his pronouncements repeated. Apparently in a bid for popularity some emperors chose to act as their own heralds. Nero enjoyed making his own announcements to the crowd, although he perhaps took this practice too far by actually competing in the contest for heralds (Suet. *Nero* 24). Augustus also usually seems to have made his own proclamations and only employed a herald when he had a sore throat (Suet. *Aug.* 84). Late in his life when he had lost the ability to project his voice effectively, he still avoided using a herald by having Germanicus read his speeches for him (Dio 56.26.2). The profession of herald or crier is certainly well attested in both literary and epigraphic evidence. However, even the use of heralds was not enough to overcome this problem of distance. Another strategy, which was used in the amphitheater, was to circulate around the audience large placards on which were written the pronouncements of the emperor (Dio 60.13.5; Suet. *Claud.* 21).

An interesting variant on the use of another to read one's own oration occurs in a letter of Pliny, although this time for aesthetic rather than practical reasons. Pliny starts by saying that because he considers himself a bad reader he is considering having one of his freedmen read for him (Pliny *Ep.* 9.34.1–2). He then asks if he should sit passively during the reading or if he should imitate the practice of some people who accompany the reader in a low voice together with appropriate looks and gestures. Since orators were communicating in two languages simultaneously, one verbal and one nonverbal, this comment represents a natural development to split the tasks with each person performing the task for which he is best suited. It is worth noting that Pliny's phrasing clearly implies that some orators actually do have others read their works while they themselves follow along performing the gestures. Pliny ends with the quip that perhaps he will not do this after all, since he is no better at dancing mime than he is at reading. It is hard to tell how serious Pliny is in this entire letter, and the situation he is discussing is a private recitation before friends rather than a formal public oration, but at the least this final remark once again emphasizes the close similarities between actor and orator and the uncomfortable self-consciousness that this relation created in the minds of Roman elites.

The various permanent buildings constructed at Rome to house public entertainments during the early empire attest not only to the size of crowds that gathered, but to the architects' efforts to ensure that the audience could hear. The impressive acoustic properties of ancient theaters are well known, yet many of the most notable speeches and assemblies did not occur in such specially designed structures.[72] The Campus Martius was well suited to assembling huge crowds, but it was not a space with favorable acoustics. The Roman Forum itself was certainly the site of famous orations, yet it too was ill suited for this role in terms of acoustics. The multistory marble-faced structures surrounding the open space of the Forum would have helped somewhat by reflecting sound, but their arrangement would have caused confusing and contradictory echoes, obscuring and mingling with an orator's own words.[73]

Often, therefore, the orator could count on the help of neither heralds nor specialized architecture, but had to rely solely on his own abilities. Much of the discussions of delivery in the rhetorical handbooks of Cicero and Quintilian is concerned with exercises and advice to strengthen an orator's voice and endurance. Modern actors can confirm that speaking for several hours at the volume and intensity demanded of Roman orators is a physically draining task.[74] When one considers the physical demands placed on an orator, Quintilian's claims that by the end of a speech an orator should be drenched in sweat and have his clothing disordered may not be rhetorical exaggerations. The carrying ability of an individual's voice is not entirely dependent on volume, but is a combination of natural tonal quality and training, a fact recognized by ancient rhetoricians (Quint. *Inst.* 11.3.40).

As opera singers know, the tone of voice that will carry the furthest while retaining the most clarity employs the middle range, not bass or treble tones. This is also the type of voice best suited to performing in poor acoustical environments such as the Forum.[75] While these observations have been established by modern science, the sophistication of the ancient rhetoricians is revealed by the fact that this is precisely the tone recommended by Quintilian, who also notes that high and low voices are not well suited for public speaking, as they produce a muffled or unintelligible sound (Quint. *Inst.* 11.3.41). Male vocal ability tends not to mature until the early thirties and to begin to deteriorate in the sixties. Hortensius's decline as an orator appears to have been partly due to the natural degradation of his voice, which, as it aged, grew ill suited to his rhetorical style (Cic. *Brut.* 330). The effects of age can also be seen in the elderly Augustus's employment of Germanicus to deliver his pronouncements. Even with professional training, however, there are still fundamental limitations on the range at which one person can make himself heard.

Under most circumstances, the furthest that it is possible to hear clearly a single speaker saying anything more complex than short, simple phrases is about sixty-five meters in an open space with average background noise. The open space of the Forum was a little over one hundred meters long and approximately half that in width. The republican rostra was located at the northwest end of this space, and the frequently used speaking platform in front of the Temple of the Deified Julius Caesar was opposite it at the southeast end. If the Forum was filled with listeners, as sometimes happened according to Cicero, at least a third of the audience could not have heard much of a speech given from either location. The Flavian amphitheater was even larger, and the Circus Maximus was nearly six hundred meters in length. Within these spaces, it often would have been impossible for many, perhaps most, of the members of a large or noisy crowd to hear an oration.

None of the attempted solutions to this dilemma was wholly successful, and it is not surprising that audiences, particularly those on the edge of a crowd, often had difficulty hearing a speaker. A participant in a court case once complained to Cicero that he could not hear the orator's words (Plut. *Cic.* 26). It was reported as an unusual event that Caligula was able to be heard even by those at a distance, perhaps due to his intensive study of oratory (Suet. *Gaius* 53). Beyond fifty or sixty meters, speakers would frequently have been, as Tacitus put it, "more visible than audible," especially if there was much noise from the crowd itself (Tac. *Ann.* 13.38). If part of a widely known nonverbal vocabulary, gestures could have greatly assisted in conveying a speaker's message, since they can be seen at a greater range than words can be heard. On occasion they could even substitute for words, as when the tribune Lucius Roscius Otho was unable to make himself heard and used hand gestures alone to convey the substance of his speech. This incident occurred during the debate over giving Pompey the extraordinary command against the pirates in 67 B.C., and Roscius was able to express through his gestures the fairly complex message that he opposed the plan, that he thought one man should not have such power, and that he proposed appointing a second commander who would share power with Pompey (Plut. *Pomp.* 25).

If the gestures used were unusual ones, or if the distances were great enough, even this strategy was not always successful and could result in misunderstandings. A notorious incident involving both difficulty in hearing a speaker and a misunderstood gesture was Julius Caesar's oration to his troops before crossing the Rubicon. The soldiers "on the fringe of the assembly, who could see better than they could hear," misinterpreted Caesar's pointing gestures toward his ring to mean that he was promising to give all of them equestrian rank in exchange for their support (Suet. *Caes.* 33). Similarly, during one of Tiberius Gracchus's speeches appealing to the people for help, "those who were standing farther away . . . could not hear his voice." Becoming aware of the problem, Tiberius tried to convey his message nonverbally by pointing to his head, indicating that he was in danger. This unfamiliar gesture backfired when it was misunderstood by some as being a request for a crown, an interpretation that his enemies advertised widely (Plut. *T. Gracch.* 19).

In all of these examples, the repeated references to difficulties in hearing, particularly by those on the fringes of a crowd, emphasize the fundamental limitation in premodern oratory on the number of listeners that an orator could address at one time. In the sources, this problem seems to have been mentioned most frequently during the late republic, at precisely the time that the population of Rome had suddenly climbed to previously unknown levels. Such problems were not mentioned very often during the early empire. If Quintilian was correct in his assertion that orators were using gestures more in his own time than they had previously, perhaps this development was a response to the problems of acoustics and crowd size. Perhaps it is also no coincidence that the first in-depth discussion in Latin of the use of gesture was not written until the early empire. With the important exception of audience size, none of the problems faced by Roman orators was unique to Rome. What may be unique is their combination in such extreme forms, particularly from the late republic onward.

Evidence ranging from the accounts in the rhetorical handbooks and Roman historical and fictional writings to artistic representations in bronze and marble sculpture, on state and private reliefs, and on coinage demonstrates that the rhetorical vocabulary of gesture was an essential component of the delivery of speeches. Furthermore, the same evidence indicates that this nonverbal vocabulary was both actually used by orators in their public performances and understandable to a sizable portion of Rome's populace. The *sermo corporis*, the language of the body, at least to some degree served as a common language among the heterogeneous groups that made up the population of ancient Rome, and it was a language that cut across cultural, economic, and social barriers. Gesture permeated Roman culture and particularly its public ceremonies, whether political, religious, or ludic.

Most of the popular forms of entertainment at Rome depended heavily upon gesture, and the levels of gestural sophistication employed by the city's actors and dancers rivaled that of its orators. Actor and orator probably influenced each other as well, as exemplified by the interactions of Cicero and Roscius. Speakers spent considerable effort learning the formal art of rhetoric, and audiences, particularly at Rome, had enough exposure to such speakers to appreciate many of the nuances of their delivery. The increased use of gesture by orators was facilitated by, or was perhaps even the result of, the rapid changes in the size and composition of the populace at Rome in the middle and late republic, coupled with the need to communicate effectively at the large public gatherings that proliferated during this same period. The mass-participation rituals of ancient Rome were the focus of its urban life, and in these rituals, gesture played a vital role.

In concluding this discussion of oratorical gesture, it is perhaps appropriate to return to Cicero, the greatest of Roman orators, for one last anecdote drawn from the final episode in his own life. Cicero was not merely a gifted composer of speeches, but plainly he was also able to maximize their effect by using all the tricks of delivery, including gesture, to reach and manipulate the emotions of his audience. His last great oratorical achievement was his series of *Philippics* directed against Marcus Antonius. Unfortunately, Cicero so aroused Antonius's wrath with the *Philippics* that he eventually demanded that Cicero be placed on the list of those to be proscribed, and Cicero was subsequently murdered in a brutal fashion.

Not content with this revenge, and specifically in order to avenge the insult of the *Philippics*, Antonius ordered that Cicero's severed head be displayed on the rostra in the midst of the Roman Forum, the place from which the living Cicero's voice had denounced him. While there were precedents for the display of enemies' heads in the Forum, in the case of Cicero, Antonius ordered a very unusual addition to this grisly display. He commanded that the orator's hands should also be severed and displayed on the rostra alongside the orator's head.[76] Gestures, like words, could be used to praise or to insult. The reason for Antonius's unique revenge is debatable, but perhaps he realized that it was not only the great orator's voice that had spoken against him with such eloquence but also his hands.[77]

Three

Oratory and the Roman Emperors

One particularly vexing problem when attempting to analyze the interactions between speakers and audiences in ancient Rome is the question of who actually formed the audience at a given speech or public event. Throughout this work, I use general terms such as audiences and crowds when referring to those who were present at urban events and who were the immediate auditors and observers of public orations. Although one can speculate about the composition of a given crowd at a specific event, ultimately this is one aspect of urban interactions that can never be accurately reconstructed. One can make guesses based on factors such as time of day, location, and the nature of the event, and one can hypothesize about the presence of partisan elements in a crowd composed of the friends, clients, and supporters of specific individuals. Every discussion of an oration given in the Forum, for example, is rife with unanswerable yet significant questions: What percentage of the audience was citizens, or slaves, or freedmen, or women, or foreigners? How many were present because of interest in the speaker or topic, and how many were there by chance, or because their jobs or social connections compelled them to attend?

The answers to these questions are important and might well affect one's analysis of an event, but how can one answer these questions? One can only guess about the composition of a crowd in the circus or at a religious festival, since every crowd is a collection of separate individuals, each with his or her own prejudices, agendas, and opinions. Complicating this dilemma further is the fact that there is a certain psychological shift that occurs when individuals gather together in anonymous masses. Such "mob behavior" has itself become an entire field of study. Occasionally an ancient author will make comments about the composition of a given crowd, but even when this happens, such information is often highly suspect because it is usually motivated by a desire to dismiss the validity of a reaction by labeling the crowd in some derogatory way.[1] Crowds are routinely described as fickle, unruly, degenerate, and vulgar. In the end, one cannot satisfactorily solve this problem but must be content with maintaining an awareness of it.

Just as gesture developed as a way for speakers to communicate more effectively with audiences, so too there were routes by which the members of a crowd could express their reactions to a speech. The remainder of the chapters examine the most significant of these methods, acclamations. The temporal focus also now narrows to the early empire when acclamations and their contents had not yet assumed the rigid, highly stylized, and predictable form they later took. This study will concentrate specifically on the lively interactions that transpired in this period between the emperor and the urban plebs, which featured the most versatile uses of acclamations. Before turning from speakers to audiences, however, it is worth considering the most prominent speakers during the empire, the emperors themselves, and the degree to which they studied the art of rhetoric, including gesture. Just as he monopolized sources of prestige, the emperor further became the supreme orator whose words carried the greatest significance. At many of the public events over which he presided and which constituted the new loci of power during the empire, the audiences were enormous and gesture played an important role in aiding communication.

The Rhetorical Training of Emperors

The importance of oratorical skill as an imperial attribute is empha-sized in a remarkable letter of Fronto addressed to the emperor Marcus Aurelius. As has been pointed out, this letter represents "one of the few attempts . . . to define some of the duties and functions of the emperor."[2] The first two imperial duties listed by Fronto are to speak in the senate and to "address the people on many matters at public meetings" (Fron. *Ant.* 2.7).[3] Emperors did often speak to the people at assemblies and ceremonies and on other occasions, both formal and informal. In the letter, Fronto proceeded to note that all the most significant tasks of the emperor involve the use of words either spoken or written and that, as a result, the study of eloquence is the most valuable preparation for the job of being emperor. Prospective emperors were urged to prac-tice their rhetorical skills tirelessly, since their imperial duties would often call for them to deliver speeches, including ones given at important state events.

Most, if not all, of the early emperors formally studied rhetoric during their childhood and adolescence, and many pursued their rhetorical studies throughout their lives. Augustus as a youth was an enthusiastic student of oratory and even during the busy Mutina campaign made time each day to read, compose, and declaim.[4] He developed an effective oratorical style and continued to practice his composition and delivery under the tutelage of a rhetorician throughout his life. Augustus cultivated a speaking style that em-phasized simplicity and clarity of expression. He repeatedly mocked those who sprinkled their speeches with archaic words or who constructed extraordinarily convoluted sentences in order to display their erudition. Fronto's letters reflect this same goal, since he urged the emperor to speak in a plain, easily understood style and particularly to avoid "obscure words" and "difficult metaphors" (Fron. *Ad M. Caes.* 3.1). This emphasis on clarity and simplicity of expression additionally suggests that these orations were intended to be intelligible to a mass audience, not just to highly educated connoisseurs of rhetoric. Perhaps Augustus was also inspired by the style of his adoptive father, Julius Caesar, who was famous both for his skill as a speaker and for the simple yet elegant and persuasive style of his writings. Caesar was judged by his contemporaries to be among the greatest of Roman orators. His style of delivery was characterized by the use of "impassioned motion and gestures, not lacking in elegance" (Suet. *Caes.* 55).[5]

The rest of the Julio-Claudians also devoted considerable attention to learning the art of rhetoric. Tiberius in his youth studied oratory and, at the age of nine, had already delivered the elegy for his father from the rostra (Suet. *Tib.* 6). He studied under the rhetorician Theodore of Gadara both as a child and as an adult, and the extent of his oratorical interests was revealed by the not entirely implausible reason he gave to explain his retreat to Rhodes: that he wished to devote himself to rhetorical studies (Suet. *Tib.* 57; Dio 55.9.5). His style of speaking was described as being highly ornate and mannered, and his delivery employed "eloquent movements of the fingers" (Suet. *Tib.* 68). Despite the erudition of his oratory, however, he was infamous for his use of ambiguous phrasing and convoluted syntax, which drew the censure of Augustus (Suet. *Tib.* 68, 70; *Aug.* 86).[6]

The "theatrical" emperors Gaius and Nero were particularly keen students of rhetoric. Gaius neglected his literary studies, but devoted considerable effort to mastering oratory and was an excitable and eloquent speaker who was able to project his voice clearly to those at a distance, a useful trait in an emperor (Suet. *Gaius* 53). He was said to be enormously persuasive, a talent that he cultivated with great diligence. In general, Gaius was judged to be a superlative public speaker who could use both Greek and Latin fluently, and who had the ability to compose and deliver impromptu orations of impressive length and complexity with ease (Josephus *AJ* 19.2.5 (208)). Tacitus added that Gaius's oratorical talents never decayed, even when his sanity did (Tac. *Ann.* 13.3.2). Nero's success as an orator was more uneven. Interestingly, one of his earliest tutors was a dancer who would have instructed him how to use gesture most effectively (Suet. *Nero* 6). Later, of course, his education was entrusted to Seneca, who began tutoring him at the age of eleven (Tac. *Ann.* 12.8; Suet. *Nero* 7, 52). Soon afterward he received his first opportunity to give a public oration in a speech to the people in the Forum, followed by another to the senate, although his early speeches were at least partially written by his tutor, and perhaps his later ones as well (Suet. *Nero* 7).[7] While criticizing this failing in Nero, Tacitus noted that all previous emperors had been skilled composers of orations and that many were powerful speakers whose delivery possessed great eloquence (Tac. *Ann.* 13.3). Nero's later obsessive devotion to singing, reciting, and performing before crowds is well known, as are the sometimes bizarre lengths to which he went to try to improve his voice, including lying under heavy lead weights to strengthen his diaphragm, fasting, purging, following strange diets, and drinking dried boars' dung in water (Suet. *Nero* 20, 25; Pliny *Hist. Nat.* 19.108, 28.237).

Claudius's literary talents are well attested, but he was hampered as a speaker by his infirmities, which sometimes led him to employ a reader to recite his orations (Suet. *Claud.* 41–42). When he had carefully prepared his text, however, even Claudius was said to be capable of considerable eloquence (Tac. *Ann.* 13.3.2). Considering the number of situations at which the emperor was required to address crowds, the sophistication of the Roman art of rhetoric, and the complexity of some of its components such as gesture, the attention that emperors gave to studying rhetoric hardly seems excessive.[8] It is obvious that the emperors fully recognized the importance of rhetoric and the central role that public speaking played in the performance of their duties as emperor.

Gesture in Interactions between Emperors and Plebs

As the vocabulary of gestures was one of the main components of the system of rhetoric that emperors expended so much effort mastering, they could be expected to have used gestures in their public orations. A variety of incidents in the primary sources bear out this assumption. Despite the presence of heralds, emperors often relied on gestures in order to communicate with audiences at public entertainments. Augustus protested against and checked the flattery of the crowd with a hand gesture accompanied by a disapproving glance (Suet. *Aug.* 53). The effective use of such "gestures of command" seems to have been regarded as an important imperial attribute (Pliny *Pan.* 4.4).[9] In his encomium of Trajan's virtues, Pliny praises both the "sincerity" of Trajan's gestures and the harmony of his delivery, in which his voice tone and gestures perfectly complemented his words (Pliny *Pan.* 67.1, 71.6). Knowledge of rhetorical delivery sometimes enabled emperors to convey messages through gesture alone without verbal accompaniment. To counter criticism of his marriage legislation, Augustus chose to respond at a public spectacle during which he exhibited Germanicus's children and suggested through gestures that Germanicus's family was a model that others should emulate (Suet. *Aug.* 34). The versatility of gesture as an interactive form of communication is indicated by the actions of Titus, who was in the habit of making jokes and exchanging witticisms with the crowd solely by means of gestures (Suet. *Titus* 8).

In the early empire gestures also became an important method of communication between the emperor and the urban plebs. In these circumstances, however, gestures were not a one-way form of communication, but were employed as part of a truly interactive dialogue between ruler and ruled. As will be described in more detail, public rituals, and particularly entertainments, were approved settings for the people to make known their opinions to the emperor on a variety of subjects. While the primary method by which the people expressed themselves was acclamations, gestures were a helpful, perhaps necessary, ancillary method of communication at large gatherings. Just as speakers employed gestures in many different ways, so too the urban plebs used them for a variety of purposes.

In some specialized circumstances such as gladiatorial combats, nonverbal exchanges formed an important part of the performance itself. The most notable of these dialogues was the much copied "thumbs up" or "thumbs down" gesture used to determine whether a beaten gladiator would be slain. Hollywood has decreed that the "thumbs down" gesture meant death for the gladiators and "thumbs up" life, but the ancient sources, while confirming that some gesture involving turning the thumbs was used, are vague concerning the precise nature of this gesture. Indeed it may be that the "thumbs down," rather than denoting death, actually was the crowd's way of calling for the victorious gladiator to drop his sword and spare his vanquished foe.[10]

In addition to this famous gesture, there were others used by the emperor and the plebs to collaborate with one another in order to control the course of gladiatorial combats. One such involved the emperor lifting his hand to call for a certain fighter that the crowd had requested. In one instance when two factions were clamoring for different gladiators, in order to placate them, the emperor lifted both arms simultaneously, signifying that both fighters would appear (Mart. *De Spec.* 20). Claudius was known for counting out aloud on his left hand the number of coins awarded to the victors in the "manner of the common people" (Suet. *Claud.* 21.5).[11] The standard interpretation of this passage is that the use of this gesture demonstrates Claudius's vulgarity.[12] Claudius's actions may have been crass, but this was due to his familiar behavior with the audience, not to the gesture itself.[13] While Quintilian stressed that the left hand cannot be used alone, he explicitly stated that an orator will employ it when counting off on the fingers (Quint. *Inst.* 11.3.114). Counting gestures could also be used by the plebs for material benefit. When Marcus Aurelius returned to Rome in A.D. 177 after a long absence, the people anticipated that he would give a *congiaria*, a cash distribution to all citizens. They greeted him with shouts of "eight!" and accompanied the cries with the gesture of holding up eight fingers, indicating that they hoped to receive eight gold aureii apiece (Dio 72.32.1). This was a larger sum than any previous emperor had given out, but since Marcus Aurelius did later distribute exactly this amount, the people's gestures may have contributed to the size of their bounty.

Often in tandem with acclamations, gestures were utilized to make jokes aimed at the emperor as well as to voice criticisms and protests. The crowd reciprocated Titus's jokes and argued with him in a good-natured manner about the merits of different styles of gladiatorial combats using nonverbal methods of communication. Roman audiences were fond of reacting to lines in plays or farces that could be applied to the current emperor by interrupting the performance with applause or even by repeating the lines.[14] This popular form of witticism could also incorporate gesture, as when a theater audience reacted to the recent accession of Galba by repeating a line from an Atellan farce applicable to Galba and embellishing it "with appropriate gestures" (Suet. *Galba* 13). Actors themselves sometimes used gesture to add an additional level of meaning to their performances, usually at the expense of the emperor. During the reign of Nero, Datus, a performer of farces, while speaking the line, "Goodbye father, goodbye mother," made drinking and swimming motions in order to suggest the deaths of Claudius, Nero's father by adoption whom he had supposedly poisoned, and Agrippina, his mother whom he had tried to drown. Similarly, when the underworld was mentioned in the song, Datus referred to the result of Nero's persecutions of his opponents by indicating the senate with a gesture (Suet. *Nero* 39). True to his nature, Nero seems to have responded in kind. When resistance began to break out against him, he reacted by composing obscene verses about his opponents and performed them accompanied by the appropriate gestures (42).

Gestures were one of the primary means available to the urban plebs to voice their displeasure with an emperor. Late in his reign Gaius was criticized in the theaters and at games by the plebs, who demonstrated their feelings through their gestures (Dio 59.13.4). It is unfortunate that Dio did not record what gestures were employed on this occasion. However, he did note that this was an unequal contest, since Gaius retaliated by having members of the audience dragged out of the stands and thrown in prison. Keenly aware of the potential capacity of gesture to insult or criticize, Nero was said constantly to scrutinize the gestures and postures of both senators and the plebs, intently searching for signs of insubordination (Dio 62.15.2).

Emperor, Plebs, and Gestures in Art

Scholarly attention has naturally concentrated on the surviving texts of speeches rather than on their delivery, since the manuscripts survive but there are, of course, no films of Roman orators in motion. There exist, however, the equivalents of still photographs of such scenes in the form of representations on coins and sculptural reliefs that portray not only a gesticulating speaker but also his audience and physical surroundings. Among these images are several that represent the emperor addressing civilian crowds in specific settings in the city of Rome and vividly illustrate that Roman orations were not just one-sided messages but were in fact interactions among these three elements of speaker, audience, and setting.

A series of bronze sesterces of Hadrian, minted between A.D. 125 and 128, shows the emperor standing on the rostra in front of the Temple of the Deified Julius, whose facade is carefully rendered behind him (Fig. 18). He stands in the familiar posture used for orators, with his left hand holding a scroll and his right arm and hand making a gesture. Around the base of the rostra cluster between three and eleven men who raise their right arms, reciprocating the gesture of Hadrian.[15] Scholars have attempted to link this coin to a specific incident and have suggested that it commemorates a restoration of the temple, Hadrian's funeral oration for Plotina, or Hadrian's return to Rome.[16] Whatever the exact event actually was, the coin encapsulates many of the characteristics of Roman oratory. It illustrates the use of gesture by both speaker and audience, the practice of using the public monuments of Rome as settings for speeches, and the ease with which these backgrounds could be exploited by orators. The pediment and colonnades of the temple neatly frame Hadrian, forming a natural stage, and the sculptures of the pediment and facade could easily have been invoked by an orator from this position. The rostra was itself a part of the platform of the temple and was decorated with ships' beaks captured at Actium (Dio 51.19).[17]

This site was often used for imperial addresses to the people. It was from here that Augustus delivered the funeral laudation for his sister Octavia (Dio 54.35). Tiberius gave the funeral eulogy for Augustus here, and since the temple itself was built on the spot where the plebs had spontaneously cremated Caesar's body, the site may thus have retained plebeian associations, making it an appropriate location for interactions between the plebs and the emperor.[18] Interestingly, there were two orations during these ceremonies for Augustus, as Drusus gave a second laudation from the Rostra Augusti. Since Tiberius was the imperial heir, it is suggestive of the significance of the site for the Julio-Claudians that he chose to deliver his eulogy from the *rostra aedis divi Iulii*. The Hadrianic coin and the Anaglypha Traiani/Hadriani mentioned previously illustrate that this location remained a popular one for imperial addresses to the people well beyond the time of the Julio-Claudians. Since the Anaglypha is thought to depict either a generic *adlocutio*, an announcement of a *congiaria*, or an *alimenta* scene, the plebeian connection with this location also seems to have lingered. This same site was additionally used for plebeian legislative activities, as when in 9 B.C. the urban praetor presided from here over the passage of a law by the tribal assembly, the *comitia tributa*, concerning the illegal use of aqueducts by individuals who siphoned water out of them without permission (Frontin. *Aq*. 29).

Another popular location for interactions between emperors and plebs was, of course, the Circus Maximus, and this location also appears on coinage as the background for such exchanges. A sestertius of Trajan portrays the emperor standing on a platform with outstretched right arm, while below him stands a crowd of men, most of whom are raising their right arms toward the emperor.[19] In the background are three closely set cones, while in the foreground a female figure reclines against a wheel. The setting is identified by the triple cones. The turning posts at each end of the *spina* of the Circus Maximus consisted of three cones, the *metae*, arranged close together in a triangular arrangement and sharing a large common base.[20] The *metae* of the Circus Maximus were both some of the most prominent features of the structure and some of the simplest to depict, needing only three lines, thus making them a natural choice for the coin makers to use as a shorthand way of placing the *adlocutio* scene in the desired specific setting of the circus. The identity of the reclining female figure is disputed, but the presence of the wheel is suggestive of an allusion to chariot racing. Further confirmation of the location comes from a series of Hadrianic coins commemorating the Parilia celebrations that feature an almost identical figure holding a wheel and leaning against triple cones on a common base.[21] The coins' inscriptions explicitly identify the site of the festivities as the Circus Maximus.[22] The imperial *adlocutio* coin of Trajan offers a rare visual illustration of what was a frequent scene in the circus, the acclamation of the emperor by the audience and his response. The verbal aspect of such acclamations has already been described, but this coin now completes the image by adding the visual component of these interactions, including gestures and the physical setting.[23]

Similar images of imperial orations in the Roman Forum are provided by the Anaglypha of Hadrian and the Hadrianic sculptural reliefs from the Arco di Portogallo.[24] The latter is the less realistic of the two (Fig. 17). Although Hadrian himself is depicted in a veristic orator's pose with his left hand holding an open scroll and his right forming a gesture, his audience consists of symbolic representatives of Roman citizens. There are only three figures listening to his speech below the rostra, a boy, an old man, and a seminude young man believed to be a personification of the *populus Romanus*. These figures are perhaps intended as metaphorical representations of Rome's citizenry in the three stages of life. Standing behind Hadrian is another allegorical figure, a bearded man symbolizing the genius of the Roman Senate, below whom is a soldier. There are just enough figures to symbolize the three important groups whose favor the emperor had to court, the plebs, the senate, and the army. The architectural setting is similarly generic. Hadrian stands on a platform resembling the plinth of a statue, which probably is meant to represent a rostra. The overall effect is to transform Hadrian himself into a living statue, blending in with the many similar statues that cluttered the Forum. In the background is part of the facade of a temple rendered in a correspondingly undifferentiated fashion. This relief is a generic depiction of an imperial *adlocutio* in which the artist included the bare minimum of elements necessary to have a complete scene: the emperor, an audience, and some typical architecture.[25]

On the other hand, although it is still highly stylized, the Anaglypha of Hadrian offers a much more specific portrait of the emperor addressing a crowd (Fig. 16).[26] This sculptural relief presents an imperial oration not in a generic setting, but in the Roman Forum, and includes varied crowd figures as well as detailed graphic representations of the buildings lining the southern side of the Forum. The scene begins at the left with the gesticulating emperor accompanied by six lictors standing on a platform decorated with *rostra*. The emperor holds a cylindrical object, perhaps a scroll, in his left hand, and his right arm was originally extended in front of his body, although it is impossible to determine what gesture he was making since the arm and hand have been heavily damaged. In front of the emperor is gathered a crowd of thirteen listeners consisting of two rows of senators or equestrians identifiable by their togas and behind them a group of urban plebs wearing the *paenula*, the stereotypical garb of the plebs. The foremost senator has one arm raised toward the emperor in acclamation. Next is a statue consisting of a woman with two children standing before a magistrate seated on a curule chair. After these statues are four additional members of the crowd, all plebeians clad in the *paenula*, followed by two more monuments, the sacred fig tree and a statue of Marsyas. The statue group is probably a commemoration of the imperial *alimenta* scheme for feeding poor children, with the woman representing a personification of Italia.[27]

These figures compose the foreground of the relief, but in the background the artist has provided detailed architectural elements situating the *adlocutio* in the specific context of the Roman Forum. The panel offers a sweeping view along the southern side of the open space of the Forum in which the background buildings can be positively identified. Behind the emperor on the rostra is an oblique view of the Arch of Augustus followed by the facade of the Temple of Castor. The rostra itself, clearly the one in front of the Temple of the Deified Julius, was adorned with the captured ships' beaks from Actium and was known as a favorite site for imperial speeches to the people. Next, behind the senators and equestrians is an open gap, which can be identified as the Vicus Tuscus between the buildings. Filling the remaining background all the way to the right edge of the panel is the colonnade of the Basilica Julia, on which are visible the distinctive corniculated lions' head carvings on the keystones of the arches.

Overall, the Anaglypha of Hadrian neatly encapsulates many of the themes of this study. It presents a vivid view of an imperial oration replete with the emperor orating and gesticulating before a mixed crowd of senators, equestrians, and urban plebs, who themselves are intermingled with the buildings and monuments of the Forum. This relief also provides an appropriate transition point at which to turn from speakers to audiences and from gestures to acclamations, since it includes all these elements interacting with one another in an appropriate setting. The Anaglypha of Hadrian provides a reminder that when attempting to recreate Roman oratory, the place where a speech took place was of great importance and could influence both the content and the delivery of an oration. Also, while it is easier to study these methods of communication separately, in their original context they would have been happening simultaneously, as shown in this relief. During the transition from late republic to early empire, the increase in potential size of audiences, the growth of civic ceremonies, and the trend toward theatricality in oratory probably contributed to the larger role and expanded purpose of gestures in public oratory. So too the changing political identity of the plebs and the creation of the new figure of the princeps altered and expanded the functions of acclamations, a theme that will be explored in the next two chapters.

PART II

AUDIENCES

> I also do not like your festivals either: I found too
> many actors there, and the spectators also often
> behaved like actors.
> —Nietzsche, *Thus Spoke Zarathustra*

Four

Uses of Acclamations
by the Urban Plebs

In order to gauge the effectiveness of an oration, a speaker requires some form of feedback from his audience. Roman audiences often responded with one of the most direct forms, since there existed a tradition of reacting to orators by shouting out approval or disapproval during the course of a speech. These cries represented one of the functions of acclamations in Roman society. The English word *acclamation* has acquired connotations of approval or praise, but the Latin word from which it is derived, *acclamatio*, simply means any shouted comment, whether positive or negative.[1] Similarly, the first definition of the verb *acclamo* is "to shout," the second is "to protest," and only the third is "to shout approval, or applaud." The following discussion demonstrates that the Romans used acclamations for all of these purposes, and that sometimes even a single acclamation could contain elements of both praise and criticism. Thus, in the following chapters the term *acclamation* will be used in its original sense to denote any shouted comment.

In Roman society the acclamation had a long history of use as an important feature of many social occasions. The ancient cry of "Talasse" shouted by participants in wedding ceremonies, and the bystanders' shouts of "Io Triumphe" at triumphs, are two of the most venerable of these uses.[2] The most famous type of spontaneous acclamation was probably the tradition of victorious soldiers upon the battlefield hailing their commander as "Imperator."[3] Throughout Roman history the senate, people, and army had directed laudatory acclamations at prominent politicians. During the late republic the laudatory and derogatory comments that were aimed at politicians in public spaces, particularly the theater, became a significant part of politics. There was, therefore, a long and versatile tradition of the use of acclamations in Roman society. During the early empire acclamations acquired new importance, since they became a central component of ceremonies associated with the emperor, most notably in the accession process by which a new emperor was identified and legitimized. The senate, army, and plebs bestowed acclamations on the emperor not just upon his accession, but upon various occasions in the daily running of the empire, as well as at special events such as imperial birthdays.[4]

For the urban plebs to a much greater degree than for the other groups, however, acclamations became the primary means of communication and interaction with the emperor. The numerous occasions at which acclamations could be employed facilitated this development. In addition to ceremonies centered around the emperor himself, the many performances and rituals associated with various areas of the city of Rome offered plentiful opportunities for interaction between emperor and plebs. Urban events at which such interactions occurred included not only public festivals, religious processions and ceremonies, and imperial orations, but also funerals, triumphs, *contiones*, public feasts, circus races, theatrical performances, gladiatorial games, the movements of the emperor through the streets of Rome, and his arrival (*adventus*) and exit (*profectio*) from the city.[5] Thus, the urban areas that functioned as zones of interaction between emperor and plebs in the early empire ranged from obvious sites such as the Forum and the imperial fora, to specialized structures such as the amphitheaters, circuses, and theaters, as well as the walls and streets of the city. During the early empire the political topography of the city was shifting away from the formal and traditional centers such as the Forum and the voting spaces of the Campus Martius toward public spaces whose overt purpose was often ceremony and even entertainment. This shift was away from spaces associated with republican political processes such as voting, the census, and the enrollment of armies toward spaces focused on imperial ceremonies and appearances. At the public events—political, judicial, religious, and ludic—that were staged in many of these spaces, the emperor and plebs acted together as mutual participants in the social drama being performed, and on each of these occasions acclamations played a significant role. Finally, for the plebs, acclamations became a method by which they could make known their opinions on a wide range of matters from the trivial to the momentous, express pleasure or displeasure with the emperor and his actions, and present petitions to him directly.

The subsequent discussion focuses on this most flexible use of acclamations, those directed at the emperor by the urban plebs. On these occasions the basic forms that acclamations took were, in increasing order of complexity, simple applause; rhythmic applause of various types; individual shouted words or titles; brief formulaic phrases; longer, often rhythmic sentences; and, finally, entire series of phrases that were chanted or even sung. These types of acclamation were used alone or in any combination and could be delivered by any number of persons, from a single individual to tens of thousands. The urban plebs used acclamations for three basic purposes: to greet or praise, to react to a speaker, and to criticize or petition. Acclamations possess several unique features that made them versatile forms of communication between emperor and urban plebs. The existence of a body of well-known acclamation formulas and the rhythmic nature of many of the acclamation chants themselves are the two most significant of these characteristics. The rhythmic and formulaic nature of acclamations made it easy for large numbers of people not only to deliver them in unison, but also spontaneously to vary and improvise upon the standard formulas. The utility of acclamations was due to the fact that they incorporated flexibility of message within widely known structures. Therefore they could convey a variety of meanings, yet because of their formulaic nature, each side had a clearly designated role to play. Through the medium of acclamations, the emperor and the urban plebs engaged in a continuous process of negotiation by which they constantly defined and renewed their relationship to one another and their places in society. This chapter will examine the various types of acclamations that were shouted at the emperor by the urban plebs, and the sites and times at which these interactions occurred.[6]

Greeting and Praise

Imperial greeting acclamations had their origins in the spontaneous (and sometimes carefully rigged) receptions given to political figures of the late republic when they appeared in public. Cicero's much cited dictum that "the opinion and feeling of the Roman people in public affairs can be most clearly expressed on three occasions, at assemblies, at elections, and at games and gladiatorial shows," at which the people indicated their feelings by the applause (or jeers) with which they greeted the entrance of important individuals, constitutes a succinct statement of this phenomenon (Cic. *Sest.* 106). This idea was a recurrent one in Cicero's works, and he frequently included descriptions of the receptions that politicians received from the public. For example, in a letter of 59 B.C. to Atticus, when Cicero wished to indicate the current status of Pompey, Caesar, and Curio, the way he chose to convey this information was by describing in great detail the reception that each received in the theater and at public events, since, according to him, these are the best places to gauge popular opinion. He related the hostile hisses that met Pompey upon his entrance, the cheers of the audience when an actor spoke a line that could be interpreted as critical of Pompey, the feeble applause that greeted Caesar, and the thunderous accolades for Curio (Cic. *Ad Att.* 2.19). So significant did Cicero judge these crowd reactions to be, that when he was away from Rome and asked Atticus for a letter containing all the latest news, he specifically requested that Atticus include an account of how various political figures had been greeted when they entered the theater, and even wanted to hear about all of the jests made by the actors in reference to these politicians (14.3.2).

In the *Pro Sestio* Cicero offered contrasting images of the receptions awarded to popular and reviled figures in the theater. The senators and consuls were welcomed with "unanimous applause

. . . the people stood and held out their hands, giving thanks and plainly demonstrating their goodwill," while Clodius was met with a chorus of hisses and "shouts, menacing gestures, loud curses." The audience even employed the performance itself as a means of abuse, since while "speaking loudly in unison, [it] leaned forward threateningly and looked straight at the the foul wretch and loudly chanted the words, 'This . . . is the end of your vicious life!'"—a line that had just been uttered by an actor in the play (Cic. *Sest.* 115, 117–18). In Cicero's admittedly biased account, the efforts of Clodius's claque of supporters to generate applause for its leader were completely drowned out by the spontaneous negative reaction of the spectators (118). The greetings of theater audiences could have considerable influence on events, as when in 44 B.C., shortly after Caesar's death, Octavian entered the theater and was greeted with loud applause from the people, who continued to bestow on him round after round of applause throughout the program as a mark of their approval. The importance of such indications of public support is suggested by Marcus Antonius's reaction, since, evidently perceiving Octavian as a serious rival, Antonius was afterward reportedly more hostile toward Octavian as a result of this public adulation (Nic. Dam. *Aug.* 28).

Cicero's writings are a fruitful source of information concerning acclamations and other manifestations of public opinion in the setting of public entertainments, particularly the theater. He claimed that he disapproved of such accolades because often their "recipients are the sort of men who will do anything to win popularity," but Cicero frequently cited such demonstrations in his speeches when the applause was for a client of whose character he approved (Cic. *Phil.* 1.37). Even more satisfying to Cicero were occasions when he himself was the object of applause, at which times the shouts constituted "the true and uncorrupted unanimous judgement of the entire Roman people, the inmost feelings of the country" (Cic. *Pro Sest.* 119). Clearly Cicero and others perceived the acclamations with which the people greeted the entrance of important politicians as significant.[7] The most basic and common form that such greeting acclamations took was for the crowd to rise in unison and applaud the favored figure, as when a well-disposed audience greeted Pompey (Lucan 7.18). Standing up and applauding was a universal way for a crowd to express approval whether it was of a person, a comment in a speech, or a theatrical performance. This republican tradition extended into the empire, and a similar combination of standing and applauding quickly evolved as the usual method for greeting the arrival of the emperor.

During the empire, whenever the emperor appeared in public, or particularly when he entered a circus, theater, amphitheater, the Forum, or other enclosed space, his arrival was immediately acknowledged by the people rising to their feet and applauding his entrance. As early in the empire as the reign of Augustus, this tradition had become so firmly codified that whenever he made a public appearance, such as at the theater, the entire audience rose in unison and applauded him enthusiastically (Suet. *Aug.* 56). In a similar incident described by Phaedrus that took place during the reign of Tiberius, in response to the entrance of the princeps into the theater the entire audience stood up to applaud (Phaed. 5.7.25– 28). That by the end of the first century of the empire this had become the universally standard form of acknowledging the entrance of the emperor is further attested by Pliny, who favorably contrasted the stand-and-applaud greeting with less spontaneous and more ostentatious welcomes engineered by emperors such as Nero (Pliny *Pan.* 54.3). It was noted as an indication of Vespasian's unusual tolerance that when he encountered the Cynic Demetrius, Vespasian did not take offense when Demetrius failed to rise and salute him as was customary in the emperor's presence (Suet. *Vesp.* 13).[8] The people also extended this form of acclamation to the members of the imperial family. During the reign of Augustus, Marcellus was greeted in this way, as were Augustus's adoptive sons Gaius and Lucius (Prop. 3.18.18; Suet. *Aug.* 56).

In a fawning epigram dedicated to Domitian, Martial made use of this convention to flatter the emperor by claiming that the circus crowd applauded his entrance for so long that it missed four horse races (Mart. 8.11). The custom quickly became so codified that it could be parodied in satire, as when at the dinner of Trimalchio the guests were confronted by a dish so magnificent that it seemed fit only for the emperor's table. This reaction caused all of the diners instinctively to leap immediately to their feet and shout an acclamation to the emperor (Pet. *Sat.* 60; cf. Mart. 9.33). While the stand-and-applaud greeting was plainly a frequent occurrence, it is a measure of the quotidian nature of this greeting that it is only explicitly described by an ancient author in connection with some other more noteworthy event or in order to make a point about something else. Thus, in the preceding examples, the custom is mentioned by Phaedrus only as the lead-in to a joke, since a vain stage performer thought that the applause had been directed at him, resulting in much merriment among the audience. Pliny, Suetonius, and Martial mentioned such applause while relating anecdotes that illustrated or praised imperial virtues, and Petronius used the custom for satiric purposes.

In addition to its role in greeting the arrival or entrance of the emperor, applause could also be used to praise a popular emperor. If, for example, the emperor's name was mentioned by a public official, a well-disposed crowd would often spontaneously spring to its feet and applaud.[9] Such a reaction could also occur even when the emperor's name was only implied, as in the well-known incident when an actor in a comedy at which Augustus was present spoke a line about a "good and benevolent lord" (O dominum aequum et bonum), and the crowd immediately jumped up and applauded enthusiastically (Suet. *Aug.* 53).[10] These actions were so clearly identified as a mark of favor that they could be used to praise others, so that when a line from Virgil was recited in the course of a theatrical performance at which he was present, the spectators rose to their feet and applauded, giving "homage to the poet, just as they would have done to the emperor himself" (Tac. *Dial.* 13.2). Emperors were sometimes jealous of the people's applause, as when Gaius became enraged that the people applauded performers more loudly than himself, resulting in his famous wish that all the Roman people had a single neck that he could sever (Suet. *Gaius* 30; cf. *Gaius* 35, and *Nero* 53).

Applause to acknowledge the emperor's entrance seems to have been obligatory, but laudatory applause offered scope for more spontaneous expressions of opinion. A popular emperor would often have been the recipient of such unsolicited acclamations, and an unpopular one would surely have noticed their absence. Any increase or decrease in the frequency or fervor of such applause was a ready indicator of an emperor's current standing among the people and their opinion of his recent actions.

In greeting an emperor, the people's applause was often augmented by brief formulaic shouts and phrases wishing the emperor good health, a long life, happiness, or simply hailing him as ruler.[11] For example, in the incident described by Phaedrus after the crowd had risen to its feet and applauded, the chorus and presumably the audience as well shouted, "Rejoice, Rome is safe, because the princeps is safe" (Laetare incolumis Roma salvo principe; Phaed. 5.7.27). Another common acclamation was simply to shout imperial titles such as "Imperator," as did Pliny and his peers on several instances described in his panegyric to Trajan (Pliny *Pan.* 5, 23). Probably one of the most common acclamations was simply to hail the emperor as "Augustus," as did the Arval Brethren as recorded in an inscription of A.D. 213 (*CIL* 6.2086).[12]

Short stock phrases praising the emperor or his virtues or expressing goodwill toward him were another basic type of greeting acclamation. The most frequent of these brief phrases attested in the first century of the empire employ the word *feliciter* as a hortatory expression of goodwill or good luck.[13] When he appeared in public, Claudius was greeted by the people with shouts of "Good luck to the emperor's uncle" (Feliciter patruo imperatoris), and "Good luck to the brother of Germanicus" (Feliciter Germanici fratri) (Suet. *Claud.* 7). The crowd in the amphitheater acclaimed Domitian and his wife with the phrase, "Good luck to our Lord and Lady" (Domino et Dominae feliciter; Suet. *Dom.* 13). The diners at Trimalchio's table shouted, "Good luck to Augustus, the father of the country" (Augusto, patri patriae, feliciter; Pet. *Sat.* 60). Earlier in the meal the slaves acclaimed one of the courses by applauding and shouting "Good Luck to Gaius" (Gaio feliciter; Pet. *Sat.* 50).

Acclamations featuring *feliciter* were also employed by the senate. Pliny and his peers greeted Trajan with cries of "O lucky one" (O te felicem; Pliny *Pan.* 74.1). The same list of acclamations of the Arval Brethren includes the phrases, "Most Lucky One" (Felicissime), and "Good luck to Julia Augusta, mother of Augustus" (Julia

Augustae matri Augusti feliciter) (*CIL* 6.2086). *Feliciter* figures prominently in the acclamations of the senate recorded in the *Historia Augusta* as well. Pertinax, for example, was greeted with shouts that included "Hail the loyalty of the praetorians! Hail the praetorian cohorts! Hail the armies of Rome! Hail the faithfulness of the senate! . . . Hail the victory of the Roman people! Hail the loyalty of the soldiers! Hail the loyalty of the praetorian cohorts! Hail the praetorian cohorts!" (Fidei praetorianorum feliciter. Praetoriis cohortibus feliciter. Exercitibus Romanis feliciter. Pietati senatus feliciter. . . . Fidei militum feliciter. Fidei praetorianorum feliciter. Cohortibus praetoriis feliciter; SHA *Comm.* 18.11). Here, *feliciter* is applied to other persons and groups besides the emperor. All these groups, however, were closely linked to the emperor and in this instance received praise because of their recent demonstrations of loyalty to him.

In several recorded acclamations of the senate appears another obviously stock type of acclamation phrases that either commended the emperor's actions or virtues to the gods or asked the gods to protect an emperor. Pliny and his fellow senators hailed Trajan with the cry, "So great, so revered" (Tanto maior, tanto augustior; Pliny *Pan.* 71.4). Usually wishes invoking the gods' favor were built around the basic greeting "May the gods save you" (Di te servent). Thus, in the *Historia Augusta* the senate's praise for Marcus Antoninus included the phrases "Dutiful Antoninus, may the gods save you. Merciful Antoninus, may the gods save you" (Antonine pie, di te servent. Antonine clemens, di te servent), and "May the gods watch over you" (Di te tuentur) (SHA *Avid. Cass.* 13). The Arval Brethren shouted, "May the gods save you" (Di te servent), "Augustus, may the gods forever save you" (Auguste, di te servent in perpetuo), and "Augusta and Augustus, may the gods forever save you" (Di te servent in perpetuo, Augusta, Auguste) (*CIL* 6.2086).

The verb *facere*, "to do," appears in several early imperial acclamations. A speech of Nero was interrupted by cries of "You will do it, Augustus" (Tu facies, Auguste; Suet. *Nero* 46.3). Later, Pliny and his fellow senators hailed Trajan for listening to their advice with the phrase, "Let him hear this, let him do this" (Haec faciat, haec audit; Pliny *Pan.* 2.8). The use of *facere* by the senate is suggestive as an acknowledgment of the new reality of power in the empire. They praised the emperor because he hears their prayers, but only the emperor was able to take real action, and enact their recommendations and transform them into reality. The Neronian example is interesting because it illustrates the possibilities acclamations offered to an audience for subtle subversion, even when purportedly showing agreement with the speaker. Nero's speech, which was read in the senate shortly before his death, denounced the rebellious governor Vindex and included the threat that "the villains will suffer punishment and will soon meet the end which they deserve" (Suet. *Nero* 46.3). Just after this passage was read, the audience broke in with their acclamation. Suetonius cites this incident amid a description of Nero's great unpopularity and a list of signs indicating Nero's imminent downfall. Plainly, the cry of the senate had a double meaning and was meant as a suggestion that Nero, not Vindex, was the "villain" who would soon meet the fate he deserved. By interjecting a standard and seemingly innocuous acclamation at this particular point in the address, the senate was able to subvert the meaning of Nero's words and turn his own denunciation against himself.[14]

Although few examples of actual greeting acclamations survive from Rome itself in the early empire, this is probably not because they were infrequently used, but rather that they were so commonplace that they hardly seemed worth mentioning. The ancient sources tended to record unusual events rather than mundane ones, and this tendency applied to acclamations as well, so that when acclamations were quoted, they were usually atypical in content and specific to a particular occurrence.[15] Despite this scarcity, evidence from the provinces and from nonliterary sources such as inscriptions and coinage, as well as later known acclamations, suggests what early imperial greeting acclamations were like. Many of the titles and slogans stamped upon coins or carved onto public monuments were the same as those shouted at the emperor by his subjects.

Upon his entrance to the hippodrome at Alexandria, Vespasian was greeted with the following acclamations: "Lord Caesar. In good health [may you come!] Vespasian, the one savior and [benefactor!]

Son of [Amm]o[n] rising up. . . . Keep him for us [in good health. Lord] Augustus . . . Sar[apis] . . . Son of Ammon and in a word [the one god . . .] God Caesar . . . in good health! . . . God Caesar Vespasian! . . . Lord Augustus!"[16] Despite the clearly eastern influences evident in hailing Vespasian as the son of Ammon, many of the phrases in this acclamation were standard ones that would also have been used by the people of Rome to greet the emperors. As in this example, various permutations composed of the recitation of imperial titles such as Lord, Caesar, Augustus or Imperator, and benedictions of good health undoubtedly formed the major elements of greeting acclamations. While some of these acclamations may have been shouted by official or semiofficial groups such as military units, the crowd was clearly the source of many, if not most.

Cassius Dio noted the acclamations that the people and senate of Rome used to greet Nero in 68 A.D. upon his return to the city after having made the rounds of the choregic festivals in Greece. The crowds chanted in unison, "Olympian Victor! Pythian Victor! Augustus! Augustus! Nero, our Hercules! Nero, our Apollo! The only victor of the Grand Tour, the only one from the beginning of time. Augustus! Augustus! O Divine Voice! Blessed are those who hear you! (Ὀλυμπιονῖκα οὐᾶ, Πυθιονῖκα οὐᾶ, Αὔγουστε, Αὔγουστε. Νέρωνι τῷ Ἡρακλεῖ, Νέρωνι τῷ Ἀπόλλωνι. ὡς εἷς περιοδονίκης, εἷς ἀπ᾽ αἰῶνος, Αὔγουστε Αὔγουστε. ἱερὰ φωνή μακάριοι οἵ σου ἀκούοντες; Dio 62.20.5). Dio claimed that these titles and shouts were exactly those that were used on this occasion. As with the acclamations used to greet Vespasian, these are a mixture of obviously stock formulas, such as "Augustus," and shouts specific to the situation, such as that praising Nero's voice. Such a combination of standard formulas of praise with phrases specific to a given circumstance seemed to have been characteristic of many acclamations from this period. These two examples of greeting acclamations are illustrative of the versatility of acclamations in general, since they could be readily adapted to fit widely varying situations.[17]

The custom of augmenting applause with brief shouted comments offered an occasion for spontaneous expressions of the crowd's opinion and an opportunity for praise of a popular emperor. The volume and variety of shouted acclamations accompanying an emperor's entrance furnished a rough measure of his standing with the urban plebs, in the same way that figures of the late republic had used such acclamations to judge their popularity. The obligatory type of greeting acclamation continued to grow in variety and length throughout the empire and into the Byzantine period. By the later Roman Empire, the simple stand-and-applaud greeting had been transformed into a highly formalized ceremony replete with an extended series of chants and repeated recitations of imperial titles, often with musical accompaniment.[18]

Early imperial Rome did possess one specialized type of greeting ceremony centered around the emperor that could rival the later ones in complexity. This was the celebration held to welcome the emperor's return to the city after an absence, the ceremony of *adventus*. This ceremony included a variety of chants praising the emperor's virtues, enumerating his titles, and wishing him health and success.[19] A typical *adventus* consisted of throngs of people going out a short distance from the city's walls to meet the emperor and escort him to the city. Leading these crowds was an official delegation composed of representatives of the senate and equestrians dressed in elaborate finery and often accompanied by their wives and children organized by rank and age. Substantial numbers of the urban plebs accompanied the official group to view the spectacle and take part in it. After meeting the emperor, the return march into the city took on the festive character of a parade. The crowds lining the roadside shouted acclamations as the emperor passed and would even cast flowers in his path.[20] As Vespasian entered Rome for the first time as emperor in A.D. 70 after returning from the East, he was greeted by a vast and enthusiastic crowd lining the road into the city, who shouted many of the same acclamations he had received in Alexandria, including "Benefactor," "Savior," and "Only worthy emperor of Rome," and decorated his route with flowers and garlands (τὸν εὐργέτινην καὶ σωτῆρα καὶ μόνον ἄξιον ἡγεμόνα τῆς Ῥώμης; Joseph. *BJ* 7.71). Accounts of the *adventus* of other emperors, such as Augustus, Nero, Trajan, and Commodus, suggest that Vespasian's welcome was typical. Evidently not all emperors enjoyed the pomp and ceremony of the *adventus*, however; Augustus found these elaborate ceremonies tedious and often tried to avoid them by leaving and entering cities only at night (Dio 54.25; Suet. *Aug.* 53).

Probably every appearance of the emperor in public was also a chance for similar, if less elaborate, acclamations. Indeed, the everyday movements of the emperor through the streets of the city may actually have been the most common occasion for acclamations. Despite the emphasis placed on incidents at entertainments, these random street encounters would have constituted the majority of interactions between emperor and plebs. Only a relatively small number of the urban plebs could have been present at any one event in the theater or arena. The exceptions were the spectacles, most notably chariot races, held in the Circus Maximus, which eventually could seat up to a quarter of a million spectators, and it is therefore not surprising that many of the most memorable interactions between emperor and plebs took place at the circus. Nevertheless, the places where the average citizen most commonly saw his emperor (and communicated with him through acclamations) were the streets and fora of the city.

Examples of acclamations directed at the emperor by the people as he moved through the streets of the city rarely mention the actual acclamations, but do indicate that such interactions were frequent occurrences. As a gesture of informality and in order to save time, Gaius early in his reign forbade the people whom he encountered while moving through the city to salute him as had been the custom "before this for all who met the emperor in the streets" (Dio 59.7). Generosity to the plebs could increase the zeal of such acclamations, as when Tiberius distributed money after a fire and as a result was hailed and praised by the people in the streets of the city with more than usual ardor (Tac. *Ann.* 4.64). When the emperor was known to be appearing in public, the people would often gather in the streets along his anticipated path in order to shout acclamations and hope for largess in return (Pliny *Pan.* 26). An insight into how knowledge of appropriate acclamations was passed from one generation of urban plebs to another is offered by Pliny, who described parents teaching acclamation formulas to their children as they waited in the street for the emperor to pass by on such an occasion (ibid.). Once again, these encounters offered an opportunity for the urban plebs to praise a favored emperor through the frequency and fervor of their cries and to criticize an unpopular one through a lack of enthusiasm or even the total absence of such shouts.[21]

If acclamations represented a way by which the people could identify their favorites, it is perhaps no coincidence that in keeping with his image as a particularly beloved figure, an unusual number of quoted acclamations praising Germanicus were reported by the ancient sources. When in A.D. 19 an erroneous rumor spread that Germanicus had recovered from his illness, Tiberius was awakened by a jubilant crowd who gathered around the Capitol and in unison repeatedly sang the verses, "Rome is safe, our country is safe, for Germanicus is safe" (Salva Roma, salva patria, salvus est Germanicus; Suet. *Gaius* 6). Upon the accession of his son Gaius, the adoring crowd, supposedly on account of the memory of his father, hailed Gaius with the affectionate appellations of "Star, Chick, Boy, and Nursling" (Sidus, pullum, pupum, alumnum; *Gaius* 13). His popularity even caused his brother, Claudius, to be greeted by the people at public entertainments with the acclamation, "Good luck to the brother of Germanicus" (Feliciter Germanici fratri; Suet. *Claud.* 7). Such incidents indicated not only the enduring popularity of Germanicus, but also the creativity of the plebs in devising acclamations appropriate to a variety of occasions. These three examples of actual acclamations, particularly the list of nicknames, were all seemingly spontaneous ones used by the plebs to honor a favorite and are indicative of the use of a wide range of acclamations both in terms of content and familiarity of tone.

Reaction

One significant aspect of imperial acclamations is that they were not simply one-sided expressions of praise honoring the emperor, but often constituted half of a two-sided dialogue between emperor and people. They functioned in several ways. The people routinely punctuated the speech of the emperor or his representatives with short, reactive acclamations that both encouraged the speaker and signaled the audience's assent to, or agreement with, the speaker's message. This was probably also a very frequent form of interactive acclamation (although again this is not reflected in the surviving sources, given their focus on unusual events rather than common-place ones). As the emperor or his representative spoke, the crowd would interrupt his speech not only with applause, but also with formulaic interjections of their own, to which the emperor in turn responded. These interjections were often prompted by some com-ment that had been made by the emperor. For example, if the emperor made a reference to his age or health, the people might break in with cries of "Long life to the emperor!" Often the acclama-tions were simply affirmations of what was being said.

Certainly crowds often broke into applause during the course of an oration when the speaker said something with which they strongly agreed. In a list of rhetorical questions describing the ideal orator, Cicero asked, "Who is interrupted by applause?" (Cic. *De Orat.* 3.14.53). Although officially disapproving, Tacitus conceded that "public speakers cannot get along without shouts and ap-plause, as if on the stage" (Tac. *Dial.* 39.4). All speeches to the public were thus periodically interrupted by applause and shouts express-ing the audience's assent. Crowd participation of all sorts was an integral part of public speeches, but while ancient sources often mentioned in a general way that such interruptions occurred, they rarely recorded the actual acclamations of the audiences. In recon-structing speeches as they were actually delivered rather than as they were later written down or paraphrased, the loss of the interac-tions with the crowd and of the interruptions and reactions of the audience constitutes the greatest difference. An accurate account of any ancient speech would need to resemble a modern stenogra-pher's transcript of a courtroom trial, complete with interruptions and notations indicating the audience's applause. While such literal transcripts of ancient speeches are rare, at least one exists and is worthy of detailed examination as an illustration of this type of spontaneous interaction between speaker and audience.

A papyrus found at Oxyrhynchus contains a scribe's transcript of an apparently impromptu speech given by Germanicus upon his arrival in Alexandria in A.D. 19.[22] Germanicus had been dis-patched to the eastern provinces on a special mission during which he stopped at Egypt.[23] The papyrus recorded not just the words of Germanicus and the local official, but also the shouted comments of the audience. After receiving some honorary decrees from the local exegetes, Germanicus gave a short speech, during the course of which he was periodically interrupted by interjections from the crowd. He had barely begun to talk when upon his first mention of the citizens of Alexandria, the crowd broke in and, according to the scribe, shouted, "Ha! Lord! Good luck! May you receive good things!" ([οἱ] ὄχλοι ἐφώνησαν, οὐά, κύρι'. ἐπ' ἀγαθῶι. [δ]έξηι τῶν ἀγαθῶν; lines 4–5). These interruptions were in the form of standard acclamations of greeting and praise, and their outbreak at this point in Germanicus's remarks was probably in reaction to his reference to the citizens themselves. It is unclear whether these phrases were chanted by the entire crowd in unison or represent the shouts of a few individuals. Different groups may have shouted a variety of such acclamations, and the scribe simply wrote down a representative sample. Germanicus, in turn, thanked the people for their kind wishes, asked them to restrain their enthusiasm, and then continued his speech. As soon as he mentioned their city, the people again interrupted with a cry of "Good Luck!" (οἱ ὄχλοι ἐφώυησαν, ἐπ' ἀγαθῷ; line 17). Finally, after praising the splendors and history of Alexandria, Germanicus seems to have made references to imperial benefactions, causing the audience to interrupt a third time with cries of "Ha! May your life be longer!" ([οἱ ὄχλ]οι ἐφώνησα[ν], ἰὼ, ζώης ἐπὶ πλεῖον; line 24). After a few more comments by Germanicus, the remainder of the speech is lost.

Throughout this exchange, stock acclamation formulas were used to praise Germanicus, and he responded with frequent laudatory remarks about his audience and their city. These compliments seem to have provoked the crowd's responses so that the dialogue took on the nature of a mutual exchange of flattery, with each side playing off the other. The same papyrus also contained on the verso the minutes of an audience at Rome given by Augustus to envoys from Alexandria in A.D. 12. On the only occasion when Augustus himself spoke, his speech was interrupted with shouts of "Good Luck!" from the bystanders (ἐπ' ἀγαθῶι. ἐπ' ἀγαθῶι; *P. Oxy.* 2435 verso, line 54). On both these occasions, it is plain that the crowd was accustomed to interrupting the speaker with brief shouts in reaction to what was being said. Such a back-and-forth exchange between speaker and audience was the typical structure for imperial speeches to the people.

This was also a common structure for speeches to the senate. In the *Historia Augusta* the author of the "Life of Severus Alexander" preserved what he claimed was a verbatim extract from the *Acta Urbis* recording a speech by the emperor to the senate (*Sev. Alex.* 6–12; see also SHA, *Max.* 16). In the course of this very brief address, the emperor's comments were interspersed with senatorial acclamations. While the veracity of the exact words spoken on this occasion is highly questionable, there is no reason to doubt the general nature of the exchange. It began with a lengthy list of stock acclamations expressing the hope that the emperor would enjoy a long life and the favor of the gods, as well as a few shouts that denigrated his predecessor, Elagabalus. The emperor then replied with a few platitudes thanking the senate, but had barely spoken a few sentences when they burst in with another set of acclamations urging him to adopt the name Antonius. He thanked them and attempted to decline, but again the senators broke into acclamations. This back-and-forth exchange was repeated several more times, so that ultimately during his short oration the emperor was interrupted no fewer than ten times.[24]

This interactive form of communication has received much attention in the field of literary criticism, in which this form of dialogue is labeled as *call-and-response*. One linguist defines the call-and-response format as "spontaneous verbal and nonverbal interaction between speaker and listener in which all the speaker's statements (calls) are punctuated by expressions (responses) from the listener."[25] Another important characteristic is that "there is no sharp line between performers or communications and the audience, for virtually everyone is performing and everyone is listening."[26] In call-and-response dialogues, "the audience not only aids a speaker's performance but also performs in its own right. Every member of the . . . audience is required to participate actively in communication. The audience in fact is a speaker, and the speaker, thriving on the response of the audience is [him]self a listener."[27]

These descriptions are certainly reminiscent of the interactions between the speaker and his audience in the examples cited earlier. While the senate's responses were plainly prearranged to some degree, in some instances they were reacting to specific comments made by the emperor.[28] The exchange between Germanicus and the Alexandrian crowd seems to have been more spontaneous on both sides and closely fits the call-and-response model. Members of the audience constantly interrupted him, but in a way that simultaneously praised him and signaled their approval of his message. In turn, Germanicus directly responded to their interruptions and was encouraged to continue his accolades of the Alexandrians and their city. In this instance, the acclamation ritual does indeed blur the line between speaker and audience, since both were speaking, listening, and reacting.

Criticism or Petition

Occasionally an acclamation was coupled with an additional message, usually a petition, so that under the guise of praising the emperor, the people were actually making a demand or sometimes even a criticism of him. Although such acclamations happened much less frequently than greeting or reactive acclamations, they are the type most commonly mentioned by ancient authors. Because these were exceptions to the rule, they were memorable and therefore noted. Such petitions in the form of acclamations have drawn the attention of many scholars and have resulted in a substantial secondary literature. Usually, however, these petitions are treated as an independent phenomenon and are not considered within their larger context as a type of acclamation. Many, but not all, of these petitions were delivered by the audiences at public entertainments, and there certainly was a strong tradition that at the circus, arena, and theaters the populace was tacitly allowed or even encouraged to petition the emperor with requests, to express its displeasure about imperial activities (whether serious or trivial), and finally to make jokes and witticisms about the emperor, both complimentary and derogatory. Before examining these acclamations, it is necessary to describe this tradition and the expectations for behavior that accompanied it.[29]

In the empire, proximity and access to the emperor became all important. The routes of communication between the emperor and his subjects were often, at least from a modern point of view, rather ill defined and nebulous. Frequently these links were informal and personal. Like the patronage system, most petitions to the emperor worked on the basis of unspoken understandings, not formal, explicitly stated rules.[30] Petitions to the emperor from members of the upper classes or from those who had contacts with them were, as demonstrated in the letters of Pliny, often routed through friends of the emperor.[31] Individuals of high status were able, from a distance, to petition the emperor directly by letter.[32] One of the emperor's duties, however, was to be responsive to petitions not only from the elite, but also from Roman citizens from all sectors of society, including the lowest.[33]

Particularly for the urban plebs who lacked aristocratic links, the ability to petition the emperor was contingent upon direct access to him. The only places in which the plebs could, in substantial numbers, personally interact with the emperor were the public spaces of Rome: the streets, fora, theaters, and circus. Because the emperor had to traverse the streets, participate in festivals, and preside over games, such encounters were frequent, and therefore the very presence of the emperor in the city of Rome made the urban plebs a privileged group simply because these meetings provided them with routine access to him. The routes of communication between emperor and plebs that developed were, not surprisingly, informal, nonbureaucratic, and personal.

At least in the early empire emperors felt compelled to attend the games, even when they did not enjoy them. For an emperor, attending the games did not simply constitute entertainment, but was a duty and a part of the job of being emperor. So great was the expectation that the emperor would be present at games that his absence required some sort of explanation. Augustus was always careful to send apologies when he could not attend a performance, even if he was only delayed for a few hours. When he was unable to preside at the games, he appointed an official substitute, usually a member of his own family, to take his place (Suet. *Aug.* 45). Similarly, when Gaius did not wish to attend, he often required his uncle Claudius to go in his place (Suet. *Claud.* 7). Emperors who did not appear at the games, such as Tiberius, incurred considerable displeasure (Suet. *Tib.* 47).

The compulsion for emperors to attend entertainments seems to have been quite strong. Even while Augustus was sick with his fatal illness, he dragged himself from his sickbed to watch some local games at Naples (Suet. *Aug.* 98). Being present at the games was not all that was required of the emperors. They also had to pay close attention to the spectacle. Caesar was severely criticized for reading and answering letters while at the games, and Marcus Aurelius was later guilty of the same offense and, as a result, suffered much ridicule from the people (Suet. *Aug.* 45; SHA *M. Aur.* 15).

Not only was the emperor expected to attend, but there were also expectations about how he should behave. Many of these expectations revolved around the idea that the emperor and the audience were coparticipants in the performance. At the games, the emperor and the people were psychologically linked by both being spectators of the performance. More than this, however, they joined together to take an active role in directing the performance, particularly in those entertainments involving violence.[34] The most obvious form that this interaction took was at gladiatorial games when the emperor and the spectators played a role in deciding the outcome of the combats. When a wounded fighter dropped his shield and raised a finger of his left hand in submission, the people made gestures and shouted to indicate whether the unfortunate man should be spared or dispatched. Although the decision was the emperor's, only rarely would he disagree with the consensus of the crowd. The awards given to the victor were also determined by an exchange of gestures and mutual consultation between the emperor and the rest of the crowd.[35]

Despite their poverty and an apparent low status, the urban plebs were able to enhance their standing through their literal life-and-death control over the yet-lower-status combatants. The urban plebs symbolically shared in the Roman domination of the Mediterranean by watching barbarians and foreigners die at their command and for their amusement. They also had their identities reaffirmed and their rank as citizens enhanced by observing and participating in the disciplining of criminals and other stigmatized individuals within the Roman state. Within the arena, the gulf between emperor and plebs was narrowed, and their common identity as Romans was stressed. Through these various forms of interaction, the urban plebs and the emperor acted together as Romans controlling and punishing foreigners, criminals, and barbarians.

The emperor was just another onlooker at the games, and he shared the same emotions and responses as the rest of the crowd. One important imperial virtue was *civilitas*, which can be defined as showing deference to the people and acting as a fellow citizen rather than an absolute ruler.[36] The games, because of the way in which they linked emperor and people as fellow spectators, certainly offered plentiful opportunities for an emperor to display his *civilitas*. Claudius amply demonstrated this trait. His demeanor was informal, and he emulated the plebs by counting aloud on the fingers of his outstretched left hand the monetary awards given to the victors—"as the commoners did." Furthermore, he directly spoke to his fellow spectators, telling jokes, urging them to enjoy themselves, and even referring to them as *dominus* (Suet. *Claud.* 51). *Dominus* was a usual form of address with which the people hailed the emperor, and it was a term particularly associated with him. It was also the term that slaves used when addressing their master. Therefore, this habit of Claudius represented a dramatic inversion of the social order, since the highest-status member of Roman society was addressing one of the lowest-status sectors with this term of extreme deference. Claudius was often criticized for his vulgarity, so perhaps he took the idea of *civilitas* to an extreme. Suetonius's life of Titus, however, was in many ways the portrait of an ideal ruler, so it is instructive to see how his interactions with the plebs at the games are portrayed. He too behaved toward his fellow spectators with indulgence and openly declared that he wished to conduct the show "not after his own inclinations, but rather those of the spectators." He was also depicted as arguing in a good-natured manner with his cospectators at the games about the virtues of Thracian gladiators, who were his favorites (Suet. *Tit.* 8.2).[37]

While the people were pleased if the emperor shared their enthusiasm for the games, he could not abuse his power as emperor, but rather had to remain just another spectator. At a horse race, Caracalla became very upset when the crowd jeered at a charioteer that he favored. Rather than accepting this as part of the spectacle, as other emperors had, he took personal offense and ordered soldiers into the crowd to arrest those who had insulted his favorite. This immediately destroyed the illusion of equality and incurred the wrath of the plebs. Soon after this incident, he found it prudent to take a holiday away from the city (Herodian 4.6–7). More often, if the emperor disagreed with the opinion of the people, he felt compelled to circulate placards explaining and justifying his decision. Hadrian chose this format to refuse the people's request to emancipate a charioteer; he circulated around the circus a board explaining why, for moral reasons, he felt he could not accede to their request (Dio 69.16). Such apologetic behavior at public entertainments was unusual for an individual who, in most circumstances, was the holder of absolute power.

There were evidently other unspoken rules of etiquette that the emperor was expected to observe at games and whose purpose was to support the illusion of equality. Once when Domitian was annoyed by the crowd, he brusquely ordered a herald to demand silence from the people (Suet. *Dom.* 13.2). Evidently this was such a breach of unspoken etiquette that, decades later, this action was still remembered with disapproval. When the people were aggressively demanding of Hadrian something he did not wish to grant, in a moment of impatience he ordered his herald to call for silence. When the herald managed to quiet the crowd without recourse to "Domitian's rude order," Hadrian rewarded the herald for saving him from such a serious faux pas (Dio 69.6.2). Even the use of a herald, however, seems to have been frowned upon; Claudius, for example, was singled out for praise because he very seldom used an intermediary to address the people (60.13.5). The stigma attached to the use of a herald at the arena (at least in the early empire) is suggestive. The use of a herald shattered the image of the emperor as just another cospectator in the crowd. The herald was a reminder of the usual social hierarchy, which was to some degree suspended within the walls of the arena. His role as an intermediary also served to distance even more the emperor from the plebs.

Finally, another portrait of the ideal ruler, Pliny's panegyric to Trajan, also stressed both the importance of *civilitas* and the idea of emperor and plebs as cospectators. Trajan received praise for not watching from the emperor's box but instead sitting with the people and experiencing the performance in the same way as the rest of the audience. The emperor was described as exchanging glances with his fellow citizens as equals (Pliny *Pan.* 51.4–5). Such behavior creates a coherent picture of the emperor consciously attempting to appear like one of the people. By their actions, the plebs too actively joined in this fiction in order to create the illusion that the emperor was just a fellow spectator.

Clearly, there was a perception that the theater, amphitheater, circus, or wherever the entertainment was taking place was a special zone in time and space in which behavior that would have been forbidden anywhere else was permitted and where the usual social hierarchy was to some degree suspended. This was the plebs's opportunity for personal contact with the emperor, and the additional expectation developed that such occasions were the proper time for requests and petitions to be made to the emperor. Public entertainments were announced long in advance, and many games were held annually on specific religious holidays. This periodic nature of entertainments further facilitated their use as the proper and accepted route of communication between emperor and plebs. This regularity ensured that the people would have frequent and predictable opportunities to make their desires known to the emperor. The plebs certainly made use of these chances. Josephus flatly stated that there was an expectation that, at the circus, "the plebs made requests of emperors," and naturally, emperors who at least appeared to listen attentively to such petitions were highly popular (Joseph. *AJ* 19.1.4).

Not only was there pressure for the emperor to listen to requests, but he was expected to act favorably upon them. Josephus added that most emperors did not deny the requests of circus crowds but readily granted them (Joseph. *AJ* 19.1.4). Once again, Titus represents the paradigm of the good emperor, since at gladiatorial games he promised that he would grant anything that was asked of him (Suet. *Tit.* 8). Trajan exceeded even this benevolence, since not only did he grant all requests, but supposedly he strove to anticipate unspoken wishes and then urged the people to make further demands of him (Pliny *Pan.* 33.2–3). Even Tiberius, probably the emperor who took the least interest in cultivating the goodwill of the plebs, was compelled on several occasions to accede to requests by the people (Pliny *Hist. Nat.* 34.62). After these experiences he ceased to give public shows himself and rarely was present at others because he feared that requests would be made of him (Suet. *Tib.* 47).[38] This action had the predictable effect of making him very unpopular with the urban plebs. Eventually Tiberius retreated into a self-imposed exile on the island of Capri, where he avoided exposing himself both to the hostility of the people and to more petitions. These examples are striking since they show how the supposedly omnipotent emperor, even one like Tiberius, who was one of the emperors least concerned with the favor of the plebs, had at least to consider, and usually yield to, such public requests.

The petitions themselves spanned a broad spectrum of matters ranging from the course of the entertainment to affairs of state. In addition to the usual collaboration concerning the outcomes of contests, crowds could demand the manumission of slaves who were charioteers, gladiators, and actors, ask for famous gladiators, request fights featuring specific styles of fighting, and even demand the release of criminals condemned to be devoured by beasts.[39] Usually the emperor granted such petitions. Whether or not the famous story of Androcles and the lion is apocryphal, it illuminates some of the procedures by which emperor and plebs could communicate and act together to affect the outcome of a performance (Gellius 5.14). When the lion refused to maul Androcles, the audience began shouting, demanding an investigation into this remarkable occurrence. The emperor acceded to their wishes and personally conducted the interrogation, but interestingly, and realistically, most of the crowd could not hear what was being said. The emperor then had Androcles' story written on placards and circulated about the audience until everyone had been informed. By shouting, the crowd asked for Androcles to be pardoned and presented with the lion, and, again, the emperor ratified their request. Such interactions were common, and this episode illustrates that there was an expectation that the crowd could make such demands as well as some of the actual mechanisms that existed to facilitate communication among emperor, audience, and performer.

Entertainments were also the scene of requests concerning matters outside the walls of the theater or circus. Tiberius was compelled by vehement shouting in the theater to return to the public baths a well-liked statue he had appropriated for his palace (Pliny *Hist. Nat.* 34.62). The petitions of the people did not always involve such trivial subjects, however. Augustus, Tiberius, and Claudius all undertook troublesome attempts to fix corn prices after requests by the people at entertainments.[40] Nero revised the tax collection system in response to a demand from the people (Tac. *Ann.* 13.50). Perhaps he had learned from the negative example of Gaius, who refused a similar request and was murdered shortly afterward (Joseph. *AJ* 19.1.4). Sometimes the crowd would call for the execution of detested individuals such as Sabinus and Atticus under Vitellius, and Tigellinus under Galba, or the pardon of others such as Augustus's daughter, Julia (Tac. *Hist.* 3.74,75; Plut. *Galba* 17; Dio 55.13). During Augustus's reign, an outraged crowd chanted witty abuse at the freedman Sarmentius, a favorite and perhaps ex-slave of Maecenas, when he arrogantly sat in the rows reserved for equestrians (Schol. Juv. 5.3).[41] The sources contain many other examples of similar petitions.[42]

Such petitions were, in reality, one specialized type of acclamation and were often coupled with standard acclamations of praise. During the incident just cited in which an angry crowd clamored for the execution of Sabinus, their shouted threats were interspersed with phrases of flattery and praise (Tac. *Hist.* 3.74). Another illustration of this insertion of a petition into a standard acclamation of praise is the detailed eyewitness account by Cassius Dio of a demonstration at the circus in A.D. 196 (Dio 75.4). At this time, a civil war had broken out between Septimius Severus and Albinus, and the war-weary populace desired peace. A very large audience gathered to watch the last horse race before the Saturnalia, and between two races the crowd unexpectedly urged one another to silence. Once a perfect silence had been achieved, those assembled all clapped their hands in unison and shouted out a standard acclamation invoking good fortune. They followed this with another unspecified acclamation in which Rome was hailed as "Queen" and "Immortal." Thus far they were proceeding in the usual pattern for a laudatory acclamation; however, from this point on, they deviated from the normal procedure in order to combine their acclamation with a petition. The people then cried out, still in unison, "How long are we to suffer these misfortunes?" (μέχρι πότε τοιαῦτα πάσχομεν), "How long are we to be waging war?" (μέχρι ποῦ πολεμούμεθα), and a few other similar remarks. After this plea for peace, they shouted, "So much for that" (ταῦτά ἐστιν), and returned their attention to the races.

Several points are worth noting in this episode. First, what was clearly planned as a criticism directed at the emperor began initially with a standard acclamation of praise coupled with applause. Second, since this event occurred at the circus rather than at a theater, literally tens of thousands of people were involved. Dio, who stressed repeatedly that he witnessed this event himself and was reporting it accurately, marveled at how so many thousands could have coordinated their actions, and compared their shouts to a "carefully trained chorus." He was not too far off in this observation. This performance was at least somewhat prearranged, and the circus was one of the recognized sites for making such petitions. Although there was certainly a group behind this demonstration that authored the phrases to be used and may even have circulated among the public at large general knowledge of what was being planned, the chants as finally delivered in the circus involved the cooperation of many tens of thousands of people.

Several requirements were necessary for a demonstration of this scale to work. In order for the majority of the audience to join in, the expressed sentiments had to be shared by the audience as a whole and thus genuinely represent public opinion, or at least the feelings of a substantial segment of the audience. Additionally, the chants used either had to consist of widely known formulas, or else they had to be easy to pick up and repeat. These characteristics were applicable to all types of acclamations, whether greeting acclamations, acclamations of praise, reactive acclamations, or acclamations of criticism and petition. The plebs employed all of these types of acclamations according to the circumstances and often mixed them together. For the plebs, they represented not only a way of responding to a speaker, but also a means of voicing their own opinions. While acclamations of petition in particular have received much attention as a form of interaction between emperor and plebs, less notice has been paid to the functional aspects of how these and other acclamations were actually coordinated and delivered by the often huge crowds at public events at Rome. The next chapter examines the practical aspects of coordinating and delivering massed chants, as well as the implications of their use for Roman imperial society.

Five

Characteristics of the Use
of Acclamations

cclamations have several notable features that enabled them to serve as such powerful and versatile forms of interaction between emperor and urban plebs. The most significant of these qualities are the existence of a body of well-known acclamation formulas and the rhythmic nature of many acclamation chants themselves. These two attributes were vital if acclamations were to be used by large crowds without significant prior planning and if they were to be flexible forms of communication that could convey a variety of messages. The greater the number of people chanting an acclamation, the greater its force, and rhythms and formulas made possible the participation of literally thousands by rendering acclamations easy to remember and to deliver in unison. Acclamations also possessed certain characteristics that encouraged their widespread use in the early empire, and which caused them to assume an important role in the rituals associated with the new political reality of the principate. Acclamations became particularly associated with the person of the emperor. They played a fundamental part in his actual creation as emperor during the ceremonies that led to his accession, and they offered a means by which the intrinsically ill-defined nature of the emperor's position could be made more concrete. As with many other republican traditions, acclamations had to be adapted to fit imperial society and, due to the traits mentioned, acclamations not only continued to be used during the empire but also took on a new significance and gained an expanded role.

Formulas and Rhythms

The purpose of any formula is to provide a fixed structure within which are placed elements that are mutable. While a formula is by definition a rigid construct, its real function is to promote versatility and adaptability. By ordering how the information is presented, a formula offers the opportunity to use a multitude of different variables in a manageable and coherent manner. Formulas are paradoxical because they imply both a rigidity and a flexibility. The structure is rigid, but the actual content varies. A verbal formula may consist of a series of specific words or phrases that are universally regarded as a unit, or of a certain grammatical structure that is readily identifiable as a discrete unit. Acclamations of praise certainly constituted verbal formulas, since they were formed out of phrases that everyone knew were associated with the emperor, such as imperial titles. While the fixed nature of ancient acclamations is generally acknowledged, it is important not to neglect the other primary characteristic of formulas, their flexibility. The Roman plebs made use of the versatility innate to any formula in order to adapt acclamation formulas to serve more functions than just praising the emperor. Because there were so many well-known acclamation formulas, Roman acclamations were particularly ripe for exploitation in this way.

Verbal formulas allowed large numbers of people to communicate directly with a minimum of prior planning. In the circus demonstration of A.D. 196 described by Dio, the participation of so many thousands was made possible because everyone in the audience knew the basic formulas. Thus they easily joined together in shouting the laudatory acclamations that began the exchange. The flexibility of the acclamation formulas also made it easily possible for a few cheerleaders to adapt some of these formulas to the specific situation and express an additional message. Since the basic acclamation formulas were so well known, once these cheerleaders began the new chant, it was easy to incite the rest of the crowd to join in. As modern football or soccer fans know, people tend to join readily in collective behaviors, such as chants or motions. Even when the demonstration is not of vital interest to a particular individual, he often participates to be part of the group action. An illuminating example from antiquity of this tendency involves a partisan of Piso who was able to goad bystanders in the crowd to chant acclamations praising Piso. Tacitus specifically noted that many of those who participated in these acclamation chants were either completely ignorant of the political situation or did not have a strong allegiance to Piso (Tac. *Hist.* 4.49).[1] Many of the crowd members joined in out of habit, simply because others were shouting. This is vivid evidence of the ease with which large numbers of people could spontaneously take up a chant without any prior planning as long as it was composed of widely known formulas.

The fundamental importance of formulas in organizing mass acclamations was strikingly revealed by the disaster that ensued when Nero compelled a group of Italians from rural Italy to attend one of his theatrical performances, where they were forced at sword point to praise his thespian skills. The frightened rustics were ignorant of the acclamation formulas used in Rome and of the various types of rhythmic applause that the urban plebs were accustomed to employ. Attempting to imitate the complex verbal acclamations of the locals, the Italians merely created chaos in the theater with their confused, disjointed shouting, and with their "inexperienced hands" they disrupted the smooth rhythms of the urban applauders (Tac. *Ann.* 16.5). This incident interestingly suggests that many of the acclamations used by the urban plebs were specific to the city of Rome, and stresses that the utility of acclamations as a flexible form of dialogue was contingent upon knowledge of a shared body of common formulas and structures. Once this knowledge was widespread, however, acclamations could serve as powerful vehicles of spontaneous expression because, within the basic structures of acclamations, words could easily be altered to convey a variety of messages.

The adaptability of acclamation formulas was further demonstrated by the acclamations with which the plebs celebrated the death of the despised Commodus and hailed his successor. They transformed the standard imperial acclamations of praise and changed these laudatory chants into abuse of the dead emperor. Utilizing the same basic acclamation formulas, they simply replaced the positive epithets with negative ones, so that instead of saluting him with such standard titles as "Imperator" or "the benefactor," they reviled him as "the gladiator," "the charioteer," "the left-handed," and "the ruptured" (τὸν μονομάχον, τὸν ἁρματηλάτην, τὸν ἀριστερόν, τὸν κηλήτην; Dio 74.2.2).[2] Dio commented that "all the chants that the people were accustomed to utter with a kind of rhythmic swing in the amphitheaters, in order to praise Commodus, now they shouted with various changes that made them utterly ridiculous" (Dio 74.2.3). At this time, the senate also indulged in exactly the same sort of negative acclamations, consisting of cries such as "The enemy of the fatherland, the murderer, the gladiator, let him be mangled in the *spoliarium*! Let the murderer be dragged! Let the slayer of citizens be dragged! Let him be dragged by a hook!" (Hostis patriae, parricida, gladiator, in spoliario lanietur! Parricida trahatur! Necator civium trahatur! Unco trahatur!; SHA *Com.* 18).

Although these acclamations are abusive, their form and structure are very close to those of standard complimentary ones. The recitation of imperial titles was the most basic, and perhaps most common, sort of senatorial acclamation, so instead of shouting complimentary titles such as "Imperator" or "Augustus," they bestowed upon him the derisive titles of "murderer" and "gladiator." Similarly, one common type of acclamation formula was to commend the emperor to the gods or to identify him as their favorite, as in the senate's cries of "Merciful Antonius, may the gods protect you" (Antonine clemens, di te servent; SHA *Avid. Cass.* 13.2), and "The gods have given you to us, may they keep you safe" (Di te nobis dederunt, di conservent; *Sev. Alex* 6.3). In order to condemn Commodus, this formula was reversed, and he was labeled as one who had been spurned by the gods: "[He is] the enemy of the gods, the murderer of the senate, the enemy of the gods, the enemy of the senate" (Hostis deorum, parricida senatus, hostis deorum, hostis senatus; SHA *Com.* 18.5). The hortatory construction of the repeated shouts of "Let him be dragged" corresponded to the conventional form for laudatory imperial acclamations, such as "Let him live longer" or "Let him receive blessings."

Negative acclamations seem to have been a custom much earlier as well, since, although the actual acclamations are not recorded, the senate celebrated Domitian's demise in the same way (Suet. *Dom.* 23). During the confusion after the death of Nero, a pro-Galba crowd called for the condemnation of Otho and his supporters "in exactly the manner" that they would have called for certain types of entertainment in the circus or theaters (Tac. *Hist.* 1.32). In the same way that the senate and people created and legitimized emperors by labeling them with positive acclamations, they could destroy and delegitimize an emperor by relabeling him with the titles reserved for criminals.

Commodus was reviled and distanced from society by being named as a member of two of the most despised and ostracized groups: criminals and gladiators. Ironically, in Commodus's case the term gladiator was not an exaggeration but rather was an accurate description of his behavior. In most contexts, however, it was a standard term of degradation. Further, one of the most repeated cries of the senate called for his corpse to receive the treatment accorded executed criminals of being savagely dragged away with a hook. In Roman society the mutilation of a corpse was one of the greatest demonstrations of contempt, and the emphatic reiteration of this phrase stressed the senate's total rejection of Commodus. Although specific examples do not survive, there may well have been a standard set of negative acclamations that were used to condemn criminals or to deride defeated gladiators, and the anti-Commodus chants may have borrowed from these traditions. The senate's specific demand that Commodus's body be mutilated in the *spoliarium*, the room in an amphitheater where dead gladiators were stripped of their equipment, reinforces the parallels between Commodus and a gladiator. Just as a dead gladiator was stripped of the distinctive arms that marked him as a gladiator, the acclamations of the senate stripped Commodus of the special titles that identified him as emperor. These cries also drew the sharpest contrast with the customary treatment of an emperor's corpse in which it was revered and carefully prepared for a ritual cremation, a ceremony that often represented his deification and enshrinement among the gods. Thus, in the negative acclamations directed at Commodus, many of the usual sentiments were expressed in inverted form, and the emperor, identified by his labels as the highest-status figure in society, was relabeled as that society's lowest-status and most contemptible figure.

While acclamations are usually viewed as a way of granting titles and honors, the reverse process of stripping away titles through negative acclamations can be seen most clearly in the shouts of the senate following the death of Elagabalus. Their shouts reviling him included the sequence: "[You are] neither an imperator, nor an Antonine, nor a citizen, nor a senator, nor a nobleman, nor a Roman" (Nec imperator, nec Antoninus, nec civis, nec senator, nec nobilis, nec Romanus; SHA *Sev. Alex.* 7.4). The senate methodically strips Elagabalus of every shred of his identity, not merely revoking his rank of emperor, senator, and citizen, but also refusing even to acknowledge his very Romaness. These acclamations constitute a kind of ultimate ostracism in which every link that once joined Elagabalus to Roman society is systematically severed and he is denied even the most basic recognition as a member of society.

Another stock type of acclamation took the format of praising an emperor by stating that he is even better in some way than a previous emperor who had been regarded as an exemplary ruler. An example of this is the acclamation "Luckier than Augustus, Better than Trajan" (Felicior Augusto, melior Traiano; Eutropius 8.5.3).[3] This formula offered another opportunity for adapting a positive acclamation in order to condemn a hated emperor. This formula was parodied in the senate's denunciation of Commodus when the senators chanted the memorable phrase, "Crueler than Domitian, filthier than Nero" (Saevior Domitiano, impurior Nerone; SHA *Com.* 19.2). This acclamation simply takes the structure of a positive acclamation formula and inverts it. Instead of praising an emperor by comparing him favorably to acknowledged good emperors, this one draws negative comparisons with the most despicable rulers. The archetypal good emperor was Augustus, so that when the Arval Brethren wished to praise an emperor, they naturally included the phrase "Greater than Augustus" (Maior Augusto) in their shouts (*CIL* 6.2086). When the senators wanted to find the most extreme way to condemn Elagabalus, they just as naturally compared him unfavorably with the worst emperor they could think of, resulting in their labeling him "Elagabalus alone [was] worse than Commodus" (Peior Commodo solus Heliogabalus; SHA *Sev. Alex.* 7.4).

As in these examples, within the framework of the basic formulas there was considerable room for spontaneous improvisation and adaptability of message. They also emphasize the fact that acclamations did not exclusively express praise, and that there were conventions for negative acclamations as well as positive ones. The flexibility inherent in the structure of all acclamations seems to have been particularly pronounced in the early and middle empire before acclamations had assumed the much more rigid form and more highly stylized content that they acquired in the later Roman Empire. It is this quality of acclamations in particular that facilitated their use as an avenue of communication for the urban plebs of Rome.

A second important characteristic of acclamations was their rhythmic nature.[4] As with formulas, the basic purpose of rhythm is to provide a structure. The repetition of similar sounds or stresses is one of the most fundamental ways of creating structure. There is a strong innate appeal to anything rhythmic, and associating specific words or ideas with a certain rhythm renders them both easier to remember and to repeat. In light of these tendencies, it is not surprising that many acclamations incorporated some form of rhythm and sometimes even resembled verse. Often it is impossible neatly to segregate formulas from rhythms, since verbal formulas frequently incorporated rhythms. Therefore, in the subsequent section, the two are discussed together.

As mentioned previously, one sort of acclamation consisted not merely of applause but also of various types of rhythmic clapping. Nero's tendency to indulge in extreme forms of theatricality provided the most obvious example of the elaborate types of applause that were employed as acclamations. He not only actively sought the applause of the people, but even organized a professional cheerleading section: "He was greatly taken with the rhythmic applause of some Alexandrians who had flocked to Naples from a fleet that had lately arrived, and summoned more men from Alexandria. Not content with that, he selected more than five thousand sturdy young plebeians to be divided into groups and learn the Alexandrian style of applause, and to employ these styles vigorously at all his performances. The different groups are labeled *the bees*, the *roof tiles*, and the *bricks*" (Suet. *Nero* 20). The "bees" may have not actually applauded but instead probably made some sort of humming sound. The "bricks" and "tiles" seem to have been named in accordance with the way they held their hands while clapping; the "tiles" clapped with their hands rounded or hollowed so that they resembled the concave roof tiles used in construction, and the "bricks" applauded with their palms held flat and rigid like the surfaces of bricks.[5] Each method would have produced a distinctive sound, and it is easy to see how a highly trained claque could produce an array of impressive aural effects by combining the different styles in various patterns.

Nero also organized an elite cheerleading claque known as the Augustani, composed either of soldiers or of young equestrians whose methods and organization were similar to those of the claque of plebeians (Tac. *Ann.* 14.15; Dio 62.20; Suet. *Nero* 20). The members of these groups had distinctive attire, and their importance to Nero was indicated by the fact that their leaders received a salary of HS 400,000, the amount required for equestrian rank (Suet. *Nero* 20). Regardless of whether the official claque consisted of plebeians, soldiers, or knights, all sources agree that their function was to initiate applause and cheers when the emperor performed, and that the rest of the audience was expected to join in. This expectation presumes that the general public at Rome knew, or could easily emulate, the complex acclamation forms used by Nero's claque. The experience of the rural Italians demonstrates the outcome when novices attempted to copy such specialized acclamations.

Semiprofessional cheerleading sections, or claques, were not new; actors in the theater had employed such claques to encourage applause at least since the late republic and probably earlier. The earliest explicit mention of theatrical claques appeared in the prologue to Plautus's *Amphitruo* in which the god Mercury urged that inspectors patrol the theater and punish claquers in order that true artistic skill may receive the praise it deserves (Pl. *Am.* 65–85). The claque members would distribute themselves throughout the audience and attempt to stimulate the audience to applaud for their actor.[6] The most basic technique was for the claque members to begin clapping and hope that the rest of the audience would join in. They could try both to start applause when it was lacking and to lengthen the duration of naturally occurring accolades. More ambitious manipulation of the audience could consist of the claquers trying to initiate chants or gestures among the rest of the onlookers. The goal of such claques was simultaneously to produce the most enthusiastic display possible while making it appear to be completely spontaneous. Thus the most proficient claquers were those whose activities went unnoticed by the audience members who were being manipulated. These techniques for inciting a crowd reached a high level of sophistication, and the best claque leaders were regarded as skilled professionals. A soldier named Percennius, who prior to his military career had been the leader of a theater claque, was blamed for fomenting mutiny among the Pannonian troops after the death of Augustus. Percennius used his experience in the art of inciting an audience gained in the rivalries of actors to bring the soldiers methodically and almost scientifically to the point of open rebellion (Tac. *Ann.* 1.16–18).[7]

Orators also employed claques. When a politician gave a speech, his friends and particularly his clients would have infiltrated the audience and acted as an amateur claque, provoking and encouraging applause and favorable shouts. As previously described, such behavior was rampant at trials and speeches in the late republic. Clodius's claquers are the most famous, but others employed them as well.[8] Some claquers had no real allegiance to a politician, but had instead sold their applause for a specific occasion. At games held soon after the assassination of Julius Caesar, a group "hired for this purpose" shouted for Brutus and Cassius to be recalled (App. *BC* 3.24). The strategy could backfire if the claquers began their demonstration and no one else followed their cue, thus exposing the claque and revealing that their applause was rigged. Cicero noted that "it is common for some feeble and scanty applause to be started at theatrical and gladiatorial shows by a hired claque, and yet when that happens it is easy to see how, and by whom, it is started, and what the honest part of the audience does" (Cic. *Sestio* 115).

Such behavior continued into the empire. Toward the end of the first century, Pliny vividly described how forensic orators would hire claquers to pack the audience and loudly applaud their speeches (Pliny *Ep.* 2.14.4–8). Some of these people, whom he noted are called in Latin *laudiceni*, dinner clappers, or in Greek, σοφοκλεῖς, clever callers, would openly receive their bribes in the court itself and would shamelessly spend the day going from one case to another applauding for anyone who would pay.[9] He indignantly related that two of his attendants, "barely old enough to wear the toga," were lured by greed to accept three denarii apiece to contribute their applause. This is a surprisingly large sum and, if accurate, easily explains why people readily served as *laudiceni*. The passage paints an image of claque leaders prowling among the audience at trials and hiring people on the spot to applaud. The claque leaders who organized the acclamations are also described. They would indicate to their hired followers when to clap by giving them a prearranged signal upon which they all would burst into noisy applause. Pliny noted that the claquers did not even pay attention to the oration but merely watched for their leader's signal.

Although Nero appears to have been unique among emperors of the early empire in organizing an official claque of applauders, an emperor's retainers, attendants, and bodyguards would always have constituted a natural claque, although a highly visible one. The emperor Titus took a more subtle approach. When he wished to proscribe someone, he supposedly sent members of the praetorian guard in disguise to the theaters of Rome where they mingled with the audiences and called for the punishment of the targeted individual. The goal was to make the demands appear to emanate "as if from the common consensus of the crowd" (Suet. *Titus* 6.1). In this way Titus could act and make it seem that he was merely bowing to popular pressure. At some later point (at least by the sixth century), an official group of trained applauders such as that organized by Nero became a standard element of the imperial entourage, and similar claques are well attested in late Roman and Byzantine sources.[10] So indispensable a part of the imperial retinue had the acclamation claque become in the later Roman Empire that when Heraclius went to bargain with an Avar king threatening his land, he did not take the army with him, but instead took his professional claquers, presumably hoping to impress and intimidate the Avars by means of their complex and impressive acclamation rituals.[11]

Not only applauded acclamations possessed rhythmic qualities, however; verbal acclamations often shared this characteristic. Rhythm by definition relies on the repetition of certain sounds in a discernible pattern. One of the most obvious characteristics of acclamations and their formulas was their repetitiveness. Entire phrases were frequently chanted over and over. The most extreme example of this, although admittedly from both a late and a questionable source, occurs in the *Historia Augusta*, where the author listed senatorial acclamations together with the number of times each phrase was shouted (SHA *Claud.* 4).[12] These repetitions range in number from a modest five times to an astounding eighty iterations. While there are no reliable accounts of repeated acclamations from the early empire, this strategy is a near universal feature of verbal acclamations and was probably practiced at Rome as well.

Not only were whole phrases repeated, but within a single acclamation, individual words often appeared multiple times. Anaphora, the use of the same word at the beginning of successive clauses, was used in the chant of the crowds praising Germanicus: "Salva Roma, Salva patria, Salvus est Germanicus" (Safe is Rome, safe is the country, because Germanicus is safe). The triple repetition of *salva* both reinforced the message and made the acclamation easier to remember (Suet. *Gaius* 6). The basic equation "the country is safe, because the emperor is safe" seems to have been a popular one in the early empire, and illustrates both the formulaic and flexible nature of acclamations. Tiberius was praised in the theater with a variation on this phraseology when his entrance was greeted with the chant of "Laetare incolumis Roma salvo principe" (Rejoice,

Rome is safe because the princeps is safe; Phaed. 5.7.27). This line lacks the rhythm and repetition of the praise accorded to Germanicus but expresses exactly the same sentiment. Severus Alexander supposedly received nearly the same greeting when he escaped a military debacle: "Salva Roma, Salva res publica, quia salvus est Alexander" (Safe is Rome, safe is the state, because Alexander is safe; SHA *Sev. Alex.* 57.5).

The "equation" type of acclamation, in which two objects or actions were related in a cause-and-effect relationship, was a common verbal structure and appeared in multiple variations such as the senate's cries, "Tu voluisti quod licebat, nos fecimus quod decebat" (You have wished what was lawful, we have done what was appropriate; SHA *Avid. Cass.* 13), and "Haec faciat, haec audiat" (Let him hear this, let him do this; Pliny *Pan.* 2.8). These hortatory acclamations also seem to have utilized repeated words or sounds, as did the senate's cheers praising Trajan, "Crede nobis, crede tibi" (Trust us, trust yourself; Pliny *Pan.* 74.2). The "Haec faciat, haec audiat" chant is particularly effective because the anaphoric repetition of *haec* is supplemented by parallel trisyllabic verbs with identical final syllables due to their conjugated endings. The grammatical structure of Latin, with its declensions and conjugations, offers many opportunities for creating slogans whose phrases contain repeated final syllables. The foregoing acclamation using *licebat* and *decebat* is one example. A senatorial acclamation recorded by Pliny features a combination of anaphora and repeated grammatical endings: "Tanto maior, tanto augustior" (So great, so revered; Pliny *Pan.* 71.4). The comparative acclamations, "Felicior Augusto, melior Traiano" and "Saevior Domitiano, impurior Nerone" have very similar structures (Eutropius 8.5.3; SHA *Com.* 19.2). These shouts were able to make use of the comparative *-ior* ending and repeated case endings to create euphonic and memorable acclamations. Many of the extant acclamations from the early empire took advantage of the opportunities inherent in Latin grammar for repetition.

The lists of senatorial acclamations recorded in the *Historia Augusta* also exploit this characteristic, as in a list of imperial virtues recited by the senators: "philosophiae tuae, patientiae tuae, doctrinae tuae, nobilitati tuae, innocentiae tuae" ([we praise] your phi-

losophy, your patience, your principles, your excellence, your inno-
cence; SHA *Avid. Cass.* 13). The repeated *-ae* ending lends a definite
cadence to this chant, as does the alternation of the short word *tuae*
with the longer words. Also, four out of five of the listed virtues
have five syllables, further adding to the rhythmic qualities of this
line.

Similarly, the negative acclamations abusing Commodus, many
of which ended with variations on the demand that his corpse
should be dragged away, achieved a certain rhythm from the repetition of the word *trahatur* at the end of each phrase. Of the approximately fifty acclamation phrases listed in this passage, over half end
with some variant of "Let him be dragged." As in many of the earlier
acclamations, most of these phrases have two linked parts. Sometimes these were explicitly in the cause-and-effect equation format,
such as "He who murdered everyone, let him be dragged by a hook.
He who murdered people of all ages, let him be dragged by a hook.
He who murdered both sexes, let him be dragged by a hook," or "As
he did [to others], let him suffer [the same]" (Sic fecit, sic patiatur;
SHA *Com.* 19.4, 2).

The recurrence of similar words and sounds in these phrases
made them both easier to learn and to remember, qualities that
would have enabled them to be disseminated quickly and used by
large numbers of people. Rhyming and rhythmic lines also seem to
appeal to people because of their very catchiness and their potential
for capturing humor. The witty cry of the plebs celebrating the
death of the despised Tiberius, "Tiberium in Tiberim" ([Throw]
Tiberius into the Tiber; Suet. *Tib.* 75), relied on the homonymic
reiteration of the two names for its effect, as did the people's praise
of Domitian and his wife, "Domino et Dominae feliciter" (Good
Luck to our Lord and Lady; Suet. *Dom.* 13). It is certainly no
accident that modern marketers center the advertisements for their
products around a musical "jingle," which often incorporates just
such rhyming or witty slogans. The ideal jingle is one that can be
remembered after a single hearing and that has euphonic appeal,
the same qualities found in many Roman acclamations. Rhymed
phrases that encapsulate a key argument are not foreign to modern
courtrooms either. The most notorious recent example of this oc-

curred during the sensational trial of O. J. Simpson when his defense attorney, Johnny Cochrane, included in his closing arguments the phrase, "If the gloves don't fit, then you must acquit." This phrase, immediately picked up by the media and endlessly repeated, was regarded as a brilliantly effective bit of oratory directed at a mass audience.

Some Roman acclamation chants went so far as to have a formal metrical structure.[13] This characteristic seems to have become more pronounced and the metrical structure more rigid over time. Thus, the acclamations of the early empire usually had at least a crude rhythmic quality, while those of the later followed strict metrical rules. Indeed, by the Byzantine period, the acclamations had become so completely metrical that they resembled songs, and, not surprisingly, in this period acclamations were routinely delivered with musical accompaniment.[14] Even in the early empire, however, acclamations were sometimes recited in metrical form. On Augustus's return to Rome from the provinces, the people greeted him not just with the usual greeting acclamations but also with laudatory songs, which they sang as he entered the city (Suet. *Aug.* 57). The phrases rejoicing at Germanicus's supposed recovery were sung by the happy crowd (Suet. *Gaius* 6). Later, Germanicus's son Gaius was flattered by a choral ode enumerating his virtues, sung by a group of young nobles, similar perhaps to Nero's Augustani (Suet. *Gaius* 16). One hostile crowd in A.D. 70 provoked the normally tolerant Vespasian not only by their words, which "in themselves were insulting enough," but also because "there was something about their anapestic rhythm that roused his ire" (Dio 65.8).[15] The traditional use of the anapest in Greek theater for lines expressing comedic or satiric content perhaps added an additional layer of insult to its application here in an acclamation critical of the emperor.

The rhythmic qualities of acclamations greatly contributed to their versatility. Just as there was a set of standard acclamation formulas, so there were probably a few widely known rhythms used in acclamations, and it was this existence of "a certain range of easily recognized rhythms which made it possible for large assemblies throughout the empire, not only to pronounce standard acclamations, but to vary and improvise them."[16] Since it is always easier to memorize and recall the lyrics to a song or phrases that rhyme rather than nonmetrical sentences, it is natural that many acclamations were in the form of songs or at least had distinct rhythmic qualities.

The standard analogy that is almost invariably made by modern commentators to these acclamations and chants is to compare them with the chants of football fans in Europe and South America.[17] This is a useful analogy and certainly demonstrates that it is possible for very large numbers of people to act together at public events with a minimum of prior coordination. It is also a somewhat misleading analogy, however, for two reasons. First, it fails to capture the religious overtones of ancient entertainments. All gladiatorial games were originally part of funeral games, and athletic contests had a long tradition of being associated with religious festivals.[18] Most of the theaters of Rome included a temple, at which the emperor would sacrifice to open the games, and many games continued to be held on religious holidays and as an important part of the celebrations at religious festivals.[19] Therefore, in addition to overtly religious ceremonies, many other occasions at which acclamations were used contained a significant religious element. Second, and more important, these modern analogies do not reflect the interactive, participatory nature of these ancient acclamations as two-way dialogues between ruler and people. Footballers may respond in some fashion to the shouts of a crowd, but they do not usually conduct a back-and-forth exchange of messages.

Another modern parallel to ancient acclamations is the chants used at protest marches and rallies. These chants are usually based on widely known songs or on simple formulas that can be easily altered to fit the specific circumstance, and which are just as easily learned by the participants. Examples of such protest formulas include the popular chant, "1, 2, 3 (fill in appropriate slogan rhyming with "3") . . . 4, 5, 6 (fill in appropriate slogan rhyming with "6") . . . 7, 8, 9 . . . etc." This example employs both a formula and a rhyme. Since the fixed part of the chant consists simply of counting, the pattern is instantly recognized and everyone can anticipate the next phrase. The variable parts are rendered easy to remember since each phrase rhymes with the preceding number. If a chant is directed against an individual on college campuses in the United

States, a common formula is "Hey, hey, ho, ho; John Doe has got to go," in which the target's name is substituted for "John Doe." This formula similarly relies on a combination of predictable phrases and rhyme. These chants are so basic that it is extremely simple for even a very large number of people to take them up rapidly and spontaneously. Both of these formulas make heavy use of syllables that either are not directly related to the message (numbers) or are completely nonsensical (hey, hey, ho, ho). These short meaningless interjections, which are often repeated two or three times, are a common feature of acclamation formulas.

The comments of the Alexandrian crowd greeting Germanicus often began with the interjections οὐά and ἰώ, which seem to have served a purpose similar to the "ho, ho" of the protest chant by fleshing out the variable "message" portion of the acclamation with familiar but essentially meaningless structural components. In Dio Cassius's account of the acclamations with which the people of Rome greeted Nero's return to the city in A.D. 68 after his Greek tour, οὐά was similarly used to fill out and enhance the rhythmic structure of the acclamations: Ὀλυμπιονῖκα οὐᾶ, Πυθιονῖκα οὐᾶ, Αὔγουστε, Αὔγουστε (Olympian Victor, Pythian Victor, Augustus, Augustus; Dio 62.20.5). The idea that such words were employed as an easy way to add rhythm or rhyme without altering the meaning of a sentence is supported by the most common context in which they appeared—in drama. In Greek tragedies, words such as οὐά, and particularly ἰώ, occurred frequently and offered an easy way for a playwright to complete the desired rhyme scheme for a line. Just as with the "ho, ho" of the protest chant, these words were usually repeated twice in a row at the beginning of a line and sometimes even more.[20] The cry of *Io* used at triumphs, by Bacchantes, and at weddings could have served a similar purpose in Latin verse.[21] The association of these words with tragic drama was so strong that when a character in Plautus's comedy *Pseudolus* wished to give a speech in mock-tragedic form, he naturally used such an interjection: "Io! Io! Te, te, turanne, te, te, ego qui imperatas Pseudolo, quaero" (Io! Io! You, you, tyrant, I seek you, you, who orders Pseudolus; Pl. *Ps.* 702).

A more accurate and illuminating modern parallel than either the chants of sports fans or protest marchers is the preaching style of many revivalist churches. These sermons are obviously closer to Roman orations in structure and intent since both consist of a speaker attempting to persuade an audience. This type of sermon recaptures the religious overtones of many ancient occasions for speechmaking and, most important, it is also an interactive exchange between speaker and audience utilizing the call-and-response format. In this form of preaching the audience frequently interrupts the preacher with shouts and commentary, much as the crowd interrupted and commented upon Germanicus's speech at Alexandria. It also parallels the acclamations of the plebs, since these calls take many forms, ranging from brief formulaic phrases such as "Amen," which serve as affirmations of the preacher's words, to longer phrases commenting on his message. Just as the plebs could use acclamations to petition or make demands of the emperor, a congregation can shout out questions or demand elaborations from the preacher. Another characteristic of call-and-response preaching is that the speaker often makes use of rhyming phrases that the audience will pick up on and repeat, thus both reacting to the speaker's comments and signifying assent.[22] This recalls the frequent instances in the theater when the crowd would spontaneously single out and repeat certain lines, or even entire songs, from the performance. During Galba's brief reign, for example, at the staging of an Atellan farce, when the audience in the theater heard the beginning lines of a popular song that could be interpreted as alluding to the emperor, they interrupted the performance by completing the song and then singing it in unison several more times (Suet. *Galba* 13). Plays offered numerous opportunities for such references, and emperors from Augustus to Commodus had to put up with such witticisms, both laudatory and derisive.[23]

Even political and forensic speeches were often composed deliberately to rhyme and to be metrical, and even to resemble songs. Although songlike orations were universally condemned in rhetorical handbooks, this oratorical practice was clearly both widespread and popular enough to give rise to a well-known epigram: at Rome, "Orators sing and actors dance" (Tac. *Dial.* 26.2–3). This passage from Tacitus's evaluation of orators further noted that some orators boasted that their speeches were so musical that they could be danced to, a claim that is denounced as shameful and improper. In their theoretical handbooks on oratory, both Quintilian and Cicero repeatedly stressed that while speeches should ideally have a certain degree of euphonious rhythm, they must not follow strict metrical patterns or resemble songs or verse too closely. In the late republic, Cicero praised those who infused their speeches with a variety of inflections and modulations that produced a pleasing rhythm, a "sort of singing," but quickly added that he did not mean the sort of singing practiced by "Phrygian and Carian rhetoricians," which resembles that found in a play (Cic. *Orat.* 18.57). Later in the same work, he returned to the theme in more detail and again emphasized how important it was to choose one's words and phrases in order to create an agreeable rhythm, and even averred that the rhythms used in oratory were the very same as those employed in poetry (Cic. *Orat.* 56.187–90). He claimed that a great orator can arrange the structure and word choice of his speech in such a way as to create a rhythmic form distinct from poetry (Cic. *De Orat.* 1.33.151). Nonetheless he warned that the speech of an orator should not contain "actual verses." This interesting paradox is found repeatedly in Cicero's rhetorical works, and toward the end of the *De Oratore* he again attempted to explicate the distinction: "An extremely important point is that although it is a fault in oratory if the connection of the words produces verse, nevertheless we at the same time desire the word order to resemble verse in having a rhythmical cadence" (Cic. *De Orat.* 3.44.175).

By his time Quintilian admitted that while in theory there should be no more than a trace of singing in an oration, in practice there were many who overstepped the bounds of decorum and delivered almost musical speeches. He labeled this the greatest fault of contemporary oratory. To his mind, even spraying the foremost members of the audience with saliva was a lesser sin than giving an oration in the singsong cadences of the stage (Quint. *Inst.* 11.3.57–60). Compare this, however, with Cicero's assertion that the characteristic that most distinguished a superior orator from a mediocre one was that the great orator molded his phrases to have a rhythmic quality while the tyro blurted out his speech in a haphazard fashion

(Cic. *De Orat.* 3.44.175–76). Yet, as always, he added the paradoxical advice that such a rhythm should be "at once bound and free," for "the words are neither tied together by a definite metrical law nor left so free as to wander uncontrolled." In the quest to follow this difficult advice, it was plainly easier for orators who lacked Cicero's genius to err on the side of verselike speech. By the early empire such habits of delivery were prevalent, as Quintilian himself admitted, but the very vehemence of his condemnations further suggests that these orations were not only common but perhaps well received and popular with their audiences.[24] An overtly songlike speech was not only easier to compose than a more subtly rhythmic one, but such a structure may also have been a favorite of listeners for a variety of reasons.

One reason for the popularity of musical or rhythmic orations could be that they presented plentiful opportunities for the audience to notice and repeat the rhyming or metrical phrases.[25] A short and witty rhyming couplet is instantly memorable, and if an orator could include such slogans in his speech that summarized important points of his argument, he could hope that during his speech the audience would spontaneously (or with the assistance of a claque) pick up and repeat these phrases. If a crowd could be induced to do this during the speech, it would create the appearance that there was a consensus of opinion agreeing with the orator, and even if they did not make such an obvious demonstration during his delivery, there was always the possibility that catchy slogans would stick in the minds of the audience members and be repeated by them in the future. In this way an orator could hope that the substance of an oration both would be remembered more vividly by those present and might eventually reach a larger audience. However much strict rhetoricians condemned this strategy in their manuals, the temptations of and rewards for approximating verse in an oration ensured that this was a widespread practice. Through constant exposure to acclamations as well as to theatrical performances that used similar metrical structures, the inhabitants of Rome became particularly adept at learning and using complex rhythmic formulas, both those that were verbal and those that involved clapping. An example of this proficiency was recorded by

Ovid, who noted that at the festival of Anna Perenna, the people "sing whatever they have learned in the theater and move their hands easily to the words" (Ov. *Fasti* 3.535–36).

Even funeral eulogies could be presented in a rhythmic manner. During Tiberius's eulogy at the funeral of Augustus, he allegedly said to the crowd, "I, like the leader of a chorus, merely give out the leading words, while you join in and chant the rest" (Dio 56.35). Here Tiberius acted in the role of a claque leader and expected that the audience, conditioned by regular attendance at the theater and at other speeches, would know how to react appropriately. Tiberius could anticipate that those assembled would respond to his cues as claque leader with massed chanting of the desired acclamations. This incident also recalls the call-and-response structure of imperial speeches in which the audience took an active part in the performance and was itself simultaneously both speaker and listener. Heavy-handed use of repeated verb or noun endings could on occasion elicit an unwelcome form of call-and-response from an audience when it was able to predict an upcoming ending and shout it out before the orator could speak it (Demetr. 227v, I, 15).

Ancient orators routinely and deliberately composed their speeches with rhythmic phrases or even in verse, with the hope and expectation that the audience would spontaneously repeat these passages. Ideally the crowd would repeat the key phrases both during the oration as affirmatory acclamations and later to their acquaintances, thus disseminating the speaker's message beyond his immediate listeners. Together, these two characteristics, the use of formulas and rhythms, go a long way toward explaining the flexibility and power of acclamations as a truly interactive form of communication, and as one of the few ways in which the emperor and plebs were able to conduct a direct face-to-face dialogue.

Benefits: Legitimacy, Status, Participation, and Material Gain

For the Roman emperor, perhaps the most important acclamations that he received were those at his accession. Acclamations played a pivotal role in the creation and recognition of an emperor, and throughout his reign, they continued to ensure his legitimacy. The centrality of acclamations to imperial accessions was a direct result of the ambiguity of the principate itself. One of the major problems confronting Augustus after his victory over Marcus Antonius in 31 B.C. was how to keep the Roman state under his personal control when the formal political institutions that he had inherited from the republic offered no office that corresponded to his position. Furthermore, the structure of the republic, with its emphasis on single-year magistracies and multiple means of acquiring status, was the product of a social system that emphasized intense and continual competition among senators and equestrians. Once acquired, prestige was fleeting and had to be constantly and publicly renewed, and for most of republican history, these characteristics had precluded the complete monopolization of status by any one individual for more than brief intervals. Finally, this system was rooted in a society that revered tradition and was often hostile to change. After the transition from republic to empire, the emperor was faced with the dilemma of carving out a place for himself within this structure while maintaining at least the appearance that its official organization had not been substantially altered. Constrained by the weight of tradition, the emperor could not invent an entirely new office, nor could he monopolize the existing ones. Augustus and his successors met this challenge, or avoided it, by leaving their position ambiguous, ill defined, and based upon personal ties.[26]

Because of its ambiguous, if not contradictory nature, the position of Roman emperor had to be redefined and reestablished by each individual emperor. Due to the informal and personal ties that formed the basis of his power, each emperor additionally had to constantly renew his position throughout his reign. The pretenses of republicanism cherished by some senators, especially during the early empire, were most vividly torn away at the moment of succession when a new emperor had to be created. No standardized procedure existed for selecting a new emperor. Once he had been identified, there were patterns that both the novice emperor and his subjects could follow, but the moment of transition itself was always an awkward and uneasy one.

Throughout the early empire, the gaps between the death of one emperor and the accession of another were marked by moments of considerable hesitation and confusion. The awkwardness surrounding imperial accessions is best exemplified by the accounts of Tiberius's exchanges with the senate immediately following Augustus's death. While such incidents as Tiberius's statement that he would govern whatever part of the empire the senate assigned to him, to which a senator inquired, "Which part do you desire?" border on the comical, they conceal real anxieties on both sides about how to behave (Tac. *Ann.* 7–13; Suet. *Tib.* 24–25). This awkwardness, with its basis in the tensions between republican ideals and imperial realities, persisted far beyond the moment of accession, and every emperor spent his reign engaged in constantly negotiating and renegotiating his position in relation to his subjects.

A successful claimant to the throne usually had to have the backing of several influential groups in Roman society. The first and probably the most important was the army, and especially the praetorian guard, for ultimately the principate rested upon force in the literal sense and on the threat that this force might be employed. This threat was always latent in the emperors' relations with other groups. A second important group was the senators, whose approval as the representatives of tradition and civic authority was vital to an emperor's legitimacy. The recognition of the new emperor by these two groups was made manifest through the media of acclamations. No emperor could be secure until he had received the shouted acclamations of the massed bodies of the senate and the representatives of the military. Acclamations offered a ritual by which these awkward moments could simultaneously be bridged and the new relationships defined. Acclamations were uniquely well suited to delineate the positions of the constituent groups, since they consisted of words and titles that defined both the self and the other. They functioned as the public crystallization of the ongoing negotiations in which the emperor and his subjects were engaged. At such moments, acclamations were mutually beneficial rituals, since they not only confirmed approval for the new emperor, by shoring up his position, but they also reaffirmed the power and status of the groups bestowing the acclamation.

This specific use of acclamations was new, but there was a long and venerable tradition of the use of acclamations by these two groups. Therefore, acclamations fit perfectly into the changed political structure of the empire since they used an old and familiar form to carry a new message. For the senate, acclamations formed a link to the past and served as a statement that they still mattered in politics, and for the army they were an assertion of its recently apparent influence. Acclamations were also useful because they were ostentatiously public; they proclaimed the status of both recipient and bestowers in the most literal way, as shouts and chants by massed numbers of people gathered in the most visible spaces of the city. By bestowing the imperial titles—by the very act of naming a man as emperor—they created an emperor, and by paying homage to their titular master, the senate and army asserted their own importance as the groups that had the power to create such a master.[27]

The third group, the urban plebs, also had a long tradition of acclamations on which to draw. For them especially, acclamations took on a new importance during the empire. In a period when the plebs were losing whatever formal legislative powers they had once held, the bestowal of acclamations became a means by which the plebs could continue to exert influence on public events. Under Augustus, the election of magistrates, while technically in the hands of the people, seems only to have been a formality, and in A.D. 14 Tiberius transferred the election of magistrates from the *comitia* to the senate.[28] Despite this loss of input into the formal structure of politics, the plebs continued to exercise considerable informal power through their acclamations. The will of the people, formerly expressed by votes, was now made manifest through acclamations. The acclamations of the plebs were a vital ingredient in establishing the legitimacy of new emperors. Since imperial recognition depended on acclamations from all three groups, the plebs's status in society was enhanced by their role as a peer with the senate and army in this triad. The power of acclamations to identify and create emperors was exemplified by the unlikely accession of Claudius, when the acclamations of the praetorians did not merely confirm his accession, but actually caused it. Significantly, Claudius hesitated to accept until a second of the three vital groups, the urban plebs, also named him emperor (Suet. *Claud.* 10).

The importance of the acclamations of the urban plebs was partially explained by their symbolic function within the new Roman state. As the only Roman citizens with regular access to the emperor, the urban plebs served as the representatives of all Roman citizens. They were proxies for the millions of citizens who were unable to have direct input into the running of the empire. When the emperor received the acclamations of the urban plebs of Rome, he was presented not as having received the acclamations of just the inhabitants of one city, but of the Roman people as a whole.

The benefits that the emperor gained from acclamations are fairly obvious. Acclamations formed the very basis of his power, since the way he initially received his titles and was acknowledged as emperor was through the acclamations of the senate, army, and people of Rome at his accession. Throughout his reign, whenever he received acclamations he was, in the most literal way, reidentified and renamed as the emperor. Every appearance of the emperor in public, whether at a formal ceremony or simply in his travel through the streets, was accompanied by a constant chorus of acclamations listing his titles and identifying him as the emperor. It is suggestive that acclamations played such a central role in the *adventus*. This ceremony ensured that each time the emperor returned to Rome, his identity as emperor was reaffirmed, and his accession was almost literally reenacted by the senate and people gathered together to acclaim him collectively and publicly as emperor. An imperial *adventus* featuring the emperor and his train, the assembled urban magistrates and delegates, the excited crowds, the holiday atmosphere, and the festive decorations created an obvious image of a grand parade.

Even the more mundane movements of the emperor around the city, however, were accompanied by considerable pomp and display. Elaborate processions held an important place in Roman society, including not only major events such as the *adventus*, the triumph, or the funeral procession, but also miniature parades such as those made by great men each day as they marched down from their homes to the Forum, surrounded by a fawning cloud of their clients. The number and status of one's clients were an indication of one's own standing and influence. If an individual were a current officeholder, he would also have a contingent of lictors to head his entourage. The custom of having clients gather at their patron's house early in the morning so that they would be available to accompany him as he made his way to the day's business ensured that the city witnessed daily miniature parades. The lives of Roman elites, in contrast to the largely stationary lives of most of the rest of the urban populace, were structured around movement back and forth across the urban landscape as they traveled from home to forum to baths and back. One reason these sites were often located apart from one another may have been to provide frequent opportunities for "elite display," consisting of an influential man's parade through the streets with his entourage of clients.[29] To maintain status, members of the Roman elite needed to be seen by the maximum possible number of people and, further, to be seen in an impressive context that affirmed their status. The daily routine of the aristocracy required multiple trips through the streets, thus maximizing its visibility and fulfilling the need for "elite display."

As the individual with the greatest status, the emperor had to have the most grandiose processions of all. The emperor's procession would often have included lictors in their distinctive costume, an armed contingent of praetorians or select troops as a bodyguard, personal servants, imperial officials, and perhaps senators or imperial family members, each with their own corona of attendants and clients. Complementing the visual splendor of his parades was an aural component, the shouts of praise and adoration that followed his movements. In the narrow, twisting streets of Rome, an imperial procession was probably heard before it could be seen, and the emperor's arrival would have been preceded by a wave of sound as those he passed acclaimed his presence. The acclamations bestowed upon the emperor as he traversed his city played a part in solidifying and reaffirming his role as the foremost man in the state.

The greeting and laudatory acclamations he received at public entertainments also contributed to his legitimacy. The emergence of entertainments as a setting for emperor-plebs interactions was due both to the peculiar characteristics of this setting, which broke some of the usual status barriers, stressed their mutual identity as Romans, and forced them to cooperate in the performance itself, and to the fact that these entertainments were the only regularly scheduled activities at which the emperor came face to face in a confined space with significant numbers of the urban plebs. To preside over public entertainments became an important duty of the emperor. Conversely, one definition of the emperor could be simply "the person who presides over games," and imperial identity does seem to have become closely linked with public spectacles. Even in the very early empire, the first action of a new emperor often was to appear at games to receive the acclamation of the people. Their cheers ensured his legitimacy. Although after the first century of the empire, the emperor was frequently no longer physically present at Rome, this connection had already been firmly established. Rome remained the titular capital and its inhabitants retained their identity as the symbolic representatives of the Roman people. New emperors usually visited the city as soon as possible after their accession because they knew they were not completely legitimate emperors until they had personally received the acclamations not just of the senate, but also of the urban plebs of the city. Whenever the emperor did visit Rome, he made sure that some form of public entertainment was held so that he could be seen presiding over it. Over time, presiding over public spectacles and the acclamations of the people that accompanied this action became more and more identified with the official image of the legitimate emperor.

By the later Roman Empire, the circus in particular was associated with the emperor, and it is no coincidence, therefore, that when later emperors finally moved the capital of the empire away from Rome, the construction of a hippodrome was as important as, and perhaps even more so than, the construction of an imperial palace. In six of seven new imperial capitals that have been excavated, a hippodrome was built adjoining the palace.[30] This is certainly not solely due to a love of horse racing. The existence of a circus was interpreted by the locals as representing a promise that the emperor would come, and they could call their circus a "gift of the emperor's presence" (*Pan. Lat.* 7(6).22.5). The circus was the scene for imperial benefactions, so that in the aftermath of the sack of Trier, when local aristocrats requested that games be held in their city, they may really have been asking for the presence and accompanying largess of the emperor (Salvian *De Gub. Dei* 6.85).[31]

The connection between legitimacy and the acclamations of the people at public games was made most explicit in the case of usurpers. When Constantius's cousin, Gallus, gave games in Constantinople without the emperor's permission, this act constituted such a clear attempt to usurp his power that Constantius immediately had his cousin imprisoned and executed (Am. Mar. 14.11.12–13). Even foreigners and barbarians recognized this link between presiding over games and rulership. After the Persian king captured Antioch, the first thing he did was to give races and appear at them (Procop. *BP* 2.22.32). Similarly, when Totila captured Rome in 550, he too immediately held circus games (Procop. *BG* 3.37.4). Acclamations therefore greatly benefited the emperor by constantly proclaiming his status and providing rituals in which he could appear in the role of emperor, and in which his subjects could reaffirm their allegiance.

Acclamations also benefited the urban plebs. Acclamations were urban interactions in which the emperor and plebs were not just mutual participants but mutual beneficiaries, since acclamations do not just confer authority, power, and legitimacy upon a ruler; they also bestow power upon those who give them. In Roman society the act of greeting possessed a venerable history as a method of asserting the status of both bestower and recipient. Greeting ceremonies played important roles in social interactions. In the *salutatio* clients were expected to show up at their patron's house each morning to exchange greetings with him.[32] This action symbolically renewed the bonds between them and publicly asserted the existence of the relationship and its attendant obligations. The patron naturally gained status through the number and importance of his clients. On the other hand, his clients gained materially, since largess often was distributed upon these occasions, and they also improved their own status through the public confirmation of a personal relationship between themselves and the patron. The amount of status conferred on the clients was proportional to the degree of intimacy of their interaction with the patron: whether they were actually admitted into his presence, whether he greeted them personally or through an intermediary, and whether he addressed them by name or collectively. The *salutatio* defined a patron's clients by identifying them as the ones who were allowed to greet him formally in this ceremony. It was the prerogative in itself, of greeting him and receiving his acknowledgment of this greeting, that marked them as a group with a special relationship to the great man, and that therefore asserted their own importance.

During the empire, the urban plebs of Rome were an extremely privileged group because they had regular, personal, and direct access to the most powerful patron of all, the emperor. Furthermore, whenever they encountered the emperor, they had the right to greet him and to receive his acknowledgment of their salutation. Every time the urban plebs greeted the emperor, they were simultaneously proclaiming the existence of this privilege and its implications. That the action of being permitted to greet the emperor was in itself a mark of favor is exemplified by Trajan's reaction to two rival groups of envoys from Alexandria. Even before he received the delegations, Plotina, his wife, had already persuaded him to side with the first group, representing the Jews of Alexandria, in this dispute. The Jews entered first, and after they had been ushered into Trajan's presence, they hailed him, and he responded by acknowledging and warmly reciprocating their greetings. When the second group, which he had already decided was at fault, likewise entered and acclaimed him, Trajan pointedly did not return or even acknowledge their greeting, but instead responded angrily with the words, "You say 'Hail' to me as though you deserved to receive a greeting" (P. Oxy. 1242, lines 28–37).[33] This comment suggests that the very act of exchanging greetings with the emperor constituted a notable mark of favor and that, conversely, to be denied this basic recognition was a serious indication of imperial displeasure. Groups such as the urban plebs, who were freely able to acclaim the emperor in a variety of contexts with the expectation that he would reciprocate their greetings, therefore held a significant honor and privilege.

The importance attributed to the legitimacy conferred by the plebs's acclamations also solidified their standing as an important group in Roman society. Indeed, in the crucial area of choosing an emperor, they were raised to the same level as the senate and army by being classified together with them as the main groups whose acclamations were necessary to assure the legitimacy of the emperor. After Piso had been selected as Galba's successor, there was a discussion among his partisans concerning the best location for making the announcement. The three sites considered were the senate house, the rostra, and the praetorian camp (Tac. *Hist.* 1.17). Predictably, they ultimately selected the praetorian camp, but the choices neatly encapsulated the truth that the three groups whose approval mattered were the senate, the people, and the army. Laudatory acclamations could also benefit the plebs by influencing the emperor's behavior. Imperial panegyrics were not merely a form of flattery but were also a form of control over the emperor. By reminding the emperor of how he was supposed to behave and by enumerating the characteristics of an ideal ruler, a panegyric could hopefully coerce him into actually acting that way. Acclamations functioned in the same manner. They may have had even greater weight, due to the sheer numbers who shouted them and the very public settings where they were delivered.

In addition, the flexibility of acclamations gave the urban plebs the opportunity to make known their desires and opinions on issues ranging from their own comfort to important political questions. It should not be surprising, therefore, that in the early empire such initially informal rituals of mass participation seem to have acquired greater importance at the very time when the urban plebs were losing whatever vestiges of formal political power that they still possessed. In A.D. 14, the last few elections in which the people still voted had been transferred to the senate (Tac. *Ann.* 1.15). It was exactly at this time that imperial attendance at entertainments became obligatory, forcing the emperor into contact with large groups of the plebs in a setting where they could express their opinions and continue to exercise some influence upon politics. Just as the massed shouts of up to a quarter of a million people at the circus hailing an individual as the emperor were a powerful affirmation of his legitimacy, so too a petition chanted by the same quarter of a million voices carried considerable weight. These petitions could and often did bring tangible benefits to the people, such as a reduction in taxes or grain prices. Likewise, a complaint angrily shouted by a hostile crowd of tens of thousands of people would have been quite intimidating. Simply by attending the games regularly and by granting petitions, the emperors placed themselves in a vulnerable position because they had either to grant the people's petitions or to incur the enmity of the people by refusing.[34] While rejecting petitions might cause an emperor to suffer some unpopularity, the emperors who avoided this dilemma by not attending games at all, such as Tiberius, elicited real hatred.

In light of the connection between legitimacy and the acclamations of the people, it is interesting to consider Augustus's systematic monopolization of all means of gaining the favor of the plebs of Rome. In 22 B.C., Augustus imposed restrictions on games and especially on their most popular form, gladiatorial combats. He limited the amount that could be spent on them and the number of gladiators that could appear in any one show, and he imposed a limit of no more than two gladiatorial games per year. Finally, he made the permission of the senate necessary before anyone could even consider holding a gladiatorial event (Dio 54.2). Naturally, these restrictions did not apply to Augustus and the members of his family, who continued to give sumptuous spectacles. At about the same time, he made triumphs the exclusive prerogative of the emperor. Also around this time, he appears to have curtailed public works in the city of Rome by anyone other than the emperor or members of his family. The emperor already controlled the grain dole and cash distributions to the plebs. The most significant aspect of this monopolization of the means of gaining popularity with the urban plebs is that these restrictions only applied to the city of Rome itself. Outside the city, aristocrats were actually encouraged to build public works and to give games. The people of Rome were the important factor. They were the ones who acclaimed the emperor in the streets, theaters, and arenas; because of this role, Augustus saw the need to ensure that the urban plebs would be his beneficiaries and no one else's.

The inhabitants of the city became the emperor's clients, and he responded by showering them with largess. The Roman emperors lavished vast amounts of resources on the city of Rome and its inhabitants. They adorned the city with gigantic and sumptuous buildings and supplied it with water through an extensive network of aqueducts. The citizens of the capital received the monthly grain dole, supplemented by occasional distributions of oil and other foodstuffs, were feasted at public banquets, were given irregular but large cash distributions, and were provided with a variety of entertainments, including gladiatorial combats, wild beast hunts, circus races, theatrical performances, and pantomime shows. They were treated to other spectacles, such as triumphs, numerous religious festivals, and celebrations centered around the birthdays, accession dates, and other significant events in the lives of the emperor and his family.

All of these forms of largess were provided by the emperor, and its recipients were the inhabitants of the city. These entertainments were extremely expensive. Gladiatorial shows and beast hunts by definition destroyed expensive commodities that had to be replaced constantly. Major building projects were not cheap. A sum of 50 million HS was expended putting the finishing touches on the Domus Aurea, and almost 300 million HS was spent by Domitian merely to gild the Capitol (Suet. *Otho* 7.2; Plut. *Publicola* 15.3). The Claudian aqueducts cost 350 million HS (Pliny *Hist. Nat.* 36.122). The annual cost of the grain dole is estimated to have been around 60 million HS.[35] Seven times in his reign Augustus gave cash distributions to the people of Rome, and many of these distributions totaled over 100 million HS each (*Res Gest.* 15).[36] While some of these figures, such as the ones for building costs, are by no means reliable, they do indicate the order of magnitude of such expenses. Other figures, such as those for the cash distributions, are probably quite precise. Although the city of Rome absorbed a tremendous amount of the empire's resources, clearly the emperor felt that this expenditure was somehow worthwhile.

A spectacular and impressive capital city certainly had useful symbolic value for the emperor. Such a display of conspicuous expenditure may not have been as wasteful and purposeless as it appears at first glance, nor was it unique. Nineteenth-century Bali has been described as a society in which the sole purpose of the central state government was to stage massive public spectacles with elaborate ceremony.[37] In Balinese society it was the very "ability to stage productions of an eleven-roof scale, to mobilize the men, the resources, and, not least, the expertise, that made one an eleven-roof lord."[38] This recalls the definition of the emperor as the one who gives and presides over circus games and who alone is able to marshal the resources necessary to provide these games and other public spectacles. Although this is a somewhat exaggerated view, it is possible to see the purpose of the Roman Empire as being simply to feed, entertain, and adorn its capital city. Ultimately, however, the direct recipients of all this largess were the urban plebs—people who no longer had any direct role in politics. The obvious question is why the emperors would devote so much energy and so many resources to feeding, employing, and entertaining a group without formal political power. The urban plebs were a favored group for a good reason. The people may no longer have had a vote, but their applause and acclamations were even more important to the legitimacy and *auctoritas* of the emperor. Through the acclamation ritual, emperor and plebs were bound together in a symbiotic relationship where each benefited from the other, but despite this, it was a relationship marked by considerable uneasiness.

Risks: Insult, Uncertainty, Fear, and Death

Two competing images of acclamations have dominated modern scholarship. On the one hand, attention has focused largely on acclamations of greeting and praise, and acclamations in general have been interpreted as meaningless flattery that was expected and taken for granted by the emperor. According to this perspective, acclamations were empty formulas that were essentially static, and the urban plebs were shameless sycophants who lavished praise upon whomever happened to be the current emperor. In the second view, attention has almost exclusively centered on the petitions and criticisms directed at the emperor. From this standpoint, the urban plebs are portrayed as fundamentally hostile to the emperor, and discussions of these acclamations are often framed by descriptions of riots and other violent disturbances.[39] In both viewpoints, the interaction between emperor and plebs is seen as being mostly one-sided, with the plebs directing either flattery or protests at the emperor in a relationship that is predominantly either obsequious or antagonistic. These two perspectives on acclamations need to be considered together in order for a full picture of the function of acclamations to emerge. Acclamations cannot be neatly divided in this way, since even criticisms usually began as laudatory acclamations, combined censure with praise, or were constructed out of common elements of positive acclamations. More important, they cannot be separated for the basic reason that the emperor could never have known which type of acclamation he would encounter until after the acclamation had actually been delivered. A fundamental sense of uncertainty underlay all emperor-plebs interactions, and as a result, encounters between them would always have been colored by some element of anxiety.

Both sides had reasons to feel this uncertainty. Acclamations that made criticisms and petitions were the exceptions rather than the rule, but when encountered, they could certainly be awkward for the emperor. Criticisms of imperial policy expressed in highly visible public settings and by huge numbers of people would not have been very welcome. Even more undesirable were derisive observations about the emperor himself and his personal behavior. Petitions put him in the position of possibly having to perform an action or grant a favor that he did not wish to, or else risk incurring hatred by his refusal. Granting popular petitions, such as a reduction in taxes, could be quite costly in material terms as well. Even if only laudatory acclamations were expressed, because of the variety of acclamation forms, the plebs could modulate their shouts in order to indicate a wide range of enthusiasm for a ruler. By the choice of slogans and titles, the number of different acclamations used, the volume of the shouts, the total length of the acclamations, and the intensity and duration of applause, the plebs could easily deliver a greeting or laudatory acclamation that indicated anything from tepid acknowledgment of the emperor to fervid adoration of him. A lukewarm greeting could be as much of a rebuke as overt criticism and, because of the intensely public setting, highly embarrassing for an image-conscious emperor.

Some emperors could not cope with the tension produced by this element of uncertainty. Nero tried to eliminate any doubts about his reception by compelling the people to acclaim him at sword point and by organizing cheerleading sections upon whose laudations he could rely. Tiberius's solution was even more extreme, since he isolated himself at Capri in an environment that precluded any interaction with the people. At Rome, the audience for an acclamation extended far beyond the recipient at whom it was directed to include literally everyone within hearing. Because acclamations were employed at virtually every appearance the emperor made in public, from official ceremonies to travel through the alleys of the city, he was constantly receiving feedback on his popularity. Also, if others received more enthusiastic acclamations than the emperor, this could constitute not merely a rebuke but even a threat by creating a potential rival. The adulation lavished on Germanicus was a direct challenge to the legitimacy of Tiberius. Above all, the emperor could rarely have been sure what sort of reception the crowd would award to him, or what demands it might make, and for him, this uncertainty would have made every appearance an occasion for at least some degree of apprehension.

For the plebs, too, these interactions could be tinged with considerable anxiety. Issues of vital importance to their material welfare, such as the price of foodstuffs, were decided at the whim of the emperor. Just as the emperor had reason to fear the requests that could be made of him, the urban plebs had reason to fear the emperor's response. Although rare, it was not unknown for the emperor to become so offended by the people's comments or demands that he would order the praetorians to arrest or even kill members of the crowd. In the first two centuries of the empire, there were enough of these incidents to make this a valid fear. Tiberius used troops to enforce order at public entertainments. To quiet the remarks of an audience in the circus, Gaius commanded soldiers to attack those in the crowd; as a result, their comments were silenced and some were killed (Dio 59.28.11). On another occasion at the circus when the people requested the alleviation of a tax, he had many of the spectators arrested and later executed (Joseph. *Jew. Ant.* 19.24–26). Under such an emperor, the audience could even find itself becoming part of the entertainment, as in A.D. 38 when a shortage of criminals induced Gaius to have a section of the crowd thrown into the arena (Suet. *Gaius* 27; Dio 59.10).[40] Domitian had a spectator whose remarks displeased him dragged out of the stands and torn apart by dogs (Suet. *Dom.* 10).[41] During the reign of Commodus, who prided himself on his ability as an archer, audiences feared provoking him because of his wish to subject the spectators to the same technique his hero Hercules had used to kill the Stymphalian birds (Dio 73.20.2).

Despite the anxieties experienced by both emperor and plebs, the benefits that they derived from each other were substantial. While acclamations were sometimes used to protest and petition, the overwhelming majority of acclamations that the emperor received from the urban plebs were simple reactive acclamations, or acclamations of greeting and praise. The urban plebs were an inescapable part of the urban landscape of Rome, and thus there was no way that the emperor could avoid these encounters. Always present at them, however, was the latent threat that the exchange of pleasantries could veer off into acrimonious insults or open violence. An aura of genuine fear and uncertainty surrounded all of these encounters, which was not resolved until the interaction was completed and the outcome fully known. Every time the emperor entered the circus, theater, or amphitheater, presided over a religious or secular ceremony, or even went into the street, he would have experienced a brief moment of uncertainty about whether, as usual, he would be met by the adoring cheers and applause of the people, which publicly affirmed his prestige and status, or whether this would be one of the occasions when unwelcome demands or mockery would be directed at him, criticizing his rule and subverting his authority. It was this threat, minor but real, that made acclamations more than the empty ritual that they are sometimes depicted as. It infused them with the character of a continual process of negotiation in which each side risked something in order to acquire something. The emperor had his status enhanced and his legitimacy reiterated, whereas the urban plebs had their status enhanced, their position in society affirmed, and their material existence bettered. Because critical acclamations often began as laudatory ones, once the customary acclamations of praise had begun, the emperor could not feel secure that this particular interaction would end as an assertion of the harmony of the societal order until the exchange had been completed.

This period between the beginning of an emperor-plebs interaction and its conclusion was a liminal moment fraught with ambiguity and uncertainty in which the usual roles of the participants were suspended or even inverted (e.g., mockery of the emperor, and Claudius's humble behavior at the games). The conclusion of the interaction was usually marked by the reestablishment of normative stable and distinct societal roles (emperor as ruler, audience as ruled) through the reciprocal exchange of defining labels (imperial titles, recognition of citizenship). Occasionally, when demands were made or criticisms voiced, the transitional liminal moment created a new consensus or power relationship.[42] The specific characteristics of acclamations made them well suited to serve this purpose. Acclamations were rituals that by their very nature forced one side to define literally, through vocalized names and descriptions, the position of the other. Acclamations were flexible enough to convey a variety of meanings, yet structured enough to give each side a clearly designated role to play. It is easy to understand why acclamations should have been widely used in traversing moments of uncertainty.

The senate and army used acclamations as a way to traverse perhaps the most awkward and dangerous moment, the transition period between emperors. This ultimate liminal moment was recreated in miniature every time a group had to communicate with the emperor. The innate ambiguity of the emperor's position, which lay outside the traditional republican framework, placed not just the emperor in an uncertain role, but all those who had to interact with him as well. Therefore, acclamations were attractive because they forced specific titles and offices onto the emperor, creating a tangible entity with whom senate, army, and people could then interact, since for many of these individual titles and offices, comfortable procedures existed delineating appropriate behavior. During the republic, acclamations had complemented the existing institutions, but in the empire they assumed a more prominent role, sometimes even replacing earlier institutions. The emperor and the urban plebs employed acclamations in a continuous process of negotiation to define and renew their relationship to one another and their places in society. Every individual interaction between emperor and plebs created a brief moment of ambiguity and risk that had to be spanned. Acclamations provided one bridge to cross that gap.

Conclusion

"Decorate this capital with utter disregard of cost and make it magnificent with festivals of every kind" (Dio 52.31.1). Such was Maecenas's advice to Augustus in the debate contrived by Cassius Dio between Agrippa and Maecenas over the nature of the principate.[1] Coupled with his advice to spare no expense on the capital, Maecenas urged that, in contrast to Rome, other cities should be allowed to have neither impressive public buildings nor elaborate entertainments (52.30.3–8). These should be the sole prerogative of the capital city. He claimed that these recommendations stemmed from the desire to conserve funds, but revealed another motive when he observed that a sumptuous capital city inspires admiration in allies and fear among enemies and that in regards to such matters, "it is appropriate that we, who rule over many people, should surpass all men in all things" (52.30.1).

Augustus and his successors largely followed this dictum, and much of the prescribed adornment took the form of ostentatious marble theaters, amphitheaters, and circuses within which were staged all forms of public entertainments. With the exception of Pompey's theater, all the permanent structures for entertainment were not built until the empire. The city of Rome was important as the capital city, and both its buildings and ceremonies had to project magnificence commensurate with its status as the center of the empire. Admittedly, Dio was writing with the perspective of hindsight, and his comments reflect what the principate had evolved into as much as what Augustus himself did.

Maecenas further urged that the urban plebs should be prevented from gathering for political or judicial purposes, and only be allowed to come together at public entertainments. This reflects not so much a shift away from involvement in public affairs on behalf of the plebs as a change in setting. The votes of the people, cast in the Campus Martius, no longer mattered, but they had only rarely decided an election even at the height of the republic. The accolades of the people in the theaters, however, had always been a concern, and in the empire directly contributed to imperial legitimacy. From the plebs's perspective, protests organized in such settings were more likely to bring prompt results than their votes ever had. The mass public gatherings of the empire became the way that the plebs participated in the state, and the methods of interaction that evolved in the early empire to facilitate communication reflected these changes.

Both acclamations and gestures seem to have acquired greater prominence and complexity during the transition from republic to empire. Between Cicero and Quintilian, the nonverbal vocabulary available to orators became much more elaborate and the conventions of acceptable behavior grew broader so that orators were expected to gesticulate more frequently and more vigorously. Acclamations directed at the emperor grew out of the informal applause accorded to popular individuals as a token of approval whenever they appeared in public, but rapidly became a central facet of imperial identity.

Acclamations and gestures demanded that both audience and speaker share a body of knowledge specifying when and how these forms of interaction should be used. Both had to understand what individual gestures meant or what acclamations were appropriate to particular occasions. A key component of these methods of communication was that they encouraged innovation and versatility of message within a recognizable structure. An ordinary orator could memorize Quintilian's list of gestures and note what gesture was prescribed for each section of a speech, but the great orator was an artist who combined familiar gestures in an original and compelling manner. The intrinsic structure of acclamations demanded that phrases be combined in different ways and their rhythms and formulas facilitated the substitution of other phrases and the creation of new rhymes. Both acclamations and gestures heavily depended on the presence of rhythm. Probably the most frequent oratorical gesture was a metronomic one that provided a visual accompaniment to the cadences of the orator's words, and rhythm obviously was vital to the organization and effective delivery of acclamations.

I have focused on the transitional period between republic and empire when the models of behavior from the earlier period were undergoing profound transformations. Augustus made the grain dole, gladiatorial games, public services, and public works the exclusive jurisdiction of the emperor, and thereby privileged the relationship of the emperor, the plebs, and the capital city. One particularly significant precedent of Augustus was his systematic monopolization of almost all forms of interaction with, and benefactions for, the urban plebs. His actions were fundamental in creating many of the implicit but powerful rules for imperial behavior toward the plebs and the services that the emperor would provide for the plebs. During Augustus's reign, a network of expectations had evolved between the emperor and the inhabitants of the capital city. These behaviors and institutions were a mixture of practices from the late republic adapted to imperial Rome and innovations developed by Augustus, which became more formalized over time.

As Augustus set about establishing the principate, a form of government that was in many respects a thinly disguised monarchy, he liked to present himself as a new Romulus, a second founder of Rome. In light of this, it is interesting to examine the role given to acclamations in creating kings in the very early history of Rome as presented in the account of Augustus's contemporary, Livy. The power of acclamations literally to create a ruler by naming a man as one and verbally bestowing upon him the appropriate titles had its roots deep in Roman tradition and myth. Even before the foundation of the city, Romulus and Remus first rose to prominence by

overthrowing Amulius and making Numitor king. Numitor's eleva-
tion to the throne was accomplished when "the brothers advanced
through the crowd and acclaimed their grandfather as king, after
which a unanimous shout from the entire crowd confirmed the title
[*nomen*], and the authority [*imperium*] of the king" (Livy 6.2). Thus,
at least in Livy's version, the new role of acclamations in the empire
was in reality a return to Rome's earliest traditions. The next instance in Livy of acclamations creating a king ended less ideally
when after the auguries of the six and twelve vultures, Romulus and
Remus were simultaneously hailed as kings by their respective
followers. To Livy, the fratricidal outcome of this event prefigured
the civil wars of the late republic, but with hindsight, it was even
more prophetic of the later empire when provincial armies acclaimed their generals as rival emperors (Livy 7.1–3).

This study has looked backward at some of the republican precedents for gestures and acclamations in order to create a fuller under-
standing of their development in the early empire. In the opposite
direction, over time, these types of interaction became markedly
more institutionalized. This formalization resulted in an increase in
role-playing on the part of both ruler and ruled as the forms and
settings for their interactions became more clearly delineated. Ultimately, this role-playing resulted in somewhat of a loss of individu-
ality upon the part of the emperor, as his personality became sub-
merged in the various roles he was required to perform as emperor.
The more thoroughly documented interactions between emperor
and plebs in the later Roman Empire and in the Byzantine Empire
illustrate both the persistence of these models and the extreme
degree to which such behaviors became formalized. Truly spontaneous crowd demonstrations and informal claques gave way to
cheerleading organizations whose members and leaders held official positions and drew government salaries.

One recurrent theme in oratorical treatises is that oratory flourished in times of crisis and relative individual freedom and declined
or stagnated under absolute rulers. Already by the second century
of the empire, there was no longer much opportunity for great
public debates on mattters of policy in the senate or at *contiones*. As
the only person whose words really mattered, the emperor alone

had real need of oratorical training, and thus it is no surprise that the greatest orators of this age, such as Fronto, found fame not in fiery speeches before the senate or in the courts, but as the attentive teachers of rhetoric to the imperial heirs. The prototypical oratorical form was no longer the political speech such as Cicero's *Philippics* or *Catilinarians*, but the imperial panegyric exemplified by Pliny's eulogy of Trajan. The predictability of content in these panegyrics was mirrored by predictability of form.

As we have seen, two of the proofs most commonly cited by ancient critics as indicating the decline of oratory were the more frequent use of gestures and the increased flamboyance of the gestures themselves. Both these characteristics were perceived as making the orator less dignified and more like an actor. Another often mentioned symptom of degenerate oratory was singsong or overly rhythmic sentences. All these developments served to narrow the gap between oratorical delivery and theatrical performances. Orator and actor were indeed becoming more alike. These changes were for the benefit of audiences, since they had the practical effect of making the speaker's message more accessible and memorable. The large size of imperial audiences, their diversity, and their familiarity with gestures and acclamations in the context of public entertainments help to explain the role that these methods of communication assumed during the empire.

The debate of Agrippa and Maecenas was obviously a product of Dio's imagination, but it perhaps reflected Dio's own ambivalence toward the principate. He had had personal experience of the hazards of absolute rule during Commodus's reign, and the debate represents an attempt to negotiate a settlement between conflicting images of imperial rule. This theme of negotiation, of the attempt to reconcile opposing viewpoints, runs throughout this analysis of speakers and audiences and their interactions. This book is a study of forms of communication, and the ultimate goal of communication is to persuade or at least to reach an acceptable consensus. Gestures and acclamations were employed by emperors and plebs to facilitate communication in an ongoing public debate in which they negotiated their status and their places in Roman society.

Toward the end of his speech, Maecenas warned Augustus that as the emperor "you will live as it were in a theater, whose spectators are the entire world" (Dio 52.34.2). This metaphor of statecraft as a thespian art with the ruler and ruled alternatively as actor and audience or as mutual participants in a drama and with the capital city as a stage, which itself could determine or influence the performance, is a common one, and scholars have often applied this metaphor to Rome.[2] The elaborate ceremonies that occurred in the arenas and streets of the city were, in essence, theatrical performances that were often as carefully and elaborately choreographed as any drama of the stage. This observation also recalls one of the primary responsibilities of the emperor, which was to be seen in public simply being the emperor and receiving the adulation of his subjects. Dio offered an image of Augustus as an actor who was unable ever to step out of his self-assigned role as princeps. He combined this image with a vision of a sort of Roman panopticon, in which the actor-emperor was perpetually under the gaze of his audience, composed of no less than the entire world.

Some emperors were less able to bear this scrutiny than others, and less able to separate the roles required of them as emperor from reality. Not surprisingly, it is in the behavior of the "insane" emperors that we can see this metaphor manifested most clearly. Emperors such as Nero, Caligula, and Commodus were all obsessed with acting, role-playing, and performing before the people. Nero in particular took this metaphor to its logical conclusion and aspired actually to become a stage performer. He prided himself on his abilities as an actor and avidly sought opportunities to appear before the plebs in public areas. In the admittedly hostile sources, Nero is routinely depicted as being unable to distinguish between acting and reality. The ultimate example of this confusion was his behavior during the great fire of A.D. 64. This disaster appeared to Nero simply as suitable scenery for a theatrical performance. While the fires were raging, Nero allegedly donned the appropriate actor's costume and performed "The Sack of Troy" on the roof of the imperial palace (Dio 52.18.1; Suet. *Nero* 38). Thus the entire city was quite literally transformed into his stage and the panicked inhabitants became fellow actors in Nero's tragedy. Also under Nero occurred many of the most memorable examples of "fatal cha-rades," enactments of mythological scenes in which the violence was real, not faked.[3]

Even as his own death approached, Nero continued to think of himself as an actor, as reflected in his famous statement, "How great an artist dies with me" (Suet. *Nero* 49.1). Decades later, Pliny could make a pejorative mention of the "actor-emperor" (*scaenici imper-atoris*) and know that his audience would instantly understand his reference (Pliny *Pan.* 46.4). While this close identification between emperor and actor might appear to be merely one of Nero's eccen-tricities, its accuracy is revealed by the fact that even Augustus, the prototype for all later emperors, saw himself in precisely the same terms. With his last words, Augustus, like an aging actor (or orator), requested one final acclamation from his audience: "Since well I've played my part, all clap your hands and from this stage dismiss me with applause" (Suet. *Aug.* 99.1).

Notes

1. On the place of rhetoric in education and for a detailed description of the various exercises in composition and delivery that students had to master, see Bonner 1977, with extensive further bibliography.

2. Kennedy 1972. On Roman rhetoric in general and on delivery in particular, see also Kennedy 1994, Clarke 1963, Bonner 1969, Hubbel 1966, Bryant 1950, Alberte 1992, Lanham 1991, Dominik 1997, Gleason 1995, and the bibliography in Horner 1990. None of these works treats the subject of delivery in extensive detail.

3. Quint. *Inst.* 11.3.6. This story is repeated at least three times in Cicero's works: *De Orat.* 3.56, *Orat.* 56, *Brut.* 142. It is also found in Plut. *Moral.* 845a; Val. Max. 8.10.3; Dion. Hal. *De Dem.* 22; Long. *Rhet. Graec.* 1.2.194; Philodemus 1.193.

4. For basic descriptions of this system, see, for example, Cic. *De Orat.* 1.142, *Brut.* 141, *Orat.* 55; *Rhet. Her.* 1.3; Quint. *Inst.* 3.3.11.

5. This division seems to have become more definite over time. Cic. *Orat.* 55; *Rhet. Her.* 3.19; Quint. *Inst.* 11.3.1.

6. The best recent treatments of the use of gesture in Roman oratory are the commentary on Quintilian's *Inst.* 11.3.84–124 by Maier-Eichhorn (1989), containing a lengthy introduction to the topic in general, which is particularly strong on the historiography of studies of gesture, and the article by Graf (1991), which is a short but solid introduction to the subject. See also Maguire 1981, on gesture in the Byzantine period; Nadeau 1964, a brief survey of ancient rhetorical works that

mention delivery; Sittl 1890, on gesture in both Greek and Roman art; Wöhrle 1990, on oratorical delivery in Greece and Rome; Fantham 1982, an attempt to determine which elements of Quintilian's treatment of delivery were original and which were copied from earlier works; Achard 1991, containing some brief comments on gesture as a form of communication; and Sonkowsky 1959, which discusses the link between delivery and emotion in Aristotle and Cicero.

The modern theoretical literature on nonverbal communication is vast, but some useful starting points include Davies 1982, an annotated bibliography on body movement and nonverbal communication, and Schmitt 1984, an introduction to an issue of *History and Anthropology* devoted to gesture, which includes a useful bibliography. Ekman and Friesen 1972 and 1981 survey types and methods of nonverbal communication, and classify hand gestures into the categories of emblems, illustrators, and adaptors. Birdwhistell 1952 offers a written notation system for recording body movements, facial expressions, and gestures. For a psychological perspective focusing on facial expression, the gaze, speech, interpersonal distance, and kinesics, see Harper et al. 1978. Bull 1983 treats body language as an indicator of emotions and psychological state. For current debates in the study of nonverbal communication, and a survey of scholarly interest in gesture from the seventeenth century to the present, see Kendon 1981a, 1981b, 1982. Key 1982 and 1980 review articles on theories of nonverbal communication and its use in modern societies, and Key 1977 provides a bibliography of works on nonverbal communication; Argyle 1975, Hinde 1972, and Poyatos 1988 discuss nonverbal communication in various modern societies. Poyatos 1976 and 1983 treat nonverbal communication from various perspectives, including anthropological, psychological, semiotic, and linguistic, as well as in literature and on the stage, and Poyatos 1981 offers methods of cataloging gesture. Morris et al. 1979 and Morris 1994 provide a fascinating study of the variations in meaning and popularity throughout Europe of twenty common gestures, and a catalog of over six hundred gestures currently in use around the world. For a dictionary of gestures, see Bäuml and Bäuml 1975.

For an example of an elaborate non-Western "language" of gestures, see Ghosh 1957 and R. Hughes 1941 on gesture and posture in Hindu dance. Also of interest are Schmitt 1990, a survey of medieval gesture; Bremmer and Roodenburg 1991, a collection of essays on gesture from antiquity to the present; Trexler 1987, on Christian prayer in the twelfth century A.D., especially postures for worship; and Clark and Halloran 1993, on oratory in nineteenth-century America.

On treatises on gesture and oratorical delivery between the Middle Ages and the twentieth century, see Chapter 2.

7. For a good, balanced discussion of what can and cannot be surmised about the content of Theophrastus's work on delivery, see Fortenbaugh 1985.

8. On Quintilian, see note 2 above and the mammoth work by Cousin 1967.

9. On inciting the audience's emotions as being the goal of oratory, see also Cicero's comments in *De Orat.* 2.115, 121, 310–12.

   Earlier, Aristotle also stressed the power of emotion to influence an audience and he specifically linked arousing emotion with an orator's style of delivery. See especially his comments at *Rh.* 3.7.3–5, 3.7.10, 3.16.10, 3.19.3–4.

10. Cicero's linkage of gesture with strong emotions is a recurrent one throughout history. For example, modern actors are sometimes taught that in moments of extreme or heightened emotion they should make gestures, in the belief that people tend to gesticulate spontaneously at "very moments" (very angry, very sad, very happy, etc.). I owe this example to Professor A. Masson of the Theater Department, University of Michigan.

11. See, for example, the depictions of gesture in Roman art collected by Brilliant (1963) in which arm and hand gestures are emphasized. In Greek art, see Neumann 1965. On iconographic representations of Roman orators, see Chapter 2.

12. Both Cicero and Quintilian include in their lists motions of which they disapprove. Cicero cautions the orator not to direct gestures behind himself. Similarly, while acknowledging that circular motions are one of the standard types, Quintilian does not approve of their use by orators.

13. See, for example, Hill 1989, 25, pl. 30.

14. For a good brief survey of the internal arrangements of the senate house, see Talbert 1984, 121–28.

15. The statue of Victory was originally from Tarentum, and was still present in the senate house at least until the third century A.D. On the provenance, appearance, and fame of the statue, see Pohlsander 1969.

16. On this painting and its meaning, see *RE*, "Nemea." The identity of the old man is uncertain. These paintings were also part of Augustus's construction. Since the building was finished soon after Augustus's victory over Marcus Antonius at Actium, the choice of images of Victory in both painting and sculpture may be a reference to his recent success.

17. On these virtues and this shield, see Weinstock 1971, chap. 11. Valerius Maximus (3.15.2) adds that there was an *imago* of Cato the Elder also kept in the Curia.

18. Cic. *Catil.* 3.21, *Sest.* 26; Sall. *Cat.* 46, 49. Empire: Talbert 1984, 118–19.

19. Restoration: Dio 55.8.2, 56.25; Suet. *Tib.* 20; Ov. *Fasti* 640, 643–48. Vesta: Dio 55.9.6. Juno: Pliny *Hist. Nat.* 34.73. Latona and Diana: Pliny *Hist. Nat.* 34.77. Asclepius and Hygieia: Pliny *Hist. Nat.* 34.80. Mars and Mercury: Pliny *Hist. Nat.* 34.89. Ceres, Jupiter, Minerva: Pliny *Hist. Nat.* 34.90. Apollo: Pliny *Hist. Nat.* 34.73, 77. Marsyas: Pliny *Hist. Nat.* 35.66. Liber: Pliny *Hist. Nat.* 35.131. Cassandra: Pliny *Hist. Nat.* 35.144. Gems: Pliny *Hist. Nat.* 37.4. Elephants: Pliny *Hist. Nat.* 35.196. On this decorative scheme and its meaning, see Kellum 1990, 276–307.

20. With the exceptions of the Victories and Mercury, the identities of the exterior figures are disputed. Hill (1978) believes that these external statues are the ones listed by Pliny. Most other scholars think Pliny's statues were in the interior and that these are additional ones. See Kellum 1990; Richardson 1992, 99. Livy (26.23.4) mentions a statue of Victory on the roof of the temple that was struck by lightning.

21. BMC, 116, 132–34.

22. Vasaly (1983, 1993) has cataloged the verbal allusions to geographical locations both visible and nonvisible made by Cicero in his orations. Certainly many of these verbal allusions to visible objects would have been accompanied by a gesture. Vasaly is keenly aware of the possibilities offered by the symbolic landscape to add meaning to an oration. While she notes some instances when gestures were used to complement verbal allusions, her focus is primarily on the texts of the speeches rather than on their actual delivery.

23. The chronology and appearance of the early speaking platforms and their various reconstructions are extremely complex and problematic. Basic starting points on these issues include Ulrich 1994, Coarelli 1992, and Richardson 1992.

    The republican structures on the later sites of the Rostra Augusti and the Temple of the Deified Caesar are hypothetical but seem to have some literary support and are logical sites for such structures. On these, see particularly the comments by R. Ulrich 1994, chap. 2.

24. Navius: Livy 1.36.3–5; Dion. Hal. 3.71; Pliny *Hist. Nat.* 34.21. Pythagoras and Alcibiades: Pliny *Hist. Nat.* 34.26; Plut. *Numa* 8. Hermodorus: Pliny *Hist. Nat.* 34.21. Hostilius: Dion. Hal. 3.1. Horatius: Aul. Gell. 4.5; Pliny *Hist. Nat.* 34.22; Plut. *Publ.* 16.7; Dion. Hal. 3.1.

    Some of these, such as the statues of Alcibiades and Pythagoras, seem to have been destroyed or removed by the late republic, while others were still visible in Pliny's time. See Richardson 1992; Vasaly 1993, 63–68.

25. Maenius: Livy 8.14.12; Pliny *Hist. Nat.* 7.60, 34.20; Cic. *Clu.* 39; Symmachus *Ep.* 5.54.3. Duilius: Pliny *Hist. Nat.* 34.20; Quint. *Inst.* 1.7.12. Octavian: App. *BC* 5.130.

26. Tables: Diod. Sic 12.26.1; Dion. Hal. 10.57; Justin. *Dig.* 1.2.2.4. Romulus: Dion. Hal. 2.54.2. Camillus: Pliny *Hist. Nat.* 34.23; Livy 8.13.9. Hercules: Pliny *Hist. Nat.* 34.93. Minucius: Pliny *Hist. Nat.* 34.21. Tremulus: Pliny *Hist. Nat.* 34.23; Livy 9.43.22; Cic. *Phil.* 6.13. Sibyls: Pliny *Hist. Nat.* 34.22.

27. For the numerous references to the Lacus Curtius and Lapis Niger, see Richardson 1992. Marsyas: Hor. *Sat.* 1.6.120; Sen. *Ben.* 6.32.1; Pliny *Hist. Nat.* 21.8–9. Ficus Navia: Pliny *Hist. Nat.* 15.77. Vine, fig, and olive tree: Pliny *Hist. Nat.* 15.78.

28. Pliny *Hist. Nat.* 34.30–31. Some of these unauthorized statues were even melted down by the censors.

29. On the Forum of Augustus and its sculptural program, see Zanker 1968, 1988.

30. The Alban hills begin approximately twenty kilometers from Rome. While they may not have been directly visible from the low-lying Forum, they would have been a familiar sight to the inhabitants of the city. Even through today's pollution they are plainly visible from high points in Rome such as the Janiculum Hill.

31. Vasaly 1993, 40–87, has examined Cicero's use of visual symbols in the *Catilinarians* in great detail.

32. On this incident, see the comments of Corbeill 1996, 39–41, who also examines the use of humor by Roman orators in general.

33. On the development of the Forum *tabernae* and the confused terminology used to refer to them, see, as starting points, Platner and Ashby 1929, and Richardson 1992.

34. On the similarities between actor and orator, see Chapter 2.

35. On Marcus Antonius's speech on this occasion, see Kennedy 1968.

36. Another famous example of evoking pity by using a living prop was when the orator Antonius ripped open the clothes of Manius Aquilius during a trial in order to display the scars he had suffered while serving his country (Cic. *De Orat.* 2.194–96). This appeal was so dramatic that it supposedly moved Gaius Marius, who was present, to tears.

37. This story is again related by Gaius Julius Caesar Strabo, a character in Cicero's *De Oratore* whom it is tempting to see as a mouthpiece for Cicero's opinions.

38. On the power of the eyes generally, see *Inst.* 11.3.68–79.

39. On acclamations and shouts from the crowd, see Chapter 4.

40. Other examples include a gesture that when made gently indicated assent, but when performed vigorously meant praise or exhortation. Quint. *Inst.* 11.3.102.

41. The subject of intentionally rhythmic orations is treated in more detail in Chapter 5.

42. On rhythm, see also Cic. *De Orat* 1.151, 3.188, *Orat.* 175, 229; Quint. *Inst.* 10.3.9.

43. Cicero notes that some orators "sing" their speeches, a practice he deplores. Cic. *Orat.* 57.

44. Graf 1991, 46, suggests that the complicated arrangement of the toga on the left shoulder and arm may offer a partial explanation for why orators were expected to gesture primarily with the right hand, since the left arm was hampered by the fall of the garment. In addition to this pragmatic consideration, there may also have been some superstitious reasons for avoiding left-handed motions. See also Maier-Eichhorn 1989, 114–16.

Chapter Two. Gesture in Roman Society

1. See Brilliant 1963, 30–31.

2. A recurrent problem with many of these statues is that frequently the fingers, hands, and even entire arms are restorations, which may or may not reflect the originals. Where I have been able to ascertain that there is uncertainty regarding a gesture, it will be indicated. This ambiguity is one reason that in the present study I rarely discuss the meaning of specific gestures found in these statues. In future research, I hope to further explore these issues. While the precise gestures depicted in these statues may be debatable, these works plainly represent aristocratic orators, and are cited here to illustrate the limited point that an important component of the standard iconographic image of an orator was the gesticulating right arm. On these statues, see ibid., 68–69.

3. See ibid., Tiberius: 68–69, Titus: 93, Augustus: 65–68. On Augustus's gesture as oratorical, see Simon 1957 and Gross 1959.

4. On these reliefs, see Boatwright 1987, with further bibliography, 182–90, 231–33. On the Anaglypha, see also Torelli 1982, 89–118. These reliefs are discussed in more detail in Chapter 3.

5. On which parts of this relief are original, see La Rocca 1986, 24–37 and accompanying plates.

6. Augustus: BMC, 1: nos. 609–14, pl. 15.3–4; BMC Rep., 2: no. 4327; RIC, 1: nos. 2, 3; CNR 428–32. Germanicus: BMC, 1: nos. 93–100, pl. 30.9, 10; RIC, 1:119, pl. VIII.124. Vespasian: BMC, 2: no. 47, pl. 1.15; RIC, 2: no. 28, pl. 1.2. Trajan: BMC, 3: no. 347, pl. 15.2; Strack, 1:120, pl. II.123. Hadrian: BMC, 3: no. 532, pl. 57.14.

7. Soldiers—Caligula: BMC, 1: nos. 33ff., 67, 68, pls. 28.3, 29.12. Nero: BMC, 1: nos. 122–26, 303, 304, pls. 41.5, 45.18; RIC, 1:149, pl. X.166. Galba: BMC, 1:355, no. 249, pl. 58.8. Nerva: BMC, 3:xlvi, 14; RIC, 2:226, no. 50. Hadrian: BMC, 3: no. 1673, 1678, pl. 96.6, 8, 13; Bernhart pl. 89.15.

Civil—Trajan: BMC, 3: no. 827, pl. 30.6; RIC, 2: nos. 553–55; Strack, 1:32, 133, pl. V.363. Hadrian: BMC, 3: nos. 1309–11, pl. 81.10, Strack, 2:113, 114, pl. IX.599.

8. This Domitianic coin commemorates the Ludi Saeculares and shows an event from the second day, the sacrifice of a cow to Juno with prayers from 110 matrons. The coin depicts the emperor leading the prayer by reading aloud from a scroll in his left hand the ritual phrases, which are repeated by a group of kneeling women in front of the temple. On this coin and others showing the events of the Ludi Saeculares and various religious festivals, see Ryberg 1955, 174–89, pls. 63–66.

9. On the spectacular and popular nature of court trials in the late republic, see the comments by Nicolet 1980, 373–81.

10. On late republican trials, including court procedure and location, see Gruen 1968, 1974.

11. See Cic. *In Vat.* 14.34 for a lively description of a trial disrupted by the defendant and his accomplices. Trials interrupted by outbreaks of violence were frequent, and many examples are discussed by Gruen 1974, 404–48, and Nicolet 1980, 379–81. The most famous case of military intervention was the trial of Milo in 52 B.C.

12. The phrase and definition are from Pliny, *Ep.* 2.14. On the role of claques, see Chapter 5.

13. On the frequency of entertainments and their attendance, see Balsdon 1969a, 1969b.

14. On pantomime in general, see Beacham 1992, chap. 5, with recent bibliography, and Jory 1981. On riots precipitated by pantomimes in the early empire, see Jory 1984.

15. On mime shows, see Beacham 1992, 129–40; Reich 1903; Bonaria 1965; Wiemken 1972; Beare 1964; Taladoire 1951; and Balsdon 1969a, 274–79.

16. On the Atellanae, see Beacham 1992, 5–6, 128–29; Frassinetti 1953; and Beare 1964.

17. On Roman theater, see Beacham 1992, Beare 1964, Dupont 1985, Garton 1972, and Arnott 1971. On gesture in the Greek theater, see Arnott 1989, who devotes a chapter to the subject. A useful collection of primary sources on Greek and Roman theater, including crowd response, is Csapo and Slater 1995.

18. For example, Hor. *Sat.* 1.2.57; Juv. 8.187; Mart. 3.86.

19. For derogatory comments on mimes and pantomimes, see for example, Hor. *Sat.* 1.2.57; Mart. 3.86; Val. Max. 2.10.8; Juvenal *Sat.* 8.187; Quint. *Inst.* 6.3.8, 6.47.

20. On claques, see Chapter 5.

21. On these gestures and specifically on their relationship to those described in Quintilian, see Weston 1903, whose view that they are part

of a common nonverbal vocabulary shared by orator and actor is disputed by L. Jones and Morey 1931, 206–12. The miniatures can best be viewed in Jones and Morey 1931.

22. On these manuscripts, see Weston 1903; Grant 1973, 1986; L. Jones and Morey 1931; Sittl 1890; Maier-Eichhorn 1989; D. Wright 1993; and Lenz 1929. The most comprehensive analysis of the date of the manuscripts can be found in the two-volume work of L. Jones and Morey. In one volume they provide side by side representations of all the panels from the four manuscripts, and in the other describe their characteristics and provenance, and attempt to construct a stemma. Their discussion offers an excellent summary of earlier opinions on all questions relating to the miniatures.

23. L. Jones and Morey (1931) believe the most reliable illustrations are those in F. While these may be the finest from an artistic standpoint, at times the handling of the fingers seems sloppier than in C. Since my interest is solely in the gestures, I have generally relied on C, and where there are substantial differences, I will indicate them. C is also the only manuscript that I have been able to examine personally. Even in the careful photographic reproductions of Jones and Morey, much of the detail is lost and the illustrations are in black and white. Regardless of whether C or F is better, these two are plainly much superior to the other manuscripts.

24. L. Jones and Morey 1931, 35ff.

25. This enlargement is most pronounced in P and F. Fig. 19: Terence, *Phormio* act 2, scene 2, lines 315–47, as found in manuscript P, subsequently abbreviated Ter. *Ph.* 2.2, 315–47, P. Fig. 20: Ter. *Ph.* 4.4, 682–712, P.

26. L. Jones and Morey 1931, 45.

27. Ibid., 201–6. Jones and Morey do not think there is any relationship between Quintilian and the miniatures, but they base their argument on refuting Weston's identifications (206–11). Weston, however, made some errors in his reading of Quintilian, and, as I illustrate below, there does seem to be a correlation between these illustrations and Quintilian.

28. Some accounts of such attempts may be found in Ammianus Marcellinus 14.6.19. Cassiodorus *Variae* 1.32.2. Theodosian Code 15.7.8, 11, 12. On all forms of later Roman theater, see Beacham 1992, 152–53, 192–98.

29. Fig. 21: Ter. *Ad.* 5.6, 889–98, C.63.

30. L. Jones and Morey 1931, 206–11.

31. Fig. 22: Ter. *Eu.* 5.8, 1031–49, C.33v.

32. The gesture made by Demea in the *Adelphi* (5.6) and Pythias in the *Eunuchus* (4.5) may be different from the others since the thumb and

forefinger are rigid, forming a right angle with the forefinger just touching the edge of the thumb. In contrast, in all the other panels, both fingers are distinctly curved so that the tips of the fingers form the point of convergence. In the same panels from F, the actor's gestures are indistinguishable from those in the other scenes.

In general, the artists in C are more meticulous in drawing finger joints and are more consistent in drawing the same gesture exactly the same way in all panels.

33. For example, at other persons: *An.* 4.1 (made by Pamphilus), *An.* 4.5 (Mysis), *An.* 5.4 (Chremes), *Eu.* 3.5 (Chaerea), *Eu.* 4.7 (Chremes), *Eu.* 5.7 (Thraso), *Eu.* 5.8 (Gnatho, with both hands simultaneously), *Ha.* 2.3 (Syrus), *Ha.* 4.1 (Nutrix), *Ad* 3.3 (Syrus), *Ad.* 2.3 (Ctesipho), and *Hec.* 5.2 (Bacchis). In the air: *An.* 4.2 (Pamphilus) and *Hec.* 5.2 (Bacchis). Fig. 23: Ter. *Eu.* 5.7, 1025–30, C.33v. Fig. 24: Ter. *Hec.* 5.2, 767–98, C.75.

34. Fig. 25: Ter. *An.* 1.5, 236–300, C.7.

35. Fig. 26: Ter. *Ph.* 2.1, 231–314, C.80. Another usage occurs in *Ha.* 2.2, when Clinia fears that his love has been corrupted by a bad influence.

36. L. Jones and Morey 1931, 206–11.

37. This gesture is also nearly indistinguishable from the gesture for entreaty, mild surprise, or indignation, and in some of the miniatures, the meaning of entreaty could be appropriate to the context of the scene (Quint. *Inst.* 11.3.103).

38. Fig. 27: Ter. *Ad.* 4.4, 610–35, C.59.

39. Fig. 28: Ter. *Ad.* 2.2, 209–53, C.53v.

40. Fig. 29: Ter. *Hec.* 3.3, 361–414, C.70.

41. Other possible occurrences of this gesture are in the *Eunuchus* 1.1 (Phaedria), 4.2 (Phaedria), 4.3 (Phaedria), and 5.5 (Laches); *Phormio* 3.3 (Phaedria); *Andria* 1.2 (Simo); and *Adelphi* 3.3 (Demea). These identifications are more problematic and may actually represent the clenched-fist anger posture, although in some panels the actors' hands seem to be closed with just one finger extended. See, for example, Ter. *Eun.* 1.1, 46–81, C.19v. In most instances, however, the hand is raised to the level of the face as in the modesty pose. The context of the action of the scenes could support either interpretation. Perhaps the differences in gesture are due to carelessness on the part of the copyist, or the scenes may depict a third, distinct gesture with some intermediate meaning.

42. Fig. 30: Ter. *Ph.* 4.1, 567–90, C.84v.

43. Ter. *Ph.* 3.1, 465–84, C.83.

44. Weston (1903, 53) believes it to be a variant on a gesture for narration mentioned by Quintilian (11.3.94). This is possible, but while the gesture is similar, the finger position is clearly different from that

described by Quintilian. L. Jones and Morey (1931, 206–11) argues, I think correctly, that Weston's identification is wishful thinking, but they too think it is some sort of narrative gesture.

Weston also claims to see an example of the sensational thigh-striking gesture made by Phormio in act 2, scene 2 of the *Phormio* (p. 52), but I agree with Jones (pp. 206–11) that the illustration is much too ambiguous to draw such a firm conclusion, although it is possible.

45. Fig. 31: Ter. *Hec.* 4.2, 577–606, C.72v.

46. Jones 1931, 210, lists many additional examples.

47. Fig. 32: Ter. *Hec.* 2.3, 274–80, C.68. Fig. 33: Ter. *Eu.* 4.7, 771–817, C.29v.

48. It is a telling reflection on the role and voice of women in Roman society that while male orators had a vast vocabulary of gestures they could use, seemingly the only approved gesture available to women was one that emphasized their modesty and subordinate attachment to a male.

49. On funerary portraiture, see Kleiner 1977. In her catalog of funerary sculpture, there are many women shown in this posture. See catalog (and plate) nos. 11, 23, 37, 69, 91, 162–64.

50. This statue is thought to be a Roman version of a Greek original, and the pose itself may have Hellenistic origins. On the *pudicitia* pose in general, see Bieber 1959.

51. Hortensius's reply to this gibe was that he would much prefer to be a Dionysia than to be a stranger to the muse like his accuser.

52. Similarly, see Luc. *De Salt.* 65.

53. Beacham 1992, 126.

54. Another gesture that appears in Apuleius is laying the index finger across the lips to command silence (1.8). Graf (1991, 47, 56–57) believes this to be another use of the gesture for wonder with a variant finger posture, but in the context of this scene, it is clear that while the character is startled, the gesture is intended to signify silence, not surprise.

55. For an analysis of the specific fear that overly theatrical presentation could compromise an orator's masculinity, see Gleason 1995. This study has much of value to say on the deportment of orators in general.

56. Plut. *C. Gracch.* 2; Cic. *Brut.* 278; Quint. *Inst.* 11.3.123. Note also Lucian's satiric advice to an orator, "clap your thigh, lament, stride about swaying your hips." Luc. *Rhet. Praeceptor* 19.

57. The specific topic of gesture in the Middle Ages has received thorough treatment by Schmitt (1990). For a very brief introduction to this material, see also his 1991 article.

58. On changes in oratorical style in the first century and the perception

that oratory had changed for the worse by becoming more theatrical, see particularly H. Caplan 1944. More generally, see Kennedy 1972, Clarke 1963, and Bonner 1969.

59. On Roman voting procedures and the political process, see, as starting points, Nicolet 1980, Taylor 1966, and Sherwin-White 1973.

60. North 1990 offers a relatively recent and concise summary of this literature, including synopses of the major works and considerable bibliography. See also Millar 1998, and his series of articles in *JRS* 1983, 1984, 1986, 1989, and 1994.

61. Maier-Eichhorn 1989, 35–47, lists approximately fifteen other surviving treatises in various languages written between the fifteenth and the nineteenth centuries. Some of these studies, such as *Chironomia, or a Treatise on Rhetorical Delivery* (1806), by Gilbert Austin, an English clergyman, contain valuable insights.

62. Rabelais 1955, book 2, chaps. 18–20.

63. Jorio 1832.

64. Sittl 1890 to Maier-Eichhorn 1989.

65. This observation is limited to the major Western industrialized countries. Eventually, I would like to consider other societies as well.

66. For a rhetorical analysis of modern American political oratory, see Jamieson 1988. See also Atkinson 1984.

67. On the composition of Rome's populace, see Brunt 1971a.

68. For an introduction to the difficult problem of assessing Rome's population, see ibid.; Hopkins 1978, 96–98; Duncan-Jones 1982, 259–76; Salmon 1974; Packer 1967; Parkin 1992; and Hermansen 1978b.

69. Bairoch 1988.

70. On the population of Athens, see Gomme 1933.

71. See, for example, Suet. *Dom.* 13.2; Dio 69.6.1–2. This last incident, in which a herald quieted an unruly crowd by raising his hand, also reveals that heralds were versed in the language of gestures, and at least on occasion used them alone, without the accompaniment of words, to communicate with audiences.

72. On the acoustical qualities of ancient theaters, see Arnott 1989, who notes that not only could all parts of the audience clearly hear sounds from the stage, but that "the reverse is also true. Noise from any section of the auditorium can be distinctly heard in the others" (74). For audience comments to have had their intended effect, they had to be audible not merely to the performers on stage but, even more important, to fellow members of the audience. Empirical experiments I conducted at the theaters and amphitheaters at Pompeii and Alba Fucens confirm that it is easily possible to hear and be heard, between any two points in the seating and performance spaces, as well as any two points in the seats, even in high winds.

In ancient theaters there appear to have been some efforts to improve the already impressive acoustics. Vitruvius (5.5) describes in great detail one attempted architectural amplification scheme consisting of a series of bronze urns embedded at intervals around the *cavea* of the theater. These pots were supposedly tuned to different harmonic frequencies and served to somehow clarify and perhaps amplify the actors' voices. There is some achaeological evidence for the existence of such urns at over a dozen theaters around the Mediterranean. The possible extant examples are made of clay rather than bronze. How widespread such devices were, exactly how they functioned, and how effective they were remain uncertain. I owe this reference to Jean Davison who is currently investigating Vitruvius's vessels, and whose forthcoming study may elucidate these issues.

73. Vitruvius (5.5.7) states that wood provides better acoustics for performances than stone, marble, or rubble-filled structures because sound resounds better from it.

74. For a basic introduction to modern theatrical voice training and related issues, see Rodenburg 1992.

75. I owe these observations to Professor Annette Masson, voice instructor in the Theater Department at the University of Michigan.

76. There are a number of slightly differing accounts of these incidents. See Dio 47.8; App. *BC* 4.19; Plut. *Cic.* 48–49, *Ant.* 20–21; Juv. 10.120.

77. Plutarch suggests that the hands were severed because they had written the *Philippics*. Additionally, the accounts disagree concerning whether both hands were cut off, or only the right. Since the right hand was the primary hand of gesticulation, this does not help to clarify Antonius's motivations. The fame of Cicero's oratorical delivery certainly suggests that Antonius had more in mind by his order than just punishing the limbs that had transcribed the speeches.

Chapter Three. Oratory and the Roman Emperors

1. Yavetz (1988, 141–55) has usefully noted the frequent employment of stereotypes, often negative, by upper-class commentators when discussing the urban plebs.

2. Millar 1977, 203. See also Champlin 1980, chap. 8.

3. A similar sentiment is expressed in another of Fronto's letters. *Ad M. Caes.* 3.1.

4. On Augustus's early devotion to oratory, his later employment of a teacher of rhetoric, and his own style, see Suet. *Aug.* 84–89.

5. In this section, Suetonius also quotes Cicero's admiring comments on Caesar's skill as an orator.

6. Augustus was said to greatly dislike Tiberius's manner of speaking and

thought that it indicated arrogance. Tacitus ascribed more malevolent intentions to Tiberius's difficult style. On Tiberius's syntax and the confusion it caused for a senatorial audience, see Tac. *Ann.* 1.11, 33. On Tiberius's literary talents, see Suet. *Tib.* 70.

7. See also Suet. *De Rhet.* 1.6–7; Dio 61.3.1.

8. On the literary and grammatical schooling and knowledge of the Julio-Claudian emperors, see Billerbeck 1990. On the varied oratorical and literary abilities and studies of the emperors from Titus through Hadrian, see Orentzel 1981.

9. See also SHA *Did. Jul.* 4.

10. On the latter view, see Balsdon 1969a, 300. Relevant ancient sources include Juv. 3.36; Pliny *Hist. Nat.* 18.25; Horace *Ep.* 1.18.65–66; Prudent. *C. Symm* 2.1099.

    For the confusion surrounding this gesture, see Morris et al. 1979, 186–91, and Wiedemann 1992, 94–96.

11. For a similar later example, see SHA *Did. Jul.* 4.

12. So, for example, the note to the Loeb edition, in which J. C. Rolfe comments that Claudius's thrusting out his left hand is undignified because he should have kept it covered under his toga.

13. Claudius's actions may also have been part of a deliberate attempt to cultivate popularity. On expectations for imperial deportment at games, see Chapter 4.

14. For more on this practice, see Chapter 4.

15. BMC, 3: nos. 1309–11, pl. 81.10; Strack, 2:113, 114, pl. IX.599.

16. It is not clear which, if any, of these suggestions is accurate. For the arguments, and on this coin in general, see Boatwright 1987, 102–4; Pasquinucci 1973, 258–59; and Brilliant 1963, 134–35.

17. On this temple, see Ulrich 1994, 165–94; Richardson 1992; and Platner and Ashby 1929.

18. There are a number of accounts of the funeral and cremation, including Dio 47.18, 56.34; Suet. *Aug.* 100; Plut. *Caes.* 68; Livy *Ep.* 116; App. *BC* 1.4, 2.148.

19. BMC, 3: no. 827, pl. 30.6; RIC, 2: nos. 553–55; Strack, 1:32, 133, pl. V.363.

20. On the *metae* of the Circus Maximus, see Humphrey 1986, 255–59, and illustrations on pp. 178, 181, 187, 190.

21. The Parilia celebration held on April 21 originally involved purification rites for shepherds and herd animals, but by the empire the festival seems to have been transformed into a celebration of the supposed date of Rome's foundation. Thus the coin's inscription includes the phrase *(nat)alis (urb)is*. The nature of the imperial rites performed in the Circus to commemorate Rome's birthday is uncertain. See Ov. *Fasti* 4.721ff.; Varro, *Rust.* 2.1.9; Cic. *Div.* 2.98; and Scullard 1981, 103–5.

22. On this coin, see Toynbee 1934, 137–38, pls. VI.13–15.

23. Toynbee (1934, 138) believes the setting of the Trajanic coin to be the Campus Martius. She concedes that the attributes on the coin suggest the Circus, but rejects this site on the grounds that "the Campus seems to be a more probable scene than the Circus for an imperial oration." On the contrary, the Circus was one of the principal locations for emperor-plebs interactions. The exact correspondence of the three cones sharing a common base to the appearance of the *metae* in the circus, the similarities of the figure-wheel-cones combination on this coin to known representations of the Circus, and the reputation of the Circus for emperor-plebs interactions strongly indicate that the intended scene is indeed the Circus Maximus, not the Campus Martius.

24. Although these reliefs date from the early second century, and I am primarily concerned with the early empire, they have been emphasized because they include all three of the elements of orating emperor, civilian audience, and architectural setting, and as such, are more complete visual evocations of an imperial oration than any extant earlier monuments.

25. The vagueness of this relief has produced much debate concerning the identity of the figures, the buildings, and even the meaning of the scene. The only points on which there is general agreement are that the speaker is Hadrian and that the seminude man is meant to be the genius of the Roman people. Some have proposed that the boy is Lucius Verus, although the figure's features do not resemble the known portraits. Others believe he represents the beneficiaries of imperial largess schemes for children, thus making the panel a commemoration of Hadrian's *alimentaria*. Whatever the exact circumstances, it is clear that the relief is an allegorical depiction of the emperor addressing the people somewhere in the Forum.

    For introductions to these issues, see Kleiner 1992, 253–54 and bibliography on p. 265; Boatwright 1987, 226–29, 231–34; and La Rocca 1986, 24–37.

26. The Anaglypha of Hadrian was originally labeled the Anaglypha Traiani, and whether it is Trajanic or Hadrianic in date is still disputed. On this debate and other controversial issues concerning the relief, including its provenance and original setting, see Hammond 1953; Boatwright 1987, 182–90; Rüdiger 1973; Torelli 1982, 89–118, with good illustrations; and Kleiner 1992, 248–53, 265.

27. The entire panel is variously identified as a Trajanic *alimenta* scene (Hammond), a Hadrianic *alimenta* scene (Rüdiger), or a Trajanic *congiarium* (Torelli). Although the *alimenta* statue group is prominent, the principal element found in all *alimenta* scenes, a crowd of children, is absent from this relief, strongly suggesting that it is not an *alimenta*

scene. Ultimately, the problem of the exact situation represented by this panel is probably insoluble without further evidence, but it is certainly possible that it depicts an imperial oration in the Forum before a cross section of Rome's populace.

Chapter Four. Uses of Acclamations by the Urban Plebs

1. The *OLD* entry for *acclamatio* offers this definition: "1. Shouting, bawling. 2. A shout of comment. (spec.) b. of disapproval. c. of approval." Strictly speaking, the formal primary definition of the English word "acclamation" is still simply "a shout," but in practice it is used almost exclusively for expressions of approval.

2. Acclamations at weddings: Livy 1.9.12; Mart. 12.42.4; Plut. *Pomp.* 4 (used ironically). At triumphs: Varro 1.1.6.68; Ov. *Trist.* 4.2.48. On triumphs, see Versnel 1970 and Payne 1962. For these and other instances of the use of acclamations in Roman society, see Klauser 1950 and Schmidt 1958.

3. Examples include Caesar *B.C.* 2.26.1; Tac. *Ann.* 3.74. Other examples of actual acclamations by soldiers include Tac. *Hist.* 2.46; Dio 62.10; SHA *Ant. Diad.* 1–2.

4. For senatorial acclamations, see Alföldi 1934, and 1970, 85–87; Hirschfeld 1913, 682–702; Talbert 1984, 297–302.

   The largest collection of actual senatorial acclamations occurs in the *Historia Augusta*, where dozens of senatorial acclamations are directly quoted (*Avid. Cass.* 13; *Com.* 18–19; *Sev. Alex.* 6–12, 56; *Maxim.* 16.3–7, 24; *Max. Balb.* 2.9–12). Although doubts have been expressed regarding the authors' apparently exact knowledge of what was said on these occasions, many of the cited acclamations are certainly standard ones, and even if they are not what was said on a given occasion, they are probably representative of senatorial acclamations in general. On this issue, see B. Baldwin 1981, 138–49; Syme 1971, 61.

   Other examples of senatorial acclamations include Pliny, *Pan.* 2, 71–75; Suet. *Aug.* 58, *Nero* 46, *Dom.* 23; Dio 60.32.2, 62.20, 63.20.4, 74.2.1, 75.5.1, 76.6.2. See also the similar acclamations of the Arval Brethren (*ILS* 541; *CIL* 6.2086, 2104).

5. On Roman urban rituals and spectacles involving mass participation, see Beard 1987, Nicolet 1980, and Hopkins 1991. On religious festivals, see Beard and North 1990, and Scullard 1981. On rituals surrounding the emperor, see Millar 1977; Price 1984, 1987; Charlesworth 1935, 1937; and McCormick 1985, 1986. On Byzantine ceremonies, see Cameron 1987. For a perceptive analysis of rituals at Athens, see Connor 1987.

   The approach of analyzing urban public spectacles for what they reveal about society and the construction of power has been extensively employed by scholars of Italian Renaissance city-states and offers interesting comparative material for the study of antiquity. Especially relevant works include Trexler 1973, 1980, 1985; Cardini 1991; Najemy 1991; Strocchia 1992; Sznura 1991; and Weissman 1982, on Florence; Muir 1970, 1981, Romano 1987, and Brown 1990, 1991, on Venice; Ingersoll 1985, on Rome; and Martines 1972, 1988. R. Baldwin 1990 and Wirsch and Munshower 1990, vols. 1 and 2, examine artistic evidence. On Renaissance spectacle generally, see Strong 1973, 1985.

Similar works on other countries include Anglo 1966, on Tudor England; Mullaney 1988, Orgel 1975, and Phythian-Adams 1976, on Renaissance England; Cannadine 1983, on England more recently; Graham 1986, on Renaissance France; and the collection of essays in Cannadine and Price 1987. See also Bloch 1975, on the role of oratory in traditional societies.

Useful studies from a more theoretical perspective include C. Bell 1992; Bennet 1980; Cohen 1974; Geertz 1973, 1983; Goffman 1961a, 1961b; Goody 1977; Greenblatt 1988; Handelman 1990; Huizinga 1950; and Kertzer 1988.

6. It is notoriously difficult to define whom the ancient sources meant when they referred to the urban plebs. On this problem, see particularly the comments by Yavetz (1965a, 1965b, 1988) and Whittaker (1993). Other relevant discussions of the plebs include Brunt 1966, Eder 1991, Mazza 1974, Seiler 1936, Necaj 1969, and Barry 1988, on crowds in Roman Alexandria.

Discussions of the urban plebs often try to classify segments of the urban populace by economic status and living conditions. On opportunities of employment for the plebs, see Brunt 1980; Brewster 1917; Casson 1978; Garnsey 1980; Joshel 1992; Loane 1938; Treggiari 1980; Thornton and Thornton 1986, 1989; and Giglioni 1973. On various aspects of urban living conditions, see Amulree 1973, Carcopino 1968, Hodge 1989, Knapp 1925, Liversidge 1976, Rainbird 1986, and Scobie 1986. On housing, see Frier 1977, 1980, and Hermansen 1970. On food and especially the grain dole, there is a considerable bibliography. As starting points, see Chilver 1949; Garnsey 1988, 1991; Hermansen 1978a; Rickman, 1971, 1980, 1991; Sippel 1987; Sirks 1991; and Virlouvet 1985, 1991.

7. Other examples in Cicero of similar expressions of public opinion, often occurring in the theater, include *Sest.* 125–27, *Ad Att.* 1.16.11, 2.19.3, 14.2.1, *Ad Fam.* 8.2.1, *In Pis.* 3. 65. See also Suet. *J.C.* 80; Plut. *Sert.* 5, *Cic.* 13.

On Cicero and public demonstrations in the late republic in general, see Bollinger 1969, especially 24–30; Gruen 1992, chap. 5; Nicolet 1980, 343–81; Abbott 1907, 49–56; Vanderbroeck 1987.

For a perceptive analysis of the importance that being seen in public held for Roman politicians and on ways to present oneself impressively, see A. Bell 1997.

8. The chance encounter took place away from Rome after Demetrius had been banished; and not only did the Cynic fail to salute the emperor properly but he instead muttered an insult at Vespasian. Vespasian then demonstrated both his leniency and his love of witticism by responding with an insult of his own, labeling the Cynic Demetrius a dog, a play on the similarity in Greek between the words "Cynic" and "dog" (κύων).

9. See, for example, Tac. *Hist.* 2.55.

10. Other references to the "stand-and-applaud" sort of acclamation in various contexts permeate the sources. See, for example, Suet. *Aug.* 68, *Claud.* 12; Nic. Dam. *Aug.* 28; Hor. *Odes* 1.20.3, and perhaps Prop. 3.18.17.

11. Examples include Tac. *Hist.* 2.90, 3.67; Mart. 7.8; *SHA Com.* 15; Pliny *Pan.* 2; P. *Oxy.* 2435 verso.

12. On the acclamations of the Arval Brethren, see Henzen 1874, or for more recent bibliography, Law 1980.

13. While the general sense of *feliciter* in acclamations is clear, the exact translation is more difficult. In a sample of Loeb and Penguin translations, it is variously rendered as: "Success to . . ." and "All hail . . ." (Loeb, Suet. *Claud.* 7); "Long live . . ." (Penguin, Suet. *Claud.* 7); "Good fortune to . . ." (Loeb, Suet. *Dom.* 13); "God bless . . ." (Loeb, Pet. *Sat.* 50); "Fortunate" (Loeb, Pliny *Pan.* 74); "Hurray for . . ." and "God save . . ." (Penguin, Pet. *Sat.* 50, 60). The *Oxford Latin Dictionary* renders *feliciter* as "Good Luck!"

While the phrase's intended meaning probably varied with specific contexts, for clarity I have rendered most translations following the appealingly vague suggestion of the *OLD*.

14. On such "doublespeak" in general, see Bartsch 1994.

15. Quoted acclamations are often actually petitions in the form of acclamations.

16. P. *Fouad* 8: translation of restored papyrus by Sherk 1988, 123–24.

17. For a more detailed analysis of acclamation formulas and their versatility, see Chapter 5.

18. Examples of acclamations from the later Roman Empire and Byzantine Empire are much more common, and consequently have been more exhaustively studied. Basic works on this subject include Roueché 1984, 181–99, on sixth-century acclamations from Aphrodisias, which also provides the best recent survey of earlier acclamations;

McCormick 1986, on victory celebrations in late antiquity and Byzantium; MacCormack 1981, especially chap. 1, on the *adventus* ceremony; A. Cameron 1976, 157ff., on acclamations in general and particularly their use by circus factions at Rome and Constantinople; Peterson 1926, an older, but still definitive study of acclamations, particularly those with a religious component; and Robert 1960, 21–52, on Byzantine acclamations from Corinth.

Other important discussions of acclamations can be found in Klauser 1950, 216–33, the extensive *RAC* entry on acclamations that is an excellent collection of examples from all of antiquity; Whittaker 1964, 348–69, a study of one specific incident involving acclamations from A.D. 190; Colin 1965; Charlesworth 1943, 1–10; Alföldi 1970, 79–88, on acclamations as part of imperial identity; B. Baldwin 1981, on the historicity of the acclamations in the *Historia Augusta*; and Hirschfeld 1905, on senatorial acclamations (mostly from the later Roman Empire).

On some possible reasons for the disparity between amounts of evidence from the early and later empire concerning acclamations and interactions at entertainments in general, see A. Cameron 1976, 184–85.

19. For a brief description of such ceremonies, see Millar 1977, 31–32. For a more detailed discussion, see Alföldi 1970, and MacCormack 1981, 17–55. On sculptural representations of *adventus* and *profectio* ceremonies, see Koeppel 1969, 130–94. For an analysis of the theme of the imperial *adventus* in coinage, see Brilliant 1963, 173–77.

20. Vespasian: Joseph. *BJ* 7.71. Nero: Tac. *Ann.* 14.13, 16.24. Trajan: Pliny *Pan.* 22–23. Augustus: Suet. *Aug.* 57. Commodus: Herodian 1.7. Other descriptions or comments on *adventus* ceremonies include Suet. *Gaius* 4; Dio 51.4, 20; Mart. 10.6; SHA *Max.-Balb.* 13.

21. Other examples that specifically refer to acclamations in the streets and in other informal or impromptu settings include Tac. *Hist.* 3.67; *Ann.* 3.33; Dio 53.20, 56.26.

22. *Oxyrhynchus Papyri*, part XXV (1959), 2435 recto, ed. E. G. Turner. See also Weingärtner 1969, 73–90, and the translation and commentary by Sherk 1988, 60–61.

23. Germanicus's trip is described in Tac. *Ann.* 59–72; Suet. *Tib.* 52, *Gaius* 1–6. On Germanicus in the East, see Akveld 1961, Koestermann 1958, and Weingärtner 1969.

24. Another possible example of a senator interrupting an emperor's speech may have occurred during Claudius's famous rambling oration to the senate on Gallic rights, which has been preserved on two tablets from Lugdunum (*CIL* 13.1668). In the midst of this digressive speech is found the line, "Now it is time, Tiberius Caesar Germanicus, to reveal

yourself to the conscript fathers, explaining in what direction your address is heading, for already (in it) you have come to the farthest borders of Gallia Narbonensis" (trans. Sherk 1988). Commentators have disagreed as to whether this line represents the interjection of an exasperated senator demanding that Claudius come to the point, or whether Claudius is eccentrically addressing himself in the third person. Most scholars (e.g., Scramuzza 1971, 103) have concluded that Claudius is speaking to himself, although some, including Mommsen (1854, 443–50), believe that the tablets preserve the spontaneous outburst of a senator. The greatest argument against the comment being senatorial is the unlikelihood that a critical interjection such as this would not merely have been preserved but actually inscribed on an honorific monument. This is a fairly compelling argument and is probably correct. However, given the tradition of vocal reaction to orations, it is certainly possible that a senator would have made such a remark. If so, the mystery would then be how or why it ended up on the monument.

The bibliography on these tablets and their relation to Tacitus's paraphrase of them (*Ann.* 11.23–24) is extensive. Good introductions to these issues may be found in Momigliano 1934, Syme 1958, Scramuzza 1971, and Griffin 1982.

25. Smitherman 1977, 104.
26. Doob 1961.
27. Awkward 1989, 49.
28. Call-and-response exchanges between an orator and an audience could also be completely staged. In the late republic, Clodius often used a call-and-response format to torment his political opponents in public settings. At a trial in 58 B.C. at which Pompey was present, he shouted out a series of insulting questions, including; "What's the name of the lecherous imperator? What's the name of the man who's trying to find a man? Who scratches his head with one finger?" After each line, he shook the folds of his toga as a signal and his supporters among the crowd responded "like a trained chorus," shouting out in unison the reply, "Pompey!" (Plut. *Pomp.* 48).

Cicero himself records a similar later incident in a letter to his brother written in 56 B.C. On this occasion, Clodius repeated the tactic with questions and responses aimed at both Pompey and Crassus (Cic. *Ep. Q. Fr.* 2.3.2).

29. Fundamental studies on the tradition of petitioning the emperor, the expectations for his behavior at public entertainments, and emperor-plebs relations include Bollinger 1969, on all these topics; A. Cameron 1976, 155–93, a briefer but comprehensive account of the same subjects; Whittaker 1964, on a public demonstration at the circus in A.D. 190; Friedländer 1979, 1–119, 90–117, a collection of anecdotes of

emperor-plebs interactions; Yavetz 1988, the basic modern study of the relationship between emperor and plebs in the early empire, which concentrates on assessing the popularity of individual emperors with the urban populace; Gilbert 1976, 71–124; Hopkins 1983, 14–30, a short but insighful account of interactions at public entertainments; A. Cameron 1973a, on the role of circus factions that also considers the wider implications of public demonstrations; MacMullen 1967, chap. 5, on urban unrest; Yavetz 1965a, 97–110, on the urban plebs generally; Veyne 1990, a work on euergetism in antiquity which also makes interesting points concerning rulers and the symbolic function of capital cities and their inhabitants; Wallace-Hadrill 1982, on expectations for imperial public behavior; Bradley 1981, on Suetonius's accounts of public entertainments; R. Baldwin 1972, on the relationship between the emperor and his subjects in the first two centuries of the empire; and Wiedemann 1992, 165–83, a study of gladiatorial games, which concludes with a chapter on the interactions between emperors and the audiences at entertainments. The subsequent description of this tradition and expectations for imperial behavior owes much to these works.

30. On the workings of the patronage system at Rome, see, for example, Wallace-Hadrill 1989, 1–14, 63–88, and Saller 1982. See also Eisenstadt and Roniger 1984.

31. Examples of Pliny asking for imperial benefactions on behalf of friends and protégés include *Ep.* 2.9, 10.5, 10.6, 10.7, 10.10, 10.11, 10.87. Similar are requests by Fronto: *Ad Amicos* 1.6; *Ep.* 3.8.3.

32. On the ability of high-status individuals to petition the emperor directly by letter, see Millar 1977, 469–72.

33. On the emperor's obligation to address the concerns of even the lowest elements of Roman society, see Martial 8.82, and particularly the incident related in Dio 69.6.3: when Hadrian told a woman that he was too busy to hear her petition, she rebuked him with the words "then cease being emperor." The chastened emperor immediately realized his duty and granted her an audience. On this incident and the topic of the imperial obligation to listen to petitioners, see Millar 1977, 465–550.

34. On the very real violence present in all Roman entertainments, not merely in gladiatorial shows, see Hopkins 1983, chap. 1, and Coleman 1990.

35. See Wiedemann 1992, Auguet 1994, and Balsdon 1969a, 298–302, for details and further citations regarding the procedures used at gladiatorial games.

36. On *civilitas*, see particularly Wallace-Hadrill 1982, and A. Cameron 1976, 175ff.

37. On the life of Titus as an idealized portrait or panegyric, see Wallace-Hadrill 1983, 62, 114–15, and Luck 1964.
38. On Tiberius's unpopularity, see Yavetz 1965a, 103–13.
39. Manumission of charioteers, Dio 57.11; of gladiators, Mart. *De Spec.* 29.3; of actors, Suet. *Tib.* 47; requests for famous gladiators, Suet. *Gaius* 30; styles of fighting, Tac. *Hist.* 1.32; release of criminals, Fron. *Ad M. Caes.* 2.4.4.

   A mosaic from Smirat in Tunisia depicting a leopard hunt in an amphitheater records the acclamations of the crowd praising the generosity of the awards given to the gladiators. On this mosaic, see Beschaouch 1966, Dunbabin 1978, and Wiedemann 1992.
40. Augustus, Suet. *Aug.* 41; Tiberius, Tac. *Ann.* 2.87; Claudius, Tac. *Ann.* 12.43. So too later emperors, such as Julian, Libanius *Orat.* 18.195. Augustus famously resisted the cries of the people to lower the cost of wine with the admonition that Agrippa had provided them with an ample water supply. Suet. *Aug* 42, Dio 54.11.7.
41. This Sarmentius was mentioned by Horace (*Sat.* 1.5.52–70) and perhaps by Quintilian (*Inst.* 3.3.58). See also Treggiari 1969, 270–71.
42. A. Cameron 1976, 164–66, lists numerous additional examples of petitions, both successful and unsuccessful.

Chapter Five. Characteristics of the Use of Acclamations

1. Tacitus's comment may, however, be somewhat suspect, since there was a well-established literary trope of characterizing crowds as ignorant, fickle, and easily aroused. On the often pejorative adjectives routinely associated with crowds by aristocratic sources, see Yavetz 1988, 141–55.
2. Τὸν μονομάχον and τὸν ἁρματηλάτην are words with powerful negative connotations that are particularly appropriate for Commodus, since they accurately described him and his activities. Τὸν ἀριστερόν may be insulting because of the negative associations with the left side and because it implies Commodus was a masturbator. See Mart. 11.73, 9.41, and Adams 1982, 209. Τὸν κηλήτην is more difficult, but may be similarly apt, or it may be a generic insult. In any case, it is certainly meant derogatively.
3. On this acclamation, see Staehelin 1944.
4. On rhythm and rhythmic structures in Latin, see Guggenheimer 1972. Even though her ultimate interest is in Latin poetry, much of the theoretical material she describes concerning Roman attitudes and approaches to rhythm is drawn from the rhetorical handbooks of Cicero and Quintilian.

   For a technical catalog of different types of meters employed by ancient authors, see Halporn, Ostwald, and Rosenmeyer 1994.

5. These identifications are suggested by the editor of the Loeb edition of Suetonius, J. C. Rolfe (note to Suet., *Nero*, 20). They sound like reasonable explanations of Suetonius's terms, and regardless of whether these identifications are exactly correct, the point of the passage is plainly that the claque members made three different types of sounds in order to praise Nero.

6. See A. Cameron 1976 for a discussion of the color factions and their activities at Rome; on theater claques, see 235–49. He also notes a novel by J. Wechsberg, *Looking for a Bluebird* (1948), which for several chapters tells the story of a member of the Vienna Opera claque in the early twentieth century. It is fascinating reading on the role of claque leaders and their followers.

7. On claque leaders, see also Suet. *Tib.* 37.

8. On the activities of Clodius's claque, see, for example, Cic. *Sest.* 118, *Ep. Q. Fr.* 2.3.2; Plut. *Pomp.* 48.

9. *Laudiceni* is evidently a compound of *laudare* and *cena*, and Σοφοκλεῖς of σοφός and καλέω.

10. For the integration of theater claques into imperial ceremony, see A. Cameron 1976, 244–70.

11. *Chron. Pasch.* 712.15, cited in ibid., 257.

12. This tactic occurs also in the *vita* of Tacitus, 5.1–2.

13. On the rhythmic quality of some acclamations, see A. Cameron 1976, 318ff.; Roueché 1984; and Maas 1912, 31–51.

14. Roueché 1984, 189.

15. Other references to rhythmic or songlike acclamations include Tac., *Ann.* 16.4; Phaed. 5.7.27.

16. Roueché 1984, 189–90.

17. So, for example, A. Cameron 1976, 331. It is also popular to compare the riots and demonstrations that sometimes occurred at public entertainments to football "hooliganism." For an anthropological assessment of football crews and violence, see, with further bibliography, Dunning, Murphy, and Williams 1986.

18. Indeed, in his condemnation of the games, the religious component is the first aspect that Tertullian criticizes (*De Spec.* 6–8), and throughout his work it is the pagan religious rituals of the public entertainments that seem to offend him the most.

19. For example, Suetonius described Claudius opening games by offering sacrifices at the Temple of Venus Victrix and the shrines of Honor, Virtus, and Felicitas, which were located at the top of Pompey's Theater, and then walking down through the audience to his seat (Suet. *Claud.* 31).

20. A few examples of ἰώ in various plays include Soph. *O.C.* 199, 224, *Ph.* 736, *Tr.* 222, *Ant.* 850, *El.* 840; Aesc. *Ag.* 1305, *Sup.* 125; Eurip. *Ph.* 1290, *Ba.* 578.

21. For example, in Catullus (61.116–18, "Ite concinite in medum / "io Hymen Hymenaee io, / io Hymen Hymenaee" (Go on, sing in measure, io Hymen Hymenaeus, io, io Hymen Hymenaeus); or Tibullus (2.5.118) ". . . miles 'io' magna voce 'triumphe' canet" (. . . the soldiers loudly sang, "Io triumphe").

22. On the use of rhymes in churches, see Smitherman 1977, 145–47.

23. Further examples of witticisms, including lines in performances being applied to the emperor: Suet. *Aug.* 53, 68, *Nero* 39; Sen. *De Ira* 2.11.3; Dio 60.29.3; SHA *Com.* 3.4, *Maxim.* 9.3. On the intent of the actors reciting the lines, see Reynolds 1943.

24. Despite Quintilian's condemnation of overtly rhyming or rhythmic orations, he devotes considerable space (the majority of *Inst.* 9.3) to cataloging the different ways in which orators can insert a rhythmic structure into their prose.

25. See, for example, Cic. *De Orat.* 3.25.100; Mart. 3.46, 6.38.

26. On the emperor's position not being definable in constitutional terms, see Millar 1977, 616–20.

27. On the formal legal process of creating a new emperor and bestowing the appropriate powers upon him, see Brunt 1977 and Hammond 1956, 1968. The conferral of formal powers legalized and made an emperor "official," but the crucial moment of identifying the next emperor was probably accomplished through acclamations.

28. Elections under Augustus, Dio 53.21.6–7; Tiberius's action, Tac. *Ann.* 1.15. On these issues, see Yavetz 1988, 4, 103–13; A. H. M. Jones 1955; Newbold 1974; and Levick 1967. On the political role of the plebs, see also Hahn 1968, 1969; Deininger 1979; and Tengström 1977.

29. On this theory, see Laurence 1994, chap. 8. For an interesting comparative study of "parades and power" in nineteenth-century America, see S. Davis 1988.

30. These are at Antioch, Milan, Thessalonica, Trier, Constantinople, and Sirmium. See Frazer 1966, Humphrey 1986, and A. Cameron 1976, 181.

31. See Van Dam 1985, 149 and n. 34.

32. On the *salutatio*, see Saller 1982; Mohler 1931.

33. Restored and translated by Musurillo 1954.

34. See the discussion of this vulnerability by A. Cameron 1976, 8.

35. Frank 1959, 5.

36. For details regarding these and other cash distributions by the emperors, see Van Berchem 1939, and Millar 1991.

    For comparison, the annual pay of a legionary under Augustus was 900 HS, the minimum requirement for senatorial rank was only 1 million HS, and modern estimates of the annual cost of the entire

military, including legionaries, auxiliaries, retirement bounties, praetorians, urban cohorts, transport, and the navy, range from 240 to 450
million HS; see Frank 1959, 5, and Hopkins 1980, 125.

37. Geertz 1980.

38. Ibid., 120. For a recent assessment of the role of ritual in colonial and
contemporary Java, see Pemberton 1994.

39. Basic studies of violence in Roman politics and demonstrations by the
urban plebs are Africa 1971, on urban disorder during the empire, and
Heaton 1939 and Lintott 1968, on mob violence in the republic.

   Interesting comparative, anthropological, and sociological works
on mob violence and protest include Canetti 1962, N. Davis 1973,
Hobsbawm 1973, Le Bon 1896, McClelland 1989, Riches 1986, Rose
1982, Rudé 1964, Ruggiero 1980, R. Turner and Killian 1987, Waddington, Jones, and Critcher 1989, and S. Wright 1978.

40. Several other examples of Gaius tormenting spectators are related by
Suetonius; see *Gaius* 26. On such incidents, see the comments of
Scobie 1988.

41. Other examples of Domitian's abuse of spectators include Dio 68.8.2.
See also Herodian 4.6.4–5; Dio 78.1.2.

42. This description obviously reflects A. Van Gennep's (1960) definition
of "rites of passage" with their three phases of separation, transition,
and incorporation. On liminality and associated rituals, see V. Turner
1968, 1969, 1974, 1982, 1986; V. Turner and Bruner 1986. For a
recent assessment of Turner's work, see Ashley 1990.

Conclusion

1. On this debate generally, see Ruiz 1982; Millar 1964, 102–17; Hammond 1932; and P. Meyer (1891).

2. Recent examples include Bartsch 1994, and Woodman 1993, which
both concentrate on Nero, and the descriptively entitled book by Dupont 1985, *L'Acteur-Roi*. On Augustus, Nero, and the role of emperor,
see also Picard 1966.

   On theatricality and the relationship between theater and reality as
theoretical issues, see Barish 1981, Brisset and Edgley 1990, Burns
1972, Schechner and Appel 1990, and Wilshire 1982.

3. Coleman 1990.

Bibliography

Abbott, F. F. 1907. "The Theatre as a Factor in Roman Politics under the Republic." *TAPA* 38: 49–56.

Achard, Guy. 1991. *La Communication à Rome*. Paris: Les Belles Lettres.

Adams, J. N. 1982. *The Latin Sexual Vocabulary*. Baltimore: Johns Hopkins University Press.

Adler, Peter. 1981. *Momentum: A Theory of Social Action*. Beverly Hills, Calif.: Sage Publications.

Africa, T. 1971. "Urban Violence in Imperial Rome." *Journal of Interdisciplinary History* 2: 4–21.

Akveld, Willem F. 1961. *Germanicus*. Groningen: J. B. Wolters.

Alberte, Antonio. 1992. *Historia de la retorica latina: Evolucion de los criterios estetico-literarios desde Ciceron hasta Agustin*. Amsterdam: Adolf M. Hakkert.

Alföldi, Andreas. 1934. "Die Ausgestaltung des monarchischen Zeremoniells am römischen Kaiserhofe." *Röm. Mitt.* 49: 1–118.

———. 1970. *Die monarchische Repräsentation im römischen Kaiserreiche*. Darmstadt: Wissenschaftliche Buchgesellschaft.

Amulree, Lord. 1973. "Hygienic Conditions in Ancient Rome and Modern London." *Medic. History* 17: 244–55.

Anglo, Sydney. 1966. *Spectacle, Pageantry and Early Tudor Policy*. Oxford: Clarendon Press.

Argyle, Michael. 1975. *Bodily Communication*. New York: International Universities Press.

Arnott, Peter. 1971. *The Ancient Greek and Roman Theatre*. New York: Random House.

———. 1989. *Public and Performance in the Greek Theatre*. New York: Routledge.

Ashley, Kathleen, ed. 1990. *Victor Turner and the Construction of Cultural Criticism*. Bloomington: Indiana University Press.

Atkinson, Max. 1984. *Our Masters' Voices: The Language and Body Language of Politics*. New York: Methuen.

Auguet, Roland. 1994. *Cruelty and Civilization: The Roman Games*. London: Routledge.

Austin, Gilbert. [1806] 1966. *Chironomia, or a Treatise on Rhetorical Delivery*. Ed. Mary M. Robb and Lester Thonssen. Carbondale: Southern Illinois University Press.

Awkward, Michael. 1989. *Inspiriting Influences: Tradition, Revision, and Afro-American Women's Novels*. New York: Columbia University Press.

Bairoch, Paul. 1988. *Cities and Economic Development: From the Dawn of History to the Present*. Trans. Christopher Braider. Chicago: University of Chicago Press.

Baldwin, Barry. 1981. "Acclamations in the Historia Augusta." *Athenaeum*, n.s., 69: 138–49.

Baldwin, Robert. 1972. "Ruler and Ruled at Rome: A.D. 14–192." *Ancient Society*, no. 3: 149–63.

———. 1990. "Triumph and the Rhetoric of Power in Italian Renaissance Art." *Source* 9.2: 7–13.

Balsdon, J. P. V. D. 1969a. *Life and Leisure in Ancient Rome*. New York: McGraw-Hill.

———. 1969b. "Panem et Circenses." In *Hommages à Marcel Renard II*, ed. J. Bibauw, 57–60. Collection Latomus 102. Brussels.

Barish, Jonas A. 1981. *The Antitheatrical Prejudice*. Berkeley: University of California Press.

Barry, William. 1988. "Faces of the Crowd: Popular Society and Politics of Roman Alexandria, 30 B.C.–A.D. 215." Ph.D. diss., University of Michigan.

Bartsch, Shadi. 1994. *Actors in the Audience: Theatricality and Doublespeak from Nero to Trajan*. Cambridge, Mass.: Harvard University Press.

Bäuml, B. J., and N. F. H. Bäuml. 1975. *A Dictionary of Gestures*. Metuchen, N.J.: Scarecrow Press.

Beacham, Richard. 1992. *The Roman Theatre and Its Audience*. Cambridge, Mass.: Harvard University Press.

Beard, Mary. 1987. "A Complex of Times: No More Sheep on Romulus' Birthday." *Proceedings of the Cambridge Philological Society* 213: 1–15.

Beard, Mary, and John North, eds. 1990. *Pagan Priests: Religion and Power in the Ancient World*. Ithaca, N.Y.: Cornell University Press.

Beare, William. 1964. *The Roman Stage: A Short History of Latin Drama in the Time of the Republic.* 3rd ed. London: Methuen.

Bell, Andrew. 1997. "Cicero and the Spectacle of Power." *JRS* 87: 1–22.

Bell, Catherine. 1992. *Ritual Theory, Ritual Practice.* New York: Oxford University Press.

Bennet, W. L. 1980. "Myth, Ritual and Political Control." *Journal of Communication* 30: 166–79.

Beschaouch, M. Azedine. 1966. "La mosaïque de chasse à l'amphithéatre découverte à Smirat en Tunisie." *CRAI* (March): 134–57.

Bieber, Margarete. 1959. "Roman Men in Greek Himation (Roman Palliati). A Contribution to the History of Copying." *Proceedings of the American Philosophical Society* 103, no. 3: 374–417.

Billerbeck, Margarethe. 1990. "Philology at the Imperial Court." *Greece & Rome* 37, no. 2: 191–203.

Birdwhistell, Ray. 1952. *Introduction to Kinesics: An Annotation System for Analysis of Body Motion and Gesture.* Louisville: University of Louisville.

Bloch, Maurice, ed. 1975. *Political Language and Oratory in Traditional Society.* London: Academic Press.

———. 1986. *From Blessing to Violence.* Cambridge: Cambridge University Press.

Boatwright, M. T. 1987. *Hadrian and the City of Rome.* Princeton: Princeton University Press.

Bollinger, Traugott. 1969. *Theatralis Licentia: Die Publikumsdemonstrationen an den öffentlichen Spielen im Rom der früheren Kaiserzeit und ihre Bedeutung im politischen Leben.* Winterthur: Verlag Hans Schellenberg.

Bonaria, M. 1965. *Romani Mimi.* Rome.

Bonner, S. F. [1949] 1969. *Roman Declamation in the Late Republic and Early Empire.* Liverpool: Liverpool University Press.

———. 1977. *Education in Ancient Rome.* Berkeley: University of California Press.

Bradley, K. R. 1981. "The Significance of the *Spectacula* in Suetonius' *Caesares.*" *Rivista Storica dell' Antichita* 11: 129–37.

Bremmer, Jan, and Herman Roodenburg, eds. 1991. *A Cultural History of Gesture.* Ithaca, N.Y.: Cornell University Press.

Brewster, E. H. [1917] 1972. *Roman Craftsmen and Tradesmen of the Early Empire.* New York: Burt Franklin Reprints.

Brilliant, Richard. 1963. *Gesture and Rank in Roman Art.* Memoirs of the Connecticut Academy of Arts and Sciences, vol. 14. Copenhagen: Bianco Luno's Printing.

Brisset, Dennis, and Charles Edgley, eds. 1990. *Life as Theater: A Dramaturgical Sourcebook.* 2nd ed. New York: Aldine de Gruyter.

Brown, Patricia. 1990. "Measured Friendship, Calculated Pomp: The Ceremonial Welcomes of the Venetian Republic." In *All the World's a Stage:*

Art and Pageantry in the Renaissance and Early Baroque, ed. Barbara Wisch and Susan S. Munshower, 400–452. Papers in Art History from the Pennsylvania State University, vol. 6. University Park, Pa.

———. 1991. "The Self-Definition of the Venetian Republic." In *City-States in Classical Antiquity and Medieval Italy*, ed. A. Molho, K. Raaflaub, and J. Emlen, 511–48. Ann Arbor: University of Michigan Press.

Brunt, P. A. 1966. "The Roman Mob." *Past and Present*, no. 35: 3–27. Revised edition in *Studies in Ancient Societies*, ed. M. I. Finley, 74–101. London: Routledge and Kegan Paul, 1974.

———. 1971a. *Italian Manpower*. Oxford: Oxford University Press.

———. 1971b. *Social Conflicts in the Roman Republic*. New York: W. W. Norton.

———. 1977. "Lex de Imperio Vespasiani." *JRS* 67: 95–116.

———. 1980. "Free Labor and Public Works at Rome." *JRS* 70: 81–100.

Bryant, Donald C. 1950. "Aspects of the Rhetorical Tradition–II: Emotion, Style, and Literary Association." *Quarterly Journal of Speech* 36, no. 3: 326–32.

Bull, Peter. 1983. *Body Movement and Interpersonal Communication*. London: John Wiley and Sons.

Bulwer, John. 1644. *Chirologia: Or the Naturall Language of the Hand . . . Whereunto is added Chironomia: or the Art of Manuall Rhetoricke*. London. Reprint, ed. James Cleary. Carbondale: Southern Illinois University Press, 1974.

Burns, Elizabeth. 1972. *Theatricality: A Study of Convention in the Theater and in Social Life*. New York: Longman.

Cameron, Alan. 1973a. *Porphyrius the Charioteer*. Oxford: Clarendon Press.

———. 1973b. "Bread and Circuses: The Roman Emperor and His People." Inaugural Lecture in Latin Language and Literature at King's College. London: Bowman Press.

———. 1976. *Circus Factions: Blues and Greens at Rome and Byzantium*. Oxford: Clarendon Press.

Cameron, Averil. 1987. "The Construction of Court Ritual: The Byzantine *Book of Ceremonies*." In *Rituals of Royalty: Power and Ceremonies in Traditional Societies*, ed. D. Cannadine and S. Price, 106–37. Cambridge: Cambridge University Press.

Canetti, Elias. 1962. *Crowds and Power*. London: Victor Gollancz.

Cannadine, David. 1983. "The Context, Performance and Meaning of Ritual: The British Monarchy and the 'Invention of Tradition,' c. 1820–1977." In *The Invention of Tradition*, ed. Eric Hobsbawm and Terence Ranger, 101–65. Cambridge: Cambridge University Press.

Cannadine, David, and Simon Price, eds. 1987. *Rituals of Royalty: Power and Ceremonies in Traditional Societies*. Cambridge: Cambridge University Press.

Caplan, H. 1944. "The Decay of Eloquence at Rome in the First Century." In *Studies in Speech and Drama in Honor of Alexander M. Drummond*, 295–325. Ithaca, N.Y.: Cornell University Press.

Carcopino, Jérome. 1968. *Daily Life in Ancient Rome*. Ed. Henry T. Rowell, trans. E. O. Lorimer. New Haven: Yale University Press.

Cardini, Franco. 1991. "Symbols and Rituals in Florence." In *City-States in Classical Antiquity and Medieval Italy*, ed. A. Molho, K. Raaflaub, and J. Emlen, 499–510. Ann Arbor: University of Michigan.

Casson, Lionel. 1978. "Unemployment, the Building Trade, and Suetonius, Vesp. 18." *Bulletin of the American Society of Papyrologists* 15: 43–51.

Champlin, Edward J. 1980. *Fronto and Antonine Rome*. Cambridge, Mass.: Harvard University Press.

Charlesworth, M. P. 1935. "Some Observations on Ruler Cult, Especially in Rome." *Harvard Theological Review* 28: 5–44.

———. 1937. "The Virtues of a Roman Emperor: Propaganda and the Creation of Belief." *Proceedings of the British Academy* 23: 105–33.

———. 1943. "*Pietas* and *Victoria*: The Emperor and the Citizen." *JRS* 33: 1–10.

Chilver, G. 1949. "Princeps and Frumentationes." *American Journal of Philology* 70: 7–21.

Clark, Gregory, and S. Michael Halloran, eds. 1993. *Oratorical Culture in Nineteenth Century America: Transformations in the Theory and Practice of Rhetoric*. Carbondale: Southern Illinois University Press.

Clarke, M. L. 1963. *Rhetoric at Rome: A Historical Survey*. New York: Barnes and Noble.

Coarelli, Filippo. 1992. *Il Foro Romano*. 3rd ed. 2 vols. Rome: Quasar.

Cohen, A. 1974. *Two-Dimensional Man: An Essay on the Anthropology of Power and Symbolism in Complex Society*. London: Routledge and Kegan Paul.

Coleman, K. M. 1990. "Fatal Charades: Roman Executions Staged as Mythical Enactments." *JRS* 80: 44–73.

Colin, J. 1965. *Les Villes libres de l'Orient gréco-romain et l'envoi au supplice par acclamations populaires*. Collection Latomus 82. Brussels.

Connor, W. R. 1987. "Tribes, Festivals, and Processions: Civic Ceremonial and Political Manipulation in Archaic Greece." *Journal of Hellenic Studies* 107: 40–50.

Corbeill, Anthony. 1996. *Controlling Laughter: Political Humor in the Late Roman Republic*. Princeton: Princeton University Press.

Cousin, Jean. 1967. *Études sur Quintilien*. 2 vols. Amsterdam: Schippers N.V.

Csapo, E., and W. Slater. 1995. *The Context of Ancient Drama*. Ann Arbor: Univerisity of Michigan Press.

Davies, M., and J. Skupien, eds. 1982. *Body Movement and Non-Verbal Communication: An Annotated Bibliography, 1971–1981*. Bloomington: Indiana University Press.

Davis, Natalie Zemon. 1973. "The Rites of Violence: Religious Riot in Sixteenth Century France." *Past and Present* 59: 51–91.

Davis, Susan. 1988. *Parades and Power*. Berkeley: University of California Press.

Deininger, Jürgen. 1979. "Brot und Spiele: Tacitus und die Entpolitisierung der *plebs urbana*." *Gymnasium* 86, nos. 3–4: 278–303.

Dominik, William, ed. 1997. *Roman Eloquence: Rhetoric in Society and Literature*. Routledge: New York.

Doob, Leonard. 1961. *Communication in Africa: A Search for Boundaries*. New Haven: Yale University Press.

Dunbabin, Katherine M. D. 1978. *The Mosaics of Roman North Africa*. Oxford: Clarendon.

Duncan-Jones, Richard. 1982. *The Economy of the Roman Empire: Quantitative Studies*. 2nd ed. Cambridge: Cambridge University Press.

Dunning, Eric, Patrick Murphy, and John Williams. 1986. "'Casuals,' 'Terrace Crews,' and 'Fighting Firms': Towards a Sociological Explanation of Football Hooligan Behavior." In *The Anthropology of Violence*, ed. David Riches, 164–83. Oxford: Blackwell.

Dupont, Florence. 1985. *L'acteur-roi ou le théâtre dans la Rome antique*. Paris: Société d'Édition les Belles Lettres.

Eder, Walter. 1991. "Who Rules? Power and Participation in Athens and Rome." In *City States in Classical Antiquity and Medieval Italy*, ed. A. Molho, K. Raaflaub, and J. Emlen, 169–97. Ann Arbor: University of Michigan Press.

Eisenstadt, S. N., and L. Roniger. 1984. *Patrons, Clients and Friends: Interpersonal Relations and the Structure of Trust in Society*. Cambridge: Cambridge University Press.

Ekman, Paul, and Wallace Friesen. 1972. "Hand Movements." *Journal of Communication* 22: 353–74.

———. 1981. "The Repertoire of Nonverbal Behavior: Categories, Origins, Usage, and Coding." In *Non-Verbal Communication, Interaction, and Gesture: Selections from Semiotica*, ed. Adam Kendon, 57–105. New York: Mouton.

Evans, Harry B. 1982. "Agrippa's Water Plan." *AJA* 86, no. 3: 401–411.

Fantham, Elaine. 1982. "Quintilian on Performance: Traditional and Personal Elements in *Institutio* 11.3." *Phoenix* 36, no. 3: 243–63.

Firth, Raymond. 1973. *Symbols Public and Private*. Ithaca, N.Y.: Cornell University Press.

Fortenbaugh, William. 1985. "Theophrastus on Delivery." In *Theophrastus of Eresus: On His Life and Work*, ed. W. Fortenbaugh, P. Huby, and A. Long, 269–88. Rutgers University Studies in Classical Humanities 2. New Brunswick, N.J.: Transaction Books.

Frank, Tenney. 1959. *An Economic Survey of Ancient Rome*. Vol. 5. Paterson, N.J.: Pageant Books.

Frassinetti, P. 1953. *Fabula Atellana: Saggio sul Theatro Populare Latino*. Genoa: Instituto di filologia classica.

Frazer, A. 1966. "The Iconography of the Emperor Maxentius' Buildings in Via Appia." *Art Bulletin* 48, nos. 3–4: 385–92.

Freedmann, Barbara. 1991. *Staging the Gaze*. Ithaca, N.Y.: Cornell University Press.

Friedländer, L. 1979. *Roman Life and Manners under the Early Empire*. Trans. J. H. Freese and L. A. Magnus. 4 Vols. New York: Arno Press.

Frier, Bruce. 1977. "The Rental Market in Early Imperial Rome." *JRS* 67: 27–37.

————. 1980. *Landlords and Tenants in Imperial Rome*. Princeton: Princeton University Press.

Fustel de Coulanges, Numa Denis. 1980. *The Ancient City: A Study on the Religion, Laws, and Institutions of Greece and Rome*. Foreword by S. C. Humphreys and A. Momigliano. Baltimore: Johns Hopkins University Press.

Garnsey, Peter, ed. 1980. *Non-Slave Labour in the Graeco-Roman World*. Cambridge: Cambridge Philological Society.

————. 1988. *Famine and Food Supply in the Graeco-Roman World: Responses to Risk and Crisis*. Cambridge: Cambridge University Press.

————. 1991. "Mass Diet and Nutrition in the City of Rome." In *Nourrir la plèbe: Actes du colloque tenu à Genève les 28 et 29.IX.1989 en hommage à Denis Van Berchem*, ed. Adalberto Giovannini, 67–100. Basel: F. Reinhardt.

Garton, Charles. 1972. *Personal Aspects of the Roman Theatre*. Toronto: Hakkert.

Gaskell, George, and Robert Benewick, eds. 1987. *The Crowd in Contemporary Britain*. London: Sage Publications.

Geertz, Clifford. 1973. *The Interpretation of Cultures*. New York: Basic Books.

————. 1980. *Negara: The Theater State in Nineteenth-Century Bali*. Princeton: Princeton University Press.

————. 1983. *Local Knowledge: Further Essays in Interpretive Anthropology*. New York: Basic Books.

Geiger, Theodor. 1926. *Die Masse und ihre Aktion*. Stuttgart: Enke.

Ghosh, Manomohan, ed. 1957. *Nandikesvara's Abhinayadarpanam: A Manual of Gesture and Posture used in Hindu Dance and Drama*. 2nd ed. Calcutta: Firma K. L. Mukhopadhyay.

Giglioni, G. B. 1973. *Lavori Pubblici e Occupazione nell'Antichita Classica*. Bologna: Casa Editrice Patron.

Gilbert, Rolf. 1976. *Die Beziehungen zwischen Princeps und stadtrömischer Plebs im frühen Principät*. Bochum: Studienverlag Dr. N. Brockmeyer.

Giovannini, Adalberto, ed. 1991. *Nourrir la plèbe: Actes du colloque tenu à*

Genève les 28 et 29.IX.1989 en hommage à Denis Van Berchem. Basel: F. Reinhardt.

Gleason, Maud. 1995. *Making Men: Sophists and Self-Presentation in Ancient Rome.* Princeton: Princeton University Press.

Goffman, E. 1961a. *Interaction Ritual: Essays on Face-to-Face Behavior.* Chicago: Aldine Publishing Company.

———. 1961b. *Encounters: Two Studies in the Sociology of Interaction.* Indianapolis: Bobbs Merrill.

Gomme, A. W. 1933. *The Population of Athens in the Fifth and Fourth Centuries.* Oxford: Oxford University Press.

Goodwin, Charles. 1981. *Conversational Organization: Interaction between Speakers and Hearers.* New York: Academic Press.

Goody, Jack. 1977. "Against Ritual." In *Secular Ritual,* ed. S. Moore and B. Myerhoff, 25–35. Amsterdam: Van Gorcum.

Goossens, R. 1939. "Notes sur les factions du cirque à Rome." *Byzantion* 14: 205–9.

Graf, Fritz. 1991. "Gestures and Conventions: The Gestures of Roman Actors and Orators." In *A Cultural History of Gesture,* ed. Jan Bremmer and Herman Roodenburg, 36–58. Ithaca, N.Y.: Cornell University Press.

Graham, Victor. 1986. "The Triumphal Entry in Sixteenth-Century France." *Renaissance and Reformation* 22: 237–56.

Grant, John H. 1973. "G and the Miniatures of Terence." *Classical Quarterly,* n.s., 23, no. 1: 88–103.

———. 1986. *Studies in the Textual Tradition of Terence.* Toronto: University of Toronto Press.

Greenblatt, Stephen. 1988. *Shakespearean Negotiations: The Circulation of Social Energy in Renaissance England.* Berkeley: University of California Press.

Griffin, M. 1982. "The Lyons Tablet and Tacitean Hindsight." *CQ* 32: 404–18.

Gross, W. H. 1959. "Zur Augustusstatue von Prima Porta." *GöttNachr.,* no. 8: 143–68.

Gruen, Erich. 1968. *Roman Politics and the Criminal Courts, 149–78 B.C.* Cambridge, Mass.: Harvard University Press.

———. 1974. *The Last Generation of the Roman Republic.* Berkeley: University of California Press.

———. 1992. *Culture and National Identity in Republican Rome.* Ithaca, N.Y.: Cornell University Press.

Guggenheimer, Eva. 1972. *Rhyme Effects and Rhyming Figures: A Comprehensive Study of Sound Repetitions in the Classics with Emphasis on Latin Poetry.* The Hague: Mouton.

Hahn, I. 1968. "Zum Begriff der Demokratie in der politischen Theorie des Prinzipats." In *Antiquitas Graeco Romana ac Tempora Nostra*, ed. J. Burian and L. Vidman, 115–24. Prague: Academia.

———. 1969. "Zur politischen Rolle der stadtrömischen Plebs unter dem Prinzipat." In *Die Rolle der Plebs im spätrömischen Reich*, ed. V. Besevliev and W. Seyfarth, 2:39–54. Deutsche Akademie der Wissenschaften zu Berlin Schriften der Sektion für Altertumswissenschaft, no. 55. Berlin.

Halporn, James, Martin Ostwald, and Thomas Rosenmeyer. 1994. *The Meters of Greek and Latin Poetry*. Rev. ed. Indianapolis: Hackett.

Hammond, Mason. 1932. "The Significance of the Speech of Maecenas in Dio Cassius, Book LII," *TAPA* 63: 88–102.

———. [1933] 1968. *The Augustan Principate in Theory and Practice during the Julio-Claudian Period*. Enl. ed. Cambridge, Mass.: Harvard University Press.

———. 1953. "A Statue of Trajan Represented on the 'Anaglypha Traiani,'" *MAAR* 21: 127–83.

———. 1956. "Transmission of the Powers of the Roman Emperor from the Death of Nero in A.D. 68 to that of Alexander Severus in A.D. 235." *MAAR* 24: 63–133.

Handelman, Don. 1990. *Models and Mirrors: Towards an Anthropology of Public Events*. Cambridge: Cambridge University Press.

Harper, R., A. Wiens, and J. Matarazzo. 1978. *Nonverbal Communication: The State of the Art*. New York: John Wiley and Sons.

Harris, William V. 1989. *Ancient Literacy*. Cambridge, Mass.: Harvard University Press.

Heaton, John W. 1939. *Mob Violence in the Late Roman Republic,* Urbana: University of Illinois Press.

Henzen, G. 1874. *Acta Fratrum Arvalium*. Berlin: G. Reineri.

Hermansen, Gustav. 1970. "The *Medianum* and the Roman Apartment." *Phoenix* 24: 342–47.

———. 1978a. "The Bread Line through Ostia to Rome." *PACA* 14: 21–26.

———. 1978b. "The Population of Imperial Rome: The Regionaries." *Historia* 27: 129–68.

Hill, P. V. 1978. "The Temple of Concordia on Sestercii of Tiberius." *Numismatic Circular* 86, no. 2: 66.

———. 1989. *The Monuments of Ancient Rome as Coin Types*. London: Seaby.

Hinde, Robert, ed. 1972. *Non-Verbal Communication*. Cambridge: Cambridge University Press.

Hirschfeld, O. 1913. "Die römische Staatszeitung und die Akklamationen im Senat." In *Kleine Schriften*, 682–702. Berlin: Weidmannsche Buchhandlung.

Hobsbawm, Eric. 1973. *Primitive Rebels: Studies in Archaic Forms of Social Movement*. New York: Frederick A. Praeger.

————, ed. 1983. *The Invention of Tradition*. Cambridge: Cambridge University Press.

Hodge, A. Trevor. 1989. "A Plain Man's Guide to Roman Plumbing." *Échos du Monde Classique* 27, n.s. 2, no. 3: 311–28.

Holmes, T. Rice. 1931. *The Architect of the Roman Empire*. 2 vols. Oxford: Clarendon Press.

Homo, Léon. 1971. *Rome impériale et l'urbanisme dans l'antiquité*. 2nd ed. Paris: Éditions Albin Michel.

Hopkins, Keith. 1978. *Conquerors and Slaves*. Sociological Studies in Roman History, vol. 1. Cambridge: Cambridge University Press.

————. 1980. "Taxes and Trade in the Roman Empire." *JRS* 70: 101–25.

————. 1983. *Death and Renewal*. Sociological Studies in Roman History, vol. 2. Cambridge: Cambridge University Press.

————. 1991. "From Violence to Blessing: Symbols and Rituals in Ancient Rome." In *City-States in Classical Antiquity and Medieval Italy*, ed. A. Molho, K. Raaflaub, and J. Emlen, 479–98. Ann Arbor: University of Michigan Press.

Horner, Winifred Bryan, ed. 1990. *The Present State of Scholarship in Historical and Contemporary Rhetoric*. Rev. ed. Columbia: University of Missouri Press.

Hosek, Radislav. 1969. "Zur Frage der spätrömischen Plebs." In *Die Rolle der Plebs im spätrömischen Reich*, 2:19–22. Deutsche Akademie der Wissenschaften zu Berlin Schriften der Sektion für Altertumswissenschaft, no. 55. Berlin.

Hubbel, Harry M. 1966. "Cicero on Styles of Oratory." *Yale Classical Studies* 19: 173–86.

Hughes, Helen MacGill, ed. 1972. *Crowd and Mass Behavior*. Boston: Allyn and Bacon.

Hughes, Russell. 1941. *The Gesture Language of the Hindu Dance*. New York: Columbia University Press.

Huizinga, Johan. 1950. *Homo Ludens: A Study of the Play-Element in Culture*. Boston: Beacon.

Humphrey, John. 1986. *Roman Circuses: Arenas for Chariot Racing*. Berkeley: University of California Press.

Immel, Ray K. 1921. *The Delivery of a Speech: A Manual for Course I in Public Speaking*. Ann Arbor: George Wahr.

Ingersoll, Richard. 1985. "The Ritual Use of Public Space in Renaissance Rome." Ph.D. diss., University of California, Berkeley.

Jamieson, Kathleen. 1988. *Eloquence in an Electronic Age: The Transformation of Political Speechmaking*. New York: Oxford.

Jeffreys, Michael. 1974. "The Nature and Origins of Political Verse." *Dumbarton Oaks Papers*, no. 28: 141–95.

Jones, A. H. M. 1955. "The Elections under Augustus." *JRS* 45: 9–21.

Jones, Leslie W., and C. R. Morey. 1931. *The Miniatures of the Manuscripts of Terence Prior to the Thirteenth Century*. 2 vols. Princeton: Princeton University Press.

Jorio, Andrea de. 1832. *La mimica degli antichi, investigata nel gestire napoletano*. Naples: Dalla stamperia e cartiera del Fibreno.

Jory, E. J. 1970. "Associations of Actors in Rome." *Hermes* 98: 224–53.

———. 1981. "The Literary Evidence for the Beginnings of Imperial Pantomime." *Bulletin of the Institute of Classical Studies of the University of London* 28: 147–61.

———. 1984. "The Early Pantomime Riots." In *Maistor: Classical, Byzantine and Renaissance Studies for Robert Browning*, ed. Ann Moffatt, 57–66. Canberra: Australian Association for Byzantine Studies.

Joshel, S. R. 1992. *Work, Identity, and Legal Status at Rome: A Study of the Occupational Inscriptions*. Norman: University of Oklahoma Press.

Katsouris, Andreas G. 1989. *Rhetorike Hypokrise*. Ioannina: Panepistemio Ianninon.

Kellum, B. A. 1990. "The City Adorned: Programmatic Display at the *Aedes Concordiae Augustae*." In *Between Republic and Empire: Interpretations of Augustus and his Principate*, ed. K. Raaflaub and M. Toher, 276–307. Berkeley: University of California Press.

Kendon, Adam, ed. 1981a. *Non-Verbal Communication, Interaction, and Gesture: Selections from Semiotica*. New York: Mouton.

———. 1981b. "Introduction: Current Issues in the Study of Nonverbal Comunication." In *Non-Verbal Communication, Interaction, and Gesture: Selections from Semiotica*, ed. Adam Kendon, 1–53. New York: Mouton.

———. 1982. "The Study of Gesture: Some Observations on Its History." In *Recherches Semiotiques/Semiotic Inquiry* 2: 45–62.

Kennedy, George. 1968. "Anthony's Speech at Caesar's Funeral." *Quarterly Journal of Speech* 54: 99–106.

———. 1972. *The Art of Rhetoric in the Roman World, 300 B.C.–A.D. 300*. Princeton: Princeton University Press.

———. 1994. *A New History of Classical Rhetoric*. Princeton: Princeton University Press.

Kertzer, David. 1988. *Ritual, Politics and Power*. New Haven: Yale University Press.

Key, M.-R. 1980. *The Relationship of Verbal and Non-Verbal Communication*. The Hague: Mouton.

———. 1977. *Nonverbal Communication: A Research Guide and Bibliography*. Metuchen, N.J.: Scarecrow Press.

———, ed. 1982. *Nonverbal Communication Today: Current Research*. New York: Mouton.

Klauser, T. 1950. "Akklamation." In *Reallexikon für Antike und Christentum* 1:216–33.

Kleiner, Diana. 1977. *Roman Group Portraiture: The Funerary Reliefs of the Late Republic and Early Empire*. New York: Garland.

———. 1992. *Roman Sculpture*. New Haven: Yale University Press.

Kloft, Hans. 1970. *Liberalitas Principis: Herkunft und Bedeutung, Studien zur Prinzipatsideologie*. Köln: Böhlau-Verlag.

———. 1988. "Das Problem der Getreideversorgung in den antiken Städten: Das Beispiel Oxyrhynchos." In *Sozialmassnahmen und Fürsorge: Zur Eigenart antiker Sozialpolitik*, ed. Hans Kloft, 123–54. Grazer Beitrage, Zeitschrift für die Klassische Altertumswissenschaft, suppl. 3. Graz: F. Berger.

Knapp, C. 1925. "The Care of City Streets in Ancient Rome." *CW* 19: 82, 98, 114, 159.

Koeppel, G. 1969. "*Profectio* und *Adventus*." *Bonner Jahrbücher* 169: 130–94.

Koestermann, E. 1958. "Die Mission des Germanicus im Orient." *Historia* 7: 331ff.

Kuper, H. 1972. "The Language of Sites and the Politics of Space." *American Anthropologist* 74: 411–25.

Ladurie, E. Le Roy. 1979. *Carnival in Romans*. Trans. M. Feeney. New York: George Braziller.

Lane, C. 1981. *The Rites of Rulers*. Cambridge: Cambridge University Press.

Lanham, Richard. 1991. *A Handlist of Rhetorical Terms*. 2nd ed. Berkeley: University of California Press.

La Rocca, Eugenio, ed. 1986. *Rilievi storici Capitolini: Il restauro dei pannelli di Adriano e di Marco Aurelio nel Palazzo dei Conservatori*. Rome: De Luca Editore.

Laurence, Ray. 1994. *Roman Pompeii: Space and Society*. London: Routledge.

Law, V. J. 1980. "The "Acta Fratrum Arvalia" as a Source for Roman Imperial History, 23 B.C. to A.D. 243." Ph.D. diss., University of Minnesota.

Le Bon, G. [1896] 1982. *The Crowd: A Study of the Popular Mind*. 2nd ed. Atlanta: Cherokee Publishing Company.

Lenz, O. 1929. "Über das Verhältnis der frühmittelalterlichen zur antiken Terenzillustration." *Repertorium für Kunstwissenschaft* 50: 181–91.

Levick, Barbara. 1967. "Imperial Control of the Elections under the Early Principate." *Historia* 16: 207–30.

Lintott, A. W. 1968. *Violence in Republican Rome*. Oxford: Oxford University Press.

Liversidge, Joan. 1976. *Everyday Life in the Roman Empire*. New York: Putnam.

Loane, H. J. 1938. *Industry and Commerce of the City of Rome*. Baltimore: Johns Hopkins Press.

Luck, G. 1964. "Über Suetons Divus Titus." *Rhein. Mus.* 107: 63–75.

Maas, P. 1912. "Metrische Akklamationen der Byzantiner." *Byzantinische Zeitschrift* 21: 31–51.

MacCormack, Sabine. 1981. *Art and Ceremony in Late Antiquity*. Berkeley: University of California Press.

MacMullen, R. 1962. "The Emperors' Largesses." *Latomus* 21: 159–66.

———. 1967. *Enemies of the Roman Order: Treason, Unrest and Alienation in the Empire*. Cambridge, Mass.: Harvard University Press.

———. 1974. *Roman Social Relations: 50 B.C. to A.D. 284*. New Haven: Yale University Press.

———. 1986. "Personal Power in the Roman Empire." *American Journal of Philology* 107, no. 4: 512–24.

Maguire, H. 1981. *Eloquence and Gestures in Byzantium*. Princeton: Princeton University Press.

Maier-Eichhorn, Ursula. 1989. *Die Gestikulation in Quintilians Rhetorik*. Europäische Hochschulschriften, Klassische Sprachen und Literaturen, ser. 15, vol. 41. Frankfurt am Main: Peter Lang.

Maricq, A. 1950. "Factions du cirque et partis populaires." *Bulletin de L'Académie royale belgique* 26: 396–421.

Martines, Lauro, ed. 1972. *Violence and Civil Disorder in Italian Cities, 1200–1500*. Berkeley: University of California Press.

———. 1988. *Power and Imagination: City States in Renaissance Italy*. Baltimore: Johns Hopkins University Press.

Mauss, Marcel. 1990. *The Gift: The Form and Reason for Exchange in Archaic Societies*. Trans. W. D. Halls. New York: W. W. Norton.

Mazza, M. 1974. "Sul proletariato urbano in epoca imperiale." *Siculorum Gymnasium* 27: 237–78.

McClelland, J. S. 1989. *The Crowd and the Mob from Plato to Canetti*. London: Unwin Hyman.

McCormick, Michael. 1985. "Analyzing Imperial Ceremonies." *Jahrbuch der Österreichischen Byzantinistik* 35: 1–20.

———. 1986. *Eternal Victory: Triumphal Rulership in Late Antiquity, Byzantium and the Early Medieval West*. Cambridge: Cambridge University Press.

Meyer, P. 1891. "De Maecenatis Oratione a Dione Ficta." Dissertation, Berlin.

Meyer, R. 1971. "Usurpation of Status and Status Symbols." *Historia* 20: 275–302.

Millar, Fergus. 1964. *A Study of Cassius Dio*. London: Oxford University Press.

———. 1977. *The Emperor in the Roman World, 31 B.C.–337 A.D.* Ithaca, N.Y.: Cornell University Press.

———. 1983. "Empire and City, Augustus to Julian: Obligations, Excuses and Status." *JRS* 73: 76–96.

———. 1984. "The Political Character of the Classical Roman Republic." *JRS* 74: 1–19.

————. 1986. "Politics, Persuasion, and the People before the Social War." *JRS* 76: 1–11.

————. 1989. "Political Power in Mid-Republican Rome: Curia or Comitia?" *JRS* 79: 138–50.

————. 1991. "Les congiaires à Rome et la monnaie." In *Nourrir la plèbe: Actes du colloque tenu à Genève les 28 et 29.IX.1989 en hommage à Denis Van Berchem*, ed. Adalberto Giovannini, 143–58. Basel: F. Reinhardt.

————. 1998. *The Crowd in Rome in the Late Republic*. Thomas Spencer Jerome Lectures, no. 22. Ann Arbor: University of Michigan Press.

Mohler, S. L. 1931. "The *Cliens* in the Time of Martial." In *Classical Studies in Honor of John C. Rolfe*, ed. G. D. Hadzsits, 239–63. Philadelphia: University of Pennsylvania Press.

Molho, Anthony, Kurt Raaflaub, and Julia Emlen, eds. 1991. *City-States in Classical Antiquity and Medieval Italy*. Ann Arbor: University of Michigan Press.

Momigliano, A. 1934. *Claudius, the Emperor and His Achievement*. Oxford: Clarendon.

Mommsen, T. 1854. "Zur Rede des Kaisers Claudius." *Rhein. Mus.* 9: 443–50.

Morris, Desmond. 1977. *Manwatching*. New York: Harry Abrams.

————. 1994. *Bodytalk: The Meaning of Human Gestures*. New York: Crown.

Morris, Desmond, P. Collett, P. Marsh, and M. O'Shaughnessy. 1979. *Gestures: Their Origins and Distribution*. London: Jonathan Cape.

Mosse, George. L. 1971. "Caesarism, Circuses, and Monuments." *Journal of Contemporary History* 6: 167–82.

Muir, Edward. 1979. "Images of Power: Art and Pageantry in Renaissance Venice." *American Historical Review* 84: 20–21.

————. 1981. *Civic Ritual in Renaissance Venice*. Princeton: Princeton University Press.

Mullaney, Steven. 1988. *The Place of the Stage: License, Play, and Power in Renaissance England*. Chicago: University of Chicago Press.

Musurillo, H. A., ed. 1954. *Acts of the Pagan Martyrs*. Oxford: Clarendon Press.

Nadeau, Ray. 1964. "Delivery in Ancient Times: Homer to Quintilian." *Quarterly Journal of Speech* 50, no. 1: 54–60.

Najemy, John 1991. "The Dialogue of Power in Florentine Politics." In *City-States in Classical Antiquity and Medieval Italy*, ed. A. Molho, K. Raaflaub, and J. Emlen, 269–89. Ann Arbor: University of Michigan Press.

Necaj, F. M. 1969. "Concerning the Role of the Plebs in Economic, Political and Military Life at the Time of the Republic" (in Russian). In *Die Rolle der Plebs im spätrömischen Reich*, ed. V. Besevliev and W. Seyfarth, 2: 23–38. Deutsche Akademie der Wissenschaften zu Berlin Schriften der Sektion für Altertumswissenschaft, no. 55. Berlin.

Neumann, G. 1965. *Gesten und Gebärden in der griechischen Kunst.* Berlin: De Gruyter.

Newbold, R. F. 1974. "Social Tension at Rome in the Early Years of Tiberius' Reign." *Athenaeum* 52: 110–43.

―――. 1975. "The Spectacles as an Issue between Gaius and the Senate." *Proceedings of the African Classical Association* 13: 30–35.

Nicolet, Claude. 1980. *The World of the Citizen in Republican Rome.* Trans. P. S. Falla. Berkeley: University of California Press.

Nippel, W. 1984. "Policing Rome." *JRS* 74: 20–29.

North, J. A. 1990. "Democratic Politics in Republican Rome." *Past and Present*, no. 126: 3–21.

Ober, Josiah. 1989. *Mass and Elite in Democratic Athens: Rhetoric, Ideology, and the Power of the People.* Princeton: Princeton University Press.

Orentzel, Anne. 1981. "Orator Emperors in the Age of Pliny." *Classical Bulletin* 57 (Jan.): 43–48.

Orgel, Stephen. 1975. *The Illusion of Power: Political Theater in the English Renaissance.* Berkeley: University of California Press.

Packer, J. E. 1967. "Housing and Population in Imperial Ostia and Rome." *JRS* 57: 80–95.

Parkin, Tim. 1992. *Demography and Roman Society.* Baltimore: Johns Hopkins University Press.

Pasquinucci, M. Montagna. 1973. *La decorazione archittectonica del tempio del Divo Giulio nel Foro Romano.* Accademia Nazionale dei Lincei, Monumenti Antichi, Serie Miscellanea 48. Rome.

Patterson, John. 1992. "The City of Rome: From Republic to Empire." *JRS* 82: 186–215.

Payne, Robert. 1962. *The Roman Triumph.* London: R. Hale.

Pemberton, John. 1994. *On the Subject of "Java."* Ithaca, N.Y.: Cornell University Press.

Peterson, E. 1926. Εἷς Θεὸς: *Epigraphische, formgeschichtliche und religiongeschichtliche Untersuchungen.* Göttingen: Vandenhoeck und Ruprecht.

Phythian-Adams, Charles. 1976. "Ceremony and Citizen: The Communal Year at Coventry, 1450–1550." In *The Early Modern Town*, ed. Peter Clark, 106–28. New York: Longman.

Picard, Gilbert Charles. 1966. *Augustus and Nero.* Trans. Len Ortzen. London: Phoenix.

Platner, S. B., and T. Ashby. 1929. *A Topographical Dictionary of Ancient Rome.* London: Oxford University Press.

Pohlsander, H. A. 1969. "Victory: The Story of a Statue." *Historia* 18: 588–97.

Poyatos, F., 1976. *Man beyond Words: Theory and Methodology of Non-Verbal Communication.* Oswego: New York State English Council.

————. 1981. "Gesture Inventories: Fieldwork Methodology and Problems." In *Non-Verbal Communication, Interaction, and Gesture: Selections from Semiotica,* ed. Adam Kendon, 371–99. New York: Mouton.

————. 1983. *New Perspectives in Nonverbal Communication: Studies in Cultural Anthropology, Social Psychology, Linguistics, Literature and Semiotics.* New York: Pergamon.

————. ed. 1988. *Cross-Cultural Perspectives in Nonverbal Communication.* Toronto: C. J. Hogrefe.

Price, Simon. 1984. *Rituals and Power: The Roman Imperial Cult in Asia Minor.* Cambridge: Cambridge University Press.

————. 1987. "From Noble Funerals to Divine Cult: The Consecration of Roman Emperors." In *Rituals of Royalty: Power and Ceremonies in Traditional Societies,* ed. D. Cannadine and S. Price, 56–105. Cambridge: Cambridge University Press.

Raaflaub, K., and M. Toher, eds. 1990. *Between Republic and Empire: Interpretations of Augustus and His Principate.* Berkeley: University of California Press.

Rabelais, François. 1955. *Gargantua and Pantagruel.* Trans. by J. M. Cohen. New York: Penguin.

Rainbird, J. S. 1986. "The Fire Stations of Imperial Rome." *PBSR* 54: 147–69.

Reich, H. 1903. *Der Mimus.* Berlin: Weidmann.

Reynolds, R. W. 1943. "Criticism of Individuals in Roman Popular Comedy." *Classical Quarterly* 37, nos. 1–2: 37–45.

Richardson, L., Jr. 1992. *A New Topographical Dictionary of Ancient Rome.* Baltimore: Johns Hopkins University Press.

Riches, David, ed. 1986. *The Anthropology of Violence.* Oxford: Basil Blackwell.

Rickman, G. 1971. *Roman Granaries and Store Buildings.* Cambridge: Cambridge University Press.

————. 1980. *The Corn Supply of Ancient Rome.* Oxford: Clarendon Press.

————. 1991. "Problems of Transport and Development of Ports." In *Nourrir la plèbe: Actes du colloque tenu à Genève les 28 et 29.IX.1989 en hommage à Denis Van Berchem,* ed. Adalberto Giovannini, 103–16. Basel: F. Reinhardt.

Robert, Louis. 1960. "Épitaphes et acclamations byzantines à Corinthe." *Hellenica* 11–12: 21–52.

Rodenburg, Patsy. 1992. *The Right to Speak: Working with the Voice.* London: Methuen.

Romano, Dennis. 1987. *Patricians and Popolari: The Social Foundations of the Venetian Renaissance State.* Baltimore: Johns Hopkins University Press.

Rose, Jerry D. 1982. *Outbreaks: The Sociology of Collective Behavior.* New York: Free Press.

Roueché, Charlotte. 1984. "Acclamations in the Later Roman Empire: New Evidence from Aphrodisias." *JRS* 74: 181–99.

———. 1989. *Aphrodisias in Late Antiquity*. Society for the Promotion of Roman Studies, *Journal of Roman Studies* Monograph, no. 5. London.

Rudé, George. 1964. *The Crowd in History*. New York: Wiley.

Rüdiger, U. 1973. "Die Anaglypha Traiani." *Antike Plastik* 12: 161–74.

Ruggiero, Guido. 1980. *Violence in Early Renaissance Venice*. New Brunswick, N.J.: Rutgers University Press.

Ruiz, Urbano Espinosa. 1982. *Debate Agrippa-Mecenas en Dion Cassio*. Madrid: Univ. Complutense.

Ryberg, Inez. 1955. *Rites of the State Religion in Roman Art*. MAAR 22.

Rykwert, Joseph. 1988. *The Idea of a Town: The Anthropology of Urban Form in Rome, Italy and the Ancient World*. Cambridge, Mass.: MIT Press.

Saller, Richard. 1982. *Personal Patronage under the Early Empire*. Cambridge: Cambridge University Press.

Salmon, P. 1974. *Population et dépopulation dans l'empire romain*. Brussels: Latomus.

Schechner, Richard. 1985. *Between Theater and Anthropology*. Philadelphia: University of Pennsylvania Press.

Schechner, Richard, and W. Appel, eds. 1990. *By Means of Performance: Intercultural Studies of Theatre and Ritual*. Cambridge: Cambridge University Press.

Schmidt, J. [1893] 1958. "Acclamatio." In *Paulys Realencyclopädie der klassischen Altertumswissenschaft*, 1:147–50.

Schmitt, Jean-Claude. 1984. "Introduction and General Bibliography." *History and Anthropology* 1: 1–28.

———. 1990. *La raison des gestes dans l'occident médiéval*. Paris: Gallimard.

———. 1991. "The Rationale of Gestures in the West: Third to Thirteenth Centuries." In *A Cultural History of Gesture*, ed. J. Bremmer and H. Roodenburg, 59–70. Ithaca, N.Y.: Cornell University Press.

Scobie, Alex. 1986. "Slums, Sanitation, and Mortality in the Roman World." *Klio* 68.2: 399–433.

———. 1988. "Spectator Security and Comfort at Gladiatorial Games." *Nikephoros* 1: 191–243.

Scramuzza, Vincent. 1971. *The Emperor Claudius*. Edition Anastatica: Rome.

Scullard, H. H. 1981. *Festivals and Ceremonies of the Roman Republic*. London: Thames and Hudson.

Sear, Frank. 1982. *Roman Architecture*. Ithaca, N.Y.: Cornell University Press.

Seiler, Hans G. 1936. *Die Masse bei Tacitus*. Erlangen: Junge & Sohn, Universitätsbuchdruckerei.

Sherk, Robert, ed. and trans. 1988. *The Roman Empire: Augustus to Hadrian*. Cambridge: Cambridge University Press.

Sherwin-White, A. N. 1973. *The Roman Citizenship*. Oxford: Clarendon Press.

Simon, E. 1957. "Zur Augustusstatue von Prima Porta." *RM* 64: 46–68.

Sippel, Donald. 1987. "Dietary Deficiency among the Lower Classes of Late Republican and Early Imperial Rome." *Ancient World* 16: 47–54.

Sirks, Boudewijn. 1991. *Food for Rome: The Legal Structure of the Transportation and Processing of Supplies for the Imperial Distributions in Rome and Constantinople*. Amsterdam: J. C. Gieben.

Sittl, Karl. 1890. *Die Gebärden der Griechen und Römer*. Leipzig: B. G. Teubner.

Smitherman, Geneva. 1977. *Talkin and Testifyin*. Boston: Houghton Mifflin.

Sonkowsky, Robert P. 1959. "An Aspect of Delivery in Ancient Rhetorical Theory." *TAPA* 90: 256–74.

Staehelin, Felix. 1944. "Felicior Augusto, melior Traiano!" *Museum Helveticum* 1: 179–80.

Strocchia, Sharon T. 1992. *Death and Ritual in Renaissance Florence*. Baltimore: Johns Hopkins University Press.

Strong, Roy. 1973. *Splendor at Court: Renaissance Spectacle and the Theater of Power*. Boston: Houghton Mifflin.

———. 1985. *Art and Power: Renaissance Festivals, 1450–1630*. Berkeley: University of California Press.

Stylow, A. von. 1972. "Libertas und Liberalitas: Untersuchungen zur politischen Propaganda der Römer." Ph.D. diss., Munich.

Swartz, Marc, Victor Turner, and Arthur Tuden, eds. 1966. *Political Anthropology*. Chicago: Aldine Publishing.

Syme, Ronald. 1958. *Tacitus*. 2 vols. London: Oxford University Press.

———. 1971. *Emperors and Biography*. Oxford: Clarendon Press.

Sznura, Franek. 1991. "Civic Urbanism in Medieval Florence." In *City-States in Classical Antiquity and Medieval Italy*, ed. A. Molho, K. Raaflaub, and J. Emlen, 403–19. Ann Arbor: University of Michigan Press.

Taladoire, Barthélemy. 1951. *Commentaires sur la mimique et l'expression corporelle du comédien romain*. Montpellier: Impr. C. Déhan.

Talbert, Richard. 1984. *The Senate of Imperial Rome*. Princeton: Princeton University Press.

Taylor, Lily Ross. 1949. *Party Politics in the Age of Caesar*. Berkeley: University of California Press.

———. 1966. *Roman Voting Assemblies from the Hannibalic War to the Dictatorship of Caesar*. Ann Arbor: University of Michigan Press.

Tengström, E. 1974. *Bread for the People*. Stockholm: Svenska Institutet i Rom.

———. 1977. "Theater und Politik im kaiserlichen Rom." *Eranos* 75: 43–56.

Thornton, M. K., and R. L. Thornton. 1986. "Julio-Claudian Building Programs: Eat, Drink, and Be Merry." *Historia* 35: 28–44.

―――. 1989. *Julio-Claudian Building Programs: A Quantitative Study in Political Management*. Wauconda, Ill.: Bolchazy-Carducci Publishers.

Torelli, Mario. 1982. *Typology and Structure of Roman Historical Reliefs*. Ann Arbor: University of Michigan Press.

Toynbee, J. M. C. 1934. *The Hadrianic School*. London: Cambridge University Press.

Treggiari, S. M. 1969. *Roman Freedmen during the Late Republic*. Oxford: Oxford University Press.

―――. 1980. "Urban Labour in Rome: *Mercennarii* and *Tabernarii*." In *Non-Slave Labour in the Greco-Roman World*, ed. P. Garnsey, 48–64. Cambridge: Cambridge University Press.

Trexler, Richard. 1973. "Ritual Behavior in Renaissance Florence: The Setting." *Medievalia et Humanistica*, n.s., 4: 125–44.

―――. 1980. *Public Life in Renaissance Florence*. Ithaca, N.Y.: Cornell University Press.

―――. 1985. *Persons in Groups: Social Behavior as Identity Formations in Medieval and Renaissance Europe*. Binghamton, N.Y.: Center for Medieval and Renaissance Studies.

―――. 1987. *The Christian at Prayer: An Illustrated Prayer Manual Attributed to Peter the Chanter*. Medieval and Renaissance Texts and Studies, vol. 44. Binghamton, N.Y.

Turner, Ralph, and Lewis Killian. 1987. *Collective Behavior*. 3rd ed. Englewood Cliffs, N.J.: Prentice Hall.

Turner, Victor. 1968. *The Drums of Affliction*. Oxford: Oxford University Press.

―――. 1969. *The Ritual Process: Structure and Anti-Structure*, Ithaca, N.Y.: Cornell University Press.

―――. 1974. *Dramas, Fields, and Metaphors: Symbolic Action in Human Society*. Ithaca, N.Y.: Cornell University Press.

―――. 1982. *From Ritual to Theatre*. New York: PAJ Publications.

―――. 1986. *The Anthropology of Performance*. New York: PAJ Publications.

Turner, Victor, and Edward Bruner, eds. 1986. *The Anthropology of Experience*. Chicago: University of Illinois Press.

Ulrich, Roger B. 1994. *The Roman Orator and the Sacred Stage: The Roman Templum Rostratum*. Collection Latomus 222. Brussels.

Van Berchem, Denis. 1939. *Les distributions de blé et d'argent à la plèbe romaine sous l'empire*. Geneva: Georg Press. Reprint, New York: Arno Press, 1975.

Van Dam, Raymond. 1985. *Leadership and Community in Late Antique Gaul*. Berkeley: University of California Press.

Vanderbroeck, P. J. J. 1987. *Popular Leadership and Collective Behavior in the Late Roman Republic*. Amsterdam: J. C. Gieben.

Van Gennep, Arnold. [1908] 1960. *The Rites of Passage*. Trans. Monika Vizedom and Gabrielle Caffee. Chicago: University of Chicago Press.

Vasaly, Ann. 1983. "The Spirit of Place: The Rhetorical Use of Locus in Cicero's Speeches." Ph.D. diss., Indiana University.

———. 1993. *Representations: Images of the World in Ciceronian Oratory*. Berkeley: University of California Press.

Versnel, H. S. 1970. *Triumphus: An Enquiry into the Origin, Development and Meaning of the Roman Triumph*. Leiden: Brill.

Veyne, Paul. 1990. *Bread and Circuses: Historical Sociology and Political Pluralism*. Trans. Brian Pearce. London: Penguin.

Virlouvet, Catherine. 1985. *Famines et émeutes à Rome des origines de la République à la mort de Néron*. Rome: École Française de Rome.

———. 1991. "La plèbe frumentaire à l'époque d'Auguste: Une tentative de définition." In *Nourrir la plèbe: Actes du colloque tenu à Genève les 28 et 29.IX.1989 en hommage à Denis Van Berchem*, ed. Adalberto Giovannini, 43–63. Basel: F. Reinhardt.

Waddington, David, Karen Jones, and Chas Critcher. 1989. *Flashpoints: Studies in Public Disorder*. London: Routledge.

Wallace-Hadrill, Andrew. 1982. "Civilis Princeps: Between Citizen and King." *JRS* 72: 32- 48.

———. 1983. *Suetonius: The Scholar and His Caesars*. London: Duckworth.

———, ed. 1989. *Patronage in Ancient Society*. New York: Routledge.

Weber, Max. 1958. *The City*. Trans. and ed. Don Martindale and Gertrud Neuwirth. New York: Macmillan.

Wechsberg, Joseph. 1948. *Looking for a Bluebird*. Boston: Houghton Mifflin.

Weingärtner, D. G. 1969. *Die Ägyptenreise des Germanicus*. Bonn: Rudolf Habelt Verlag.

Weinstock, Stefan. 1971. *Divus Julius*. London: Oxford University Press.

Weissman, Ronald. 1982. *Ritual Brotherhood in Renaissance Florence*. New York: Academic Press.

Weston, Karl. 1903. "The Illustrated Terence Manuscripts." *Harvard Studies in Classical Philology* 14: 37–54.

Whittaker, C. R. 1964. "The Revolt of Papirius Dionysius, A.D. 190." *Historia* 13, no. 3: 348–69.

———. 1993. "The Poor." In *The Romans*, ed. A. Giardina, 272–99. Chicago: University of Chicago.

Wiedemann, Thomas. 1992. *Emperors and Gladiators*. London: Routledge.

Wiemken, Helmut. 1972. *Der griechische Mimus: Dokumente zur Geschichte des antiken Volkstheaters*. Bremen: Schünemann Universitätsverlag.

Wilshire, Bruce. 1982. *Role Playing and Identity: The Limits of Theater as Metaphor*. Bloomington: University of Indiana Press.

Wirszubski, C. 1950. *Libertas as a Political Idea at Rome during the Late Republic and Early Principate*. Cambridge: Cambridge University Press.

Wisch, Barbara, and Susan S. Munshower, eds. 1990. *All the World's a Stage: Art and Pageantry in the Renaissance and Early Baroque.* Vol. 1: *Triumphal Celebrations and the Rituals of Statecraft.* Vol. 2: *Theatrical Spectacle and Spectacular Theatre.* Papers in Art History from the Pennsylvania State University, vol. 6. University Park, Pa.

Wöhrle, Georg. 1990. "*Actio:* Das fünfte *officium* des antiken Redners." *Gymnasium* 97: 31–46.

Woodman, A. J. 1993. "Amateur Dramatics at the Court of Nero: *Annals* 15.48–74." In *Tacitus and the Tacitean Tradition,* ed. T. J. Luce, 104–28. Princeton: Princeton University Press.

Wooten, Cecil. 1976. "Petronius, the Mime, and Rhetorical Education." *Helios,* n.s., 3: 67–74.

Wright, David. 1993. "The Forgotten Early Romanesque Illustrations of Terence in Vat. lat. 3305." *Zeitschrift für Kunstgeschichte* 56, no. 2: 183–206.

Wright, Sam. 1978. *Crowds and Riots: A Study in Social Organization.* Beverly Hills, Calif.: Sage Publications.

Yavetz, Zwi. 1958. "The Living Conditions of the Urban Plebs in Republican Rome." *Latomus* 17: 500–517.

———. 1965a. "Levitas Popularis." *Atene e Roma,* n.s., 10: 97–110.

———. 1965b. "Plebs sordida." *Athenaeum,* n.s., 43: 293–311.

———. 1974. "Fama Existimatio and the Ides of March." *HSCPh* 78: 35–65.

———. 1983. *Julius Caesar and His Public Image.* London: Thames and Hudson.

———. 1988. *Plebs and Princeps.* 2nd ed. New Brunswick, N.J.: Transaction Books.

Zanker, Paul. 1968. *Forum Augustum.* Tübingen: E. Wasmuth.

———. 1988. *The Power of Images in the Age of Augustus.* Trans. Alan Shapiro. Ann Arbor: University of Michigan Press.

Index

ANCIENT SOCIETY AND HISTORY

The series Ancient Society and History offers books, relatively brief in compass, on selected topics in the history of ancient Greece and Rome, broadly conceived, with a special emphasis on comparative and other nontraditional approaches and methods. The series, which includes both works of synthesis and works of original scholarship, is aimed at the widest possible range of specialist and nonspecialist readers.

Library of Congress Cataloging-in-Publication Data

Aldrete, Gregory S.
    Gestures and acclamations in ancient Rome / Gregory S. Aldrete.
        p.   cm.
    Includes bibliographical references and index.
    ISBN 0-8018-6132-2
    1. Speeches, addresses, etc., Latin—History and criticism.
2. Rome—Politics and government.   3. Oral communication—
Rome.   4. Gesture—Rome—History.   5. Rhetoric, Ancient.
6. Oratory, Ancient.   7. Gesture in art.   8. Audiences.   I. Title.
PA6083.A44   1999
875'.0109—dc21   98-56501
                                                                        CIP